affectionately

TWENTY YEARS OF CORRESPONDENCE

BETWEEN A BOOKSELLER AND A COLLECTOR

Affectionately H

A TRIBUTE TO HELEN BURT HENNESSEY

BY JOHN H. DANIELS

WITH A PREFACE

BY WILLIAM

STEINKRAUS

To Karen and Ken
with best wishes

John Daniels (Yale '43)

august 1999.

NOTHING COULD BY FINER PRESS, CAMDEN, S.C.

1999

to Martha
with love and thanks for her advice and encouragement

Foreword

Book collection is a delightful pastime. It can be practiced on any scale, with any degree of specialization (or none at all), and with whatever monies and passion the collector chooses or can afford to commit to it. It is not such a bad profession either, though you really have to love books to justify acquiring all the knowledge you need, and selling your treasures can be very painful. Indeed, most dealers and even book scouts have certain special volumes stashed away, just as did the subject of this book.

Not surprisingly, this delightfully wide-ranging pastime/profession has been the subject of a very considerable and equally wide-ranging literature. There are bibliographies and checklists on every subject imaginable; there are practical manuals and broad surveys, there are memoirs by famous collectors and famous dealers. There are even some excellent mysteries and detective stories with a bookish background.

In all this huge literature, the narrowest category I can think of is that which is restricted to books consisting exclusively of letters exchanged between a bookseller and a client. The first of these (as far as I know) was Helene Hanff's *84, Charing Cross Road,* which comprised the correspondence between an American freelance TV writer with a taste for earlier literature and a long-established London antiquarian dealer, Marks & Co., then struggling with Britain's post-World War II austerity. Though (or perhaps, because) both the book and the idea behind it were pretty slender, *84* enjoyed a remarkable, even cultish success, earning a place on the best-seller lists on both sides of the Atlantic, and eventually enjoying the distinction of being transformed into both a play and a film.

I suspect that the present volume is only the second entrant into this category. While it covers only the same approximately two-decade span of time as did its predecessor, and I doubt that its author harbors best-seller aspirations for it, I will be so bold as to say that it seems to me to possess the significantly greater substance and intrinsic value of the two. The reason for this is that the following pages deal only partly with the education of a book collector—John Daniels—and the assistance he got from the dealer Helen Hennessey in forming an important collection of sporting books. For underlying and accompanying this process is the unfolding of a complex, interesting, and, indeed, intimate relationship (wholly innocent, I hasten to add) between two complex and interesting human beings.

The book starts, as did *84*, with a letter in response to a published advertisement, Hanff's in 1949 and Daniels's almost thirty years later, in 1978. At the beginning, Daniels presents himself very modestly, as a relatively novice collector (though someone who was already sending comprehensive want lists to some thirty dealers around the world was hardly a beginner); and as the years pass, he generously credits Helen with much of his growing sophistication about book collecting. In fact, however, as the correspondence reveals, each of them learned a good deal from the other in the course of their relationship.

For the reader who is him- or herself a collector of sporting books, the path of Daniels's "collector's progress" will largely be a familiar one, populated with old friends and acquaintances among the books, the reference sources, the auction houses, and the various other dealers referred to. But what one is left with at the end of the book is far more than all the titles and prices and names and the story of the growth of a marvelous collection. For along with this, we have watched the evolution of a human relationship from a perfunctory business level to one marked by a warmly compassionate, reciprocal rapport, and the sharing of small triumphs and serious tragedies that so often accompany advancing years. Along the way we have learned a lot about the real John Daniels and the real Helen Hennessey, and even if we have never met either of them in real life, we are richer for having known them through these letters.

The reader may wonder what has since become of the splendid sporting library formed by John Daniels with the assistance

of Helen Hennessey and many others. Some collectors, having
enjoyed all the pleasures of the hunt, choose ultimately to dis-
perse their collections so that other book lovers may enjoy the
same pleasures. In this case, however, the collection has been
kept intact, and thanks to John Daniels's munificent gift, now
forms an essential part of The National Sporting Library in
Middleburg, Virginia, where it will instruct and enchant scholars and book lovers with an interest in horses and field sports
for generations to come.

—William Steinkraus

Preface

It is difficult to pinpoint the exact time when I became a serious collector of sporting books. I had always been active in equestrian sports and enjoyed reading the books about foxhunting by Robert S. Surtees and Gordon Grand. In the early 1970s I contacted a few book search companies who advertised their services and was pleasantly surprised by how easy it was to buy so many out-of-print sporting books. Spurred by my initial success I began to dig more deeply and soon developed a system of making lists of desiderata and sending them out to a growing number of book search companies. The exact moment I realized that I was a dedicated collector was probably when I applied for a week-long course on rare books at Cornell University. The idea of going back to college and living in a dormitory may have been kindled by my nostalgia of those golden undergraduate years at Yale, which had been cut short by World War II and active military service.

The most significant outcome of my pleasant experiences at Cornell was that I learned that I had been doing all the right things as a neophyte book collector. This gave me the confidence to move forward more aggressively as a collector. I began to develop a research library of bibliographies, auction catalogues, and books about books, which made me better acquainted with the large field of sporting books that were so surprisingly available.

I simply played the field of booksellers with no specially favored suppliers and I corresponded with as many as thirty different booksellers in the United States and Great Britain. I first made contact with Helen Hennessey in 1978 at the height of this phase. The Hennesseys had run a small advertisement as book searchers in the Sunday newspaper. Although Helen was a latecomer, she survived my transitional period when it became apparent that it was more effective for me to work with a small number of antiquarian book specialists instead of playing the wide field. This very small group of five booksellers in the United States and three in the U.K. became my major source of supply. They eventually were responsible for almost eighty percent of my collection.

Helen Hennessey was good at bringing me books that I wanted and in offering me special treasures that I had never heard about. She found many of her books during her frequent buying trips to England with her daughter. We exchanged letters for twenty years, from 1978 until the year she died. Over these years we became friends and got to know each other quite well. I saved all of our correspondence, and when she died in October 1997, I re-read all of our letters. I decided to publish an edited version because these letters are a tribute to the memory of an extraordinary woman. She rose above the many tragedies that plagued her later years. Her courage and undaunted grip on life is an inspiration. This book is meant to be a tribute to my friend, Helen H.

Acknowledgments

David Acheson and Zeph Stewart, two of my Yale classmates, gave me sound advice about the possibilities and limitations of this book. James Dorsey, Darlene Burke, Paul Evans, and Bob Kearney, all from Helen's hometown of Saratoga Springs and friends of hers, have been helpful in many ways out of their loyalty to Helen. My darling wife, Martha, is my resident grammarian of the slash-and-burn school. She has done her job and has also given me essential encouragement. Bill Steinkraus has outdone himself with his generosity in not only writing the Foreword but also in giving me the benefit of his vast experience as editor of sporting books at several different publishing houses. Finally I offer my sincere thanks to Allan Kornblum and to Coffee House Press for editing, designing, and producing this book.

"For ye suffer fools gladly,
Seeing ye yourself are wise."

—The Second Epistle of Paul
the Apostle to the Corinthians

August 5, 1978
The Hennesseys
BOOKSELLERS
4th and Woodlawn
Saratoga, N.Y. 12866

Dear Sirs,

I saw your classified ad in the Sunday *New York Times Book Review*. I am a book collector and my field of interest is sporting books. I am enclosing a copy of my want list, D-78, which lists about seventy-five books that I am trying to buy. Quality and condition are important so please describe the condition of any books that you can offer. If you have any new or forthcoming catalogues on sporting books (foxhunting, polo, fishing, shooting, and Derrydale Press in particular) please send me a copy.

Yours truly,
John H. Daniels

The Hennesseys
BOOKSELLERS
4th and Woodlawn
Saratoga, N.Y. 12866

Dear Sirs,

Thank you for your reply to my list D-78. I would like to order
the following books:

> Horatio Bigelow, *Gunnerman*. Derrydale, 1939
> Harry Chamberlin, *Training Hunters, Jumpers, & Hacks*
> John Hervey, *Messenger: Great Progenitor*, 1935
> V.S. Littauer, *Jumping the Horse*, 1931
> Burton L. Spiller, *Thoroughbred*, 1936
> "Snaffles," *More Bandobast*, illus. by author

My check is enclosed.

Sincerely,
John H. Daniels

    * * *

Monday, September 1, 1978

Mr. Daniels,

Thank you very much for your order. I hope everything is
satisfactory.

Helen Hennessey

Dear Mrs. Hennessey,

The order for six books arrived in good condition today and I am well pleased with them.

If from time to time you put out a catalogue or a listing of out-of-print sporting books I would appreciate getting a copy.

Do you happen to know the real name of "Snaffles?" A. Henry Higginson's *British and American Sporting Authors* is an excellent reference book with its bibliography by Sydney Smith, but even he does not identify this interesting author and artist.

Sincerely,
John H. Daniels

* * *

Saturday, September 19, 1978

Sorry, our reference library does not tell us who "Snaffles" is. However, I am going to England Oct. 8th and I will ask my colleagues. Any English treasures you are hunting?

HBH

September 22, 1978
The Hennesseys
BOOKSELLERS

Dear Mrs. Hennessey,

Thank you for your postcard. I hope that your trip to England in October is successful.

There are a few "treasures" that I am still having difficulty in locating, although I am continuing to ask for them.

The first category is the Somerville and Ross first editions of *An Irish Cousin* and *The Real Charlotte*. According to Elizabeth Hudson's bibliography, *An Irish Cousin* was first published in 1889. The first edition consisted of 500 copies in two volumes. The publisher was Richard Bently and Son, London. The 1903 edition of *An Irish Cousin* was in one volume, published by Longman's Green and Co. and consisted of 500 copies. (I have one of these but it is in rather poor condition. *The Real Charlotte* was first published in 1894 by Ward & Downey, Ltd. and consisted of three volumes. No record of mine shows how many copies were printed. The second edition of *The Real Charlotte* was in one volume and was printed by Ward & Downey in 1895. The third edition was printed in 1900 by Longman's Green and Co. and consisted of more than 1,000 copies.

There are seven books by Lionel Edwards that I am still looking for:

My Hunting Sketch Book. London, 1930. Volume 2, 4to.
Horses and Ponies. London, N.D. 4to.
The Passing Seasons. London, N.D. 4to.
A Sportsman's Bag. London, 1937. 4to. Limited to 650 copies
Scarlet and Corduroy. London, 1941. 8vo.
Horses and Riders. London, 1946. Small oblong 4to.
and with H.F. Wallace. *Hunting and Stalking Deer.* London, 1927. 4to.

And finally two books by "Snaffles":

Gun, Rifle, and Hound. London, 1894. 8vo.
The Image of War. London, 1914. 8vo.

If you should come across any of these books I would appreciate hearing about them, their condition, and the price.

Sincerely,
John H. Daniels

* * *

October 13, 1978

Dear Mr. Daniels,

We had to postpone our trip to England, as Mr. Hennessey had a stroke last week. However, I sent your list of treasures over to my colleagues along with some things I want, so perhaps we both will be successful.

On your want list E-78 we have the following books by Cecil Aldin, all in fine condition.

I happen to be especially fond of Cecil Aldin and have quite a few of his signed prints.

Are you interested in Mordaunt's *Annals of the Warwickshire Hunt,* London, 1896?

Sincerely,
Helen Hennessey

October 20, 1978
The Hennesseys/booksellers

Dear Mrs. Hennessey,

Yes, I would like to purchase the four books by Cecil Aldin as described in your letter. My check is enclosed. We are going to be in Europe from Oct. 21 to Nov. 12, so it might be best if you would mail these books so that they arrive here about November 13 or 14.

I would be interested in getting information on the Mordaunt/Verney *Annals of the Warwickshire Hunt.*

By the way, I have learned that "Snaffles" was Robert Dunkeld, but I don't know much more about him than that.
I was very sorry to learn about Mr. Hennessey's stroke. I hope he makes a good recovery.

Sincerely,
John H. Daniels

Dear Mr. Daniels,

Received your letter of October 20th and around the end of the first week in November I will post the books to you.

Unfortunately, someone bought Aldin's *Time I Was Dead*. I am very sorry about that, it's my fault. I should have put it aside until I heard from you. Please accept my apology and our check. Regarding your request for information:

> *The Annals of the Warwickshire Hunt.* London, 1896. 2 vols, 4to. Steel engravings, and B&W illus. Binding features a red levant pattern, fabrikoid. (Sorry about that, I'm not certain that is correct.) Pictorial design of a fox in gold, also gold lettering on spine. Bookplate of Lord Durham and an inscription from Stuart Reed saying this is a Christmas gift, 1896. Fine.

My English colleague informs me that Snaffles's proper name was Charles Payne, but that is not the same Snaffles that wrote the two books you are looking for. He spelled his name Snaffle, and his proper name was Charles Dunkeld.

I hope your holiday was fun and that you found a lot of treasures.

I'm off to the Boston Book Fair next week.

Sincerely,
Helen Hennessey

November 14, 1978

Dear Mrs. Hennessey,

Just got back from Europe and found your letter. I'm glad to know the books I ordered are on their way. Also, by coincidence, I just found another source of Aldin's *Time I Was Dead,* so this presents no problem.

I was glad to get the information about Snaffle (or Snaffles). I have located both of his books, *Gun, Rifle, and Hound* and *The Image of War.*

I am enclosing my check for the two-volume *The Annals of the Warwickshire Hunt,* which I would like to add to my collection. The Boston Book Fair must have been interesting. Sounds as though everybody was there.

Sincerely,
John H. Daniels

Welcome Home,

I hope you had a nice holiday and found a lot of treasures.
I found a mint copy of Cecil Aldin's *Time I Was Dead*,
trade edition.

Sincerely,
HBH

* * *

November, 1978

Dear Mrs. Hennessey,

Thank you for your recent postcard. (Some of our correspon-
dence has crossed in the mail). Yes, we had a marvelous trip.
Partridge shooting in Spain, visiting friends in Portugal and
Provence, and searching the past (Huguenot ancestors and
World War II) in France.

Now we are back to four inches of new snow in Minnesota and
can hardly wait to start south on December fifth.

I am enclosing my check for the mint copy of Cecil Aldin's
Time I Was Dead, trade edition.

Sincerely,
John H. Daniels

November 22, 1978

Dear Mrs. Hennessey,

I would like to order two books from your catalogue number two. Incidentally, the plot thickens on "Snaffles." I think there are two writers—"Snaffle" and "Snaffles." Although the Bibliography prepared by Sidney Smith in A. Henry Higginson's *British and American Sporting Authors* only lists "Snaffles" and attributes *Gun, Rifle, and Hound* to him, the copy of *Gun, Rifle, and Hound* that I recently acquired is signed "Snaffle." The publication date for this book is 1894. In the book by "Snaffles," *More Bandobast,* the author in 1936 lists three other books that he has written and does not include *Gun, Rifle, and Hound.* What is most convincing is that the style is so different. "Snaffle" has his book illustrated by Henry Dixon while "Snaffles" illustrates his books himself in a most distinctive and attractive way.

If you have any more information on this I'd be most interested.

Sincerely,
John H. Daniels

* * *

November 23, 1978

Dear Mr. Daniels,

Have you any interest in Surtees? One of the volumes is *The Life of a Sportsman* by Nimrod. I have three volumes, large paper uniformly bound in half-red morocco, 1903. Another set of four in cloth and a first in my own library in full morocco.

Sincerely,
Helen Hennessey

November 27, 1978

Dear Mrs. Hennessey,

Thank your for your prompt reply about my F-78 list.
I would like to purchase the Edmund Smith, *The One-Eyed
Poacher of Privilege*, Derrydale, 1941.

I have so many Surtees books that I'm not sure I want to take
on any more. Could you quote me the prices and titles on the
three volumes bound in half-red morocco?

Sincerely,
John H. Daniels

* * *

December 12, 1978

Dear Mr. Daniels,

Hope you had a pleasant trip to Camden. My brother left for
Carolina on the fourth, but he only had half the distance to
travel that you had.

The books that I ordered from England are starting to come in,
and I'm terribly disappointed in their condition. The English
used to be quite honest in describing the condition of their
books, but they have picked up a nasty habit from the Americans, and the thought of returning them leaves me cold.

You mentioned tracing your family of Huguenots. If you
haven't read a book called *The Journal of John Fontaine and
His Huguenot Son in Spain & Virginia*, I would like to send
you the book as a Christmas card.

Have a nice holiday.

Sincerely,
Helen Hennessey

December 16, 1978

Dear Mrs. Hennessey,

Thank you for your nice letter. I was interested in the books you described in your letter. I am afraid I have all the Surtees that I can handle, but I would like to buy the Nimrod (Apperley) *The Life of a Sportsman,* and am enclosing my check.

I would be most interested in *The Journal of John Fontaine.* Some of my wife's relatives were Huguenots and came to South Carolina with Les Frères Gibert in the 1760s.

I hope you had a happy holiday.

Sincerely,
John H. Daniels

* * *

December 25, 1978

Dear Mr. Daniels,

Thank you for your letter and especially for the pictures of your homes. Like a child, I like to visualize people's dwellings and their professions. I suppose that is partly because I have had such a checkered career.

We are leaving tomorrow morning for South Carolina to spend the holidays. Our daughter has the week off, so we will be back New Year's Day.

Sincerely,
Helen Hennessey

Dear Mrs. Hennessey,

Thank you for your letter. I hope you had a good holiday in
South Carolina with your daughter. Where in South Carolina
do you go? I would like to buy the two books by "Snaffle."
Although the subject matter is a bit different than most of my
sporting books, I like to collect all the works of a particular
author. (My check is enclosed.)

Sincerely,
John H. Daniels

January, 1979

Dear Mr. Daniels,

Our Christmas holiday was a complete disaster. In Fayetteville a car ran a red light and made an accordion of my car and put nine stitches in my head. We limped on down to my brother's. (He stays in a small hamlet north of Georgetown.) I don't like American cars, so I was driving what my daughter calls my tank, a Peugeot station wagon. Otherwise, I think we might have all been seriously injured.

I don't know what I have to sharpen your appetite for books. You defeated me when you wrote that you collect only authors. I have some more Cecil Aldins, not the ones on your last list (F-18). *The Romance of the Road* is a beautiful book, one of two hundred copies. *Good Gun Days* and *Dog of Character,* also *An Artist's Model.*

Did you find Lionel Edwards's *Sportsman's Bag*? A. Thorburn's *Four Volumes of British Birds.* Dwight Huntington's *The True Game Birds: A Picture Book of the Shooting Fields and Feathered Game Birds of North America.* Stillman's *The Horse in Motion.* John Millais's *The Wildfowler in Scotland.*

There is a big sale this week of sporting books. I bid on quite a few. With any luck I should get a few.

Sincerely,
Helen Hennessey

Dear Mrs. Hennessey,

I was so sorry to hear about your dreadful accident, and how it made Christmas a complete disaster. Thank goodness you were in a sturdy automobile. I hope you have all recovered by now.

I'm afraid I misled you by the statement in my letter of December 25th where I said, "I like to collect all the works of a particular author." Although I do go in for this—for example, I have all of the Somerville and Ross first editions except for *An Irish Cousin* and *The Real Charlotte,* and all of the Surtees and Foote, etc.— my real purpose in collecting is to specialize in hounds, fox-hunting, polo, etc., because these are sports that I have participated in most of my life. So the real criteria is this: Does the book have something to do with these particular sports? I also have a number of good books on fishing and hunting (birds) but I'm afraid to open Pandora's box too wide on fishing, which is such a vast field.

Anyway, this is a long way of saying that I would be most inter-ested in getting more information about some of the books you mentioned in your letter.

I did find Lionel Edwards's *Sportsman's Bag.* I am still searching for his *The Passing Seasons* and *Horses and Riders.*

Your Cecil Aldin's *The Romance of the Road* etc., sound most interesting. Could you describe them for me? Also the Hunting-ton book *The True Game Birds,* Stillman's *The Horse in Motion,* and Millais's *The Wildfowler in Scotland.* So you see, you have "sharpened my appetite," at least to learn more about the books in question before making a go or no-go decision.

I look forward to hearing from you.

Sincerely,
John H. Daniels

January 24, 1979

Dear Mr. Daniels,

Nice to hear from you. The outdoors here is in a glorious mess. We had twelve hours of rain and Saratoga is one big skating rink. The yards look like a woodlot.

I'll try to describe the books to you.

> Cecil Aldin, *The Romance of the Road.* London, 1928. Written and illus. by him, 17 colored plates, folding colored map of pond inside front cover. In the back are 6 Cary's "Survey of the High Roads from London." Full parchment folio, limited to 200 copies, signed. Back cover slightly soiled. Windsor Holden White bookplate.

> Dwight W. Huntington, *The True Game Birds: A Picture Book of the Shooting Fields and Feathered Game of North America.* N.Y., 1903. Large folio, 125 pages on heavy paper. 8 color-gravure plates by Huntington, Farny McCord, & Fries, with titled tissues, numerous other illus. The contents on grouse, bobwhite, turkeys, and partridge. Extra laid-in color plate of A.B. Frost. Green cloth gilt title, "Brush, Sedge, and Stubble." First edition. Library cancelled stamp on copyright page.

> J.G. Millais, *The Wildfowler in Scotland.* 4to. With frontispiece, 8 photogravure plates, 2 colored plates by Andre and Sleigh, Ltd. and 50 illus from the author's drawings. The book deals entirely with the pursuit of ducks in Scottish waters. Boxed, vellum-backed boards. Covers slightly soiled.

Thank you very much for your interest in my quote, but please don't think I'm a pushy book dealer. I'm not, my friend. Ernest Hickok in N.J., says it's keeping our brains active that counts.

Sincerely,
Helen Hennessey

Dear Mrs. Hennessey,

Thank you for your most recent letter quoting four perfectly lovely books (Aldin, Stillman, Huntington, and Millais)—I'd love to own them, but they are a bit out of range pricewise for books that are not front and center in my range of collecting. I'd give a leg and an arm for the two elusive Somerville and Ross first editions of their first two books—*An Irish Cousin* and *The Real Charlotte*—so I have to keep my powder dry in hopes they will come along.

But please don't give up on me and keep sending me your always interesting detailed descriptions.

Best regards,
John Daniels

February 23, 1979

Dear Mr. Daniels,

The weather has been the topic of conversation around here and I didn't think you would be interested in that. I certainly wasn't. During the height of the cold, I made a voyage to Montreal where the wind-chill was -45°. Needless to say, it was stimulating. I found very little good material, one Somerville and Ross, *Wheel-Tracks*, 1923, which I feel is not a first. On the advertising page listing all her books, it doesn't mention the two books you are looking for.

I have a book for your wife. Of course, you would have to restore the side saddle and take her to your tailor for a beautiful green velvet riding habit. Allen's *Principles of Modern Riding*, 1825.

Sincerely,
Helen Hennessey

P.S. I just looked in Higginson and under Somerville and Ross. It doesn't list your two books.

Dear Mrs. Hennessey,

Our letters crossed in the mail and you should have my new list A-79 by now. It's quite a long list because I have included a lot of titles of sporting books that are in the Mulberry collection that I'd like to find for my own collection.

The Somerville-Ross books, the first and second editions of *An Irish Cousin* and *The Real Charlotte*, are well documented in the excellent bibliography of Somerville and Ross prepared by Elizabeth Hudson in 1942.

Our weather has been unspeakable, too. I spent five hours in the saddle on Saturday, herding our cattle to high ground in front of a threatened flood, which later manifested itself. Fortunately, our water is now going down and all of the cattle—including 450 little calves—have survived.

Please let me know more about *Principles of Modern Riding*, 1825.

With best regards,

Sincerely,
John H. Daniels

March 7, 1979

Dear Mr. Daniels,

Nice to hear from you. I would have thoroughly enjoyed myself herding cattle if I was on a Tennessee Walker.

The Allen is beastly expensive. However, it is a great book.

> John Allen, *Principles of Modern Riding for Ladies*. London, 1825. Large 8vo. Not found in this vol is plate titled "Parts of the Horse" (it hasn't been removed). 22 full-page steel engravings. Orig boards, newly rebacked in brown leather, leather label. First edition. Allen was the Riding Master at Seymour Place, Bryanstone Square.

You will find the book in *Book Prices Current*.

I think spring is on its way. I hope so, as I am beginning to feel as though I am in jail.

Sincerely,
Helen Hennessey

* * *

March 16, 1979

Dear Mrs. Hennessey,

Thank you for your letter about the John Allen book. I already have a copy of this so I must decline your offer.

I've been quite lucky on A-79 and have already located twenty-five of the books on the list!

Sincerely,
John H. Daniels

Dear Mr. Daniels,

I am glad you had such a success with your list A-79. I have three books coming from England, probably not before the middle of May, that are on your list, if you have not already acquired them. Brock's *The ABC of Foxhunting;* Pennell's *The Best Season on Record,* first, 1884; and Sabretache's *Shires and Provinces,* first, limited.

My daughter and I are going to do the N.Y. Book Fair (against my better judgment). Then Sherri is off to England. I can't go with her as I have no confidence in the help that I would have to hire to take care of Mr. Hennessey.

Have you any duplicates in your library you would like to sell?

My brother is expected today, after a stay in South Carolina. It will be nice to see him again. He will stay with Mr. H. while I am in New York.

Best regards,
Helen Hennessey

April 8, 1979

Dear Mrs. Hennessey,

Thank you for your good letter. It is always pleasant to hear from you. There are two books that you listed in your letter that I would be interested in:

Pennell, *The Best Season on Record.* 1864. 1st.
Sabretache, *Shires and Provinces.* (1926?) 1st, limited.

When they arrive from England, perhaps you could quote them for me and describe their condition.

I do have some duplicates in my library but I will have to wait until we get back to Minnesota to sort them out because most of my books are up there.

I hope the N.Y. Book Fair isn't too painful, and I look forward to hearing from you.

Sincerely,
John H. Daniels

May 4, 1979

Dear Mr. Daniels,

I enjoyed your letter very much. I could visualize your caravan heading north, also the meeting of the clans. I had just seen on TV a plantation meeting in Louisiana where all the members of the family were holding their yearly meeting. But it was rather sad as they raised sugar cane and the market was way off. They seemed to need money, as the plantation was not in a great state of repair.

I've just received my order of books from England. You were interested in Pennell and Sabretache.

> Capt. Elmhirst Pennell, *The Best Season on Record*. London, 1884. 8vo, 211 pp. Color and B&W illus. Half red calf. Raised gilt bands with hunting motifs. Split at the top of the front cover, but not disbound. 1st edition.

Sabretache is bloody expensive, but a very fine copy:

> *Shires and Provinces*. London, 1926. Large 4to, 195 pp. 16 mounted color plates by Lionel Edwards, tissue guards, handmade paper. Bound in full vellum. (If you have Munnings's limited signed of *Pictures of Horses and English Life*, this is a companion volume). Deluxe, limited to 100, signed by both author and artist.

Perhaps if you wait on Sabretache you may find it cheaper.

Have a fine summer, if it comes.

Sincerely,
Helen Hennessey

May 17, 1979

Dear Mrs. Hennessey,

Enclosed is my check for the Sabretache book and the Elmhirst Pennell *Best Season on Record.*

Sincerely,
John Daniels

* * *

May 21, 1979

Dear Mr. Daniels,

I'm sorry about your phone call the other day. You have to be half crazy to be in the book business and I'm all of that. I certainly should have known a Mr. Daniels after all the money you have spent with me.

I owe you an explanation on the price of the Munnings. I've had three copies of that book and have always planned to keep a copy for myself, but have sold them. So this time I decided to put such a high price on this one that no one would want it and I could keep it.

Sherri, our daughter, is in England. She phoned this morning because she had found a set of Sabretache. I was delighted, because I sort of wanted to keep the one you took. (I put them in the mail today, two packages.)

I thought you might enjoy the enclosed pictures of the book shop and the carriage house.

Sincerely,
Helen Hennessey

P.S. "The Shadow" is my Abyssinian cat, who is a very good companion. We once had eleven dogs, one belonged to Moss Hart, one to Dorothy Parker, but we lived on an island then and all you had to do was open a door. I'm selfish now. In 20° below zero, walking a dog doesn't thrill me.

May 24, 1979

Dear Mrs. Hennessey,

Thank you so much for your letter. I can see why you don't want to part with the Munnings *Pictures of Horses and English Life*. I put a bid in for $500 for the one that George Lowry sold at auction on May 10 and it went for $600. George said afterwards that if I had bid $600 it would have gone for $700. I wish I had been there to have a try at it in person. It sounds like a super book and one day I'll locate a copy to go with the Sabretache, which I am dying to see.

The photographs of your book shop and carriage house are charming. May I keep them or would you like to have them back?

I did get a carpenter to measure up a wall in our house for more bookcases (the collection keeps growing) and I did find two nice lots of books in England, but I haven't had time to start work on my next "want list."

I'm in the process of completing the editing of a somewhat long history of the Masters of Foxhounds Association that Alex Mackay-Smith started but never finished. We plan to go to press in September. It will be a limited edition of 750 numbered copies and will be in the same format as Alex Mackay-Smith's other books: *The American Foxhound, American Foxhunting,* and *The Songs of Foxhunting.* The Masters of Foxhounds Association is publishing the copies. (The book will sell for $40 and my guess is that because it is limited to 750 copies it will soon become a collector's item.) I've been working on the darned History off and on for almost two years now and I'm getting fed up with it, and will be glad to have it "locked up" and gone to press.

Please keep me posted if you come across any sporting books that you think might interest me and I shall soon get a new want list completed.

Sincerely,
John H. Daniels

June 16, 1979

Dear Mr. Daniels,

The whole family was pleased with the pictures of your home and library. It looks like a charming place to live. I liked your bronzes. I only have one, but I have some African horns!
I went to a book sale out in the western part of the state last weekend and managed to bid on some very fine hunting books in almost pristine condition. The first five volumes of the *Boone and Crockett Club* was a nice find.

I would like to have two copies of your book, one signed by the editor, of course.

Sherri is back from England with no great finds, just both volumes of Sabretache's *Shires and Provinces* and *More Shires*. She looked for some Stevens graphs for me, but unsuccessfully.

Sincerely,
Helen Hennessey

P.S. Please keep the library pictures, we did them especially for you. Have you found out that I can't spell? It puts me in a class with George Bernard Shaw, though.

June 18, 1979

Dear Mrs. Hennessey,

Thank you for your recent letter. I'm glad you liked the photographs of our house. I guess I should have added that because of my "collecting fever" we are adding a large new bookcase on the landing that goes up to the second floor of our living room. A super place that is in the dark most of the time but can be well lighted when necessary.

I was interested in your report that your daughter, Sherri, had just returned from England and had found Sabretache's *More Shires*. I don't have this one and would be interested in getting a description of the book.

"My" book, *Masters of Foxhounds*, is now ready for the printers. We plan to send out a brochure about it in July and I will be sure that you get a copy. Then you can decide if you really want one or two of them. My autograph is gladly forthcoming.

With all best regards,
Sincerely,
John H. Daniels

July 15, 1979

Dear Mr. Daniels,

Nice to talk to you yesterday. If you are a gambling man, I'll make a wager! Five dollars says that the Munnings goes for over a thousand.

The Sabretache arrived today:

> *More Shires and Provinces*. 1928. Uncut colored plates, tissue guards. Handmade paper, bound in full vellum. A companion volume to *Shires and Provinces*. Limited to 200 copies, #112, signed by author and Edwards.

Really is a beautiful book.

Best of luck,
Helen Hennessey

* * *

July 20, 1979

Dear Mrs. Hennessey,

You are on! I hope I win the five-dollar bet on the Munnings—and I hope to get the book too. I'll let you know after the auction on July 25th.

Enclosed is my check for Sabretache's *More Shires and Provinces*. It sounds like a wonderful companion piece to *Shires and Provinces*.

Sincerely,
John Daniels

July 25, 1979

Dear Mr. Daniels,

I sent *More Shires and Provinces* off today, but because of the tape on the box I was unable to insure it for its full value. I sent it first class to your office. I hope that was alright. Your letter ordering the book was on office stationery! Please drop me a card if it arrives safely. I forgot to mention that the book has a "Henry C. Taylor" bookplate. I hope that is all right also.

HBH

* * *

July 31, 1979

Dear Mrs. Hennessey,

More Shires and Provinces arrived at my office safely and it is simply beautiful! I'm delighted to have the companion piece to Sabretache's first book. The pair make a most elegant and important high point in my collection. (I think that when the Munnings comes from Phillips I'll really have a set that anybody can be proud of.) The Henry C. Taylor bookplate is nice—doesn't bother me in the least.

Many thanks for the five dollars. I was really happy to win it and get the Munnings book to boot.

All best regards,
John Daniels

August 6, 1979

Dear Mr. Daniels,

Do you have or want a copy of Guy Paget's *History of the Althorp & Pytcheley Hunt*? I also acquired, by Paget, *The Melton Mowbray of John Fernley*, with an original pencil sketch in it.

I hope the weather is kinder to you than it has been with us. It's beastly here.

Many thanks for the check.

Sincerely,
Helen Hennessey

* * *

August 10, 1979

Dear Mrs. Hennessey,

Thank you so much for your letter of the 6th. I do have a copy of Guy Paget's *The Melton Mowbray of John Fernley* but do not have the other Paget book, *History of the Althorp & Pytcheley Hunt*. Could you give a description of the book and its condition, etc?

I've just referred to Higginson's *British and American Sporting Authors* and see that there are several holes in my Paget collection. If you run across any of the following, please let me know:

> *Mr. Silas P. Mowbray Returns to Melton*, 1940.
> *Sporting Pictures of England*, 1945.
> *Life of Frank Freeman, Huntsman*, 1948.

With best regards,
Sincerely,
John H. Daniels

Dear Mr. Daniels,

I was about to write you when your letter came . . .

A lovely lady came to see me and said wonderful complimentary things about you and said you were most kind about me, and I thank you. Her name was Mrs. W. Burling Cocks. It is so nice to hear pleasant remarks made by people halfway across the continent.

The Guy Paget you asked about:

> *History of the Althrop and Pytcheley Hunt, 1634–1920.* London, 1937. Large 4to. Colored and B&W plates (5 in color). Limited to 600 copies. DJ. As-new condition.

I don't have any of the other Paget titles you asked for, but if you aren't in a hurry I'll be glad to look for them.

Sincerely,
Helen Hennessey

      * * *

August 25, 1979

Mr. Daniels,

I sent Guy Paget off this afternoon, first class, so you should get it before you leave for England.

I think I may be able to locate the Surtees for you. The Somerville and Ross will be hard to find. Will you be looking for these books in England? If not, I will start hunting.

Have a fine holiday.
HBH

August 28, 1979

Dear Mrs. Hennessey,

The Guy Paget book arrived safely yesterday and it is a lovely copy.

Please let me know if you come across either the Surtees or the Somerville and Ross first editions that I am looking for. I know that they are going to be very hard to find, especially the Somerville and Ross, as you point out. (I have all of the Somerville and Ross first editions except for *An Irish Cousin* and *Irish Memories* and have been on the prowl for them for over three years.)

We will be visiting one English bookseller up in the Lake Country during our travels. He is also Master of a pack of beagles and has invited us to hunt with him, which should be fun—and should work off some of the pasta that we will be taking on in Italy.

Sincerely,
John H. Daniels

August 31, 1979

Dear Mr. Daniels,

I think that the brochure for *Masters of Foxhounds* is very exciting. Should be a sellout, and when you return from your
English holiday I'll send you an order for two copies.

Sorry, but I have nothing on your list B-79. However, I was read-
ing a catalogue this morning and I thought of you. They had a
Somerville and Ross bibliography of the first editions, edited by
Hudson, limited and signed, and I wondered if you had it.

Also, when you get back, if you don't have it, S.F. Touchstone's
History of Celebrated English & French Stallions and Mares. I have
a fair to good copy.

Hurriedly, but with the best of wishes for a super holiday.

Sincerely,
Helen Hennessey

      * * *

September 29, 1979

Dear Mr. Daniels,

Welcome home. I don't believe I need to say, I hope you had a
wonderful holiday. I am sure you did.

I have written to England in an attempt to find some of the
books on your list: Apperley, Mills, Edwards, Horlock, Paget,
and, of course, Surtees. You can't hurry the English.

Sincerely,
Helen Hennessey

October 21, 1979

Dear Mrs. Hennessey,

I have been fortunate in locating twenty-seven titles on my list
B-79. I'm enclosing an updated copy with the titles of the ones I
have found x'd out.

The Surtees's *Handley Cross* problem has been solved by the
acquisition of *both* the 1843 and the 1854 editions.

I am still most anxious to locate Surtees's *Hawbuck Grange* in
the first edition. Also am especially interested in filling out my
Somerville and Ross collection.

With all best regards,
John H. Daniels

* * *

October 31, 1979

Dear Mr. Daniels,

Thank you very much for your check. I mailed two packages to
South Carolina today.

I wish to apologize for phoning your office. I resisted a long
time before I did, as I felt very self-conscious, fearing you might
think I was pressing over a book sale. Rest assured that was
furthest from my mind. I was concerned about you and your
family's health.

We have been working up a storm on a catalogue. It should go
to the printers next week and with any luck it should make the
post by the end of the month.

Best regards,
Helen Hennessey

Dear Mrs. Hennessey,

Thank you for your letter of October 31st. Please do not have any concern about having called me at the office in Minneapolis.

The two books that you mailed me arrived today and I am very pleased with both of them. They are lovely! Books to be very proud of.

I hope that you will send me a copy of your new catalogue when it comes back from the printers.

I believe that you told me that you visited your brother last year at Christmas-time near Georgetown, S.C. If I remember correctly you had an automobile accident in the process. Anyway, if you are going to be driving south again I do hope that you will swing by Mulberry Plantation. I'd love to show you this marvelous old house and some of its "goodies."

With best wishes,
Sincerely,
John H. Daniels

November 15, 1979

Dear Mr. Daniels,

It was nice to hear from you and I'm happy that I didn't make a faux pas. Also I am very pleased that everything is fine with you and your family.

The plantation must be wonderful. We once lived on an island that was a showplace and a curiosity to the public. Sometimes people would arrive before breakfast. The dogs helped a great deal, but I promised myself that someday I'd live in a chicken coop. But, like you, we brought the "goodies" with us and so the carriage house is inclined to draw the same traffic.
We haven't decided what to do about this winter holiday. My brother will leave for South Carolina after the Thanksgiving holiday and if I should go down, he would watch after Josy for me and I would have more freedom. But at the moment I am a monument of indecision.

I found a few books that you may or may not have, and I'm enclosing the list. Also I made up a want list of some of the items you are interested in and some books for stock, which will be published in *Bookman's Weekly*. You had wonderful luck with your list. Perhaps I will too.

I also have another copy of Betty Babcock's *Hunting Diary*, similar to the one I sent you. It's such a smart-looking book, perhaps you would like to give it as a gift to someone. Have a wonderful winter.

Sincerely,
Helen Hennessey

Dear Mrs. Hennessey,

Thank you for your good letter of the 14th. I have three of the
four books that you listed but would like to buy the Van Urk,
The Horse, the Valley, and the Chagrin Valley.

The quotation about hunting men and masters of the hounds—
"apt to be rather self-centered"—misses the mark, I hope. Being
both a hunting man and an ex-master, I'd say the master has to
be a self-starter and a good sportsman, but I'm sure it is all in
the eye of the beholder.

I am delighted to report that the new book *Masters of Foxhounds*
has been given the final okay by the Board. The printer has
started the production of the book and we are aiming for a publication date in late January, 1980.

I saw Mrs. Burling (Babs) Cocks this morning at the schooling
track where her husband was supervising the workouts of two
steeplechasers that will go in the Colonial Cup this Sunday.
Babs said that she had a wonderful time this summer visiting
you and buying books.

Please let me know if you locate any of the books on the list.

With all best wishes,
Sincerely,
John H. Daniels

November 27, 1979

Dear Mrs. Hennessey,

The Van Urk book about the Chagrin Valley arrived today and it is lovely! My wife is trying to locate several copies of a book by her great aunt, Mary Boykin Chesnut, who wrote *A Diary from Dixie* that was edited by Ben Ames Williams and was published in 1949 by the Riverside Press, Cambridge (Houghton Mifflin Company, Boston). It came out in hardcover and also in paperback. If you run across any of these, please let me know.

I have been gradually collecting the works of Archibald Rutledge. I am enclosing a list of his books that I have already acquired. My problem is that I haven't found a definitive bibliography of Rutledge's works. If you locate any of Rutledge's works that aren't on my list, please let me know.

With all best wishes,
John H. Daniels

* * *

December 6, 1979

Dear Mr. Daniels,

I went over to Skidmore Library today to research Archibald Rutledge's bibliography. My personal opinion is that there probably is something, but perhaps in pamphlet form. I found nothing over there to help you. Sometime will you send me your family name? I'm off to Montreal to visit a sick friend. An ice storm is due Saturday so I should have an exciting time.

Best regards,
Helen Hennessey

Dear Mr. Daniels,

Time has been at a premium for me this last month, but time will hang heavy on my hands from now on and I will do some researching.

I advertised in *Bookman's Weekly,* a magazine devoted to the specialist book world, for some titles you were interested in and some I was looking for. Out of sixteen titles, I had no response. I'm at a loss for an explanation. I gather the solution is perseverance.

I have been traveling quite a bit lately, as I frequently do this time of year, and the dealers seem to have no stock in my field. Only modern editions of novels that I didn't think too highly of when they were first printed. We have a few new titles that if you don't already have them you might be interested in.

I have been unable to find any Rutledge titles for you, or anything on your list B-79. However, I will continue to look.

The weather here is very strange, and I feel very sorry for Lake Placid.

Best regards,
Helen Hennessey

      * * *

January 15, 1980

Dear Mr. Daniels,

I just ordered from England C.R. Acton's *Hounds* and Snaffles's *'Osses and Obstacles.* If you haven't already found these titles, I'll quote you a month from now. I'm interested in their condition.

H.B. Hennessey

January 18, 1980

Dear Mrs. Hennessey,

Thank you for your letter (1/13/80) and your postcard (1/15/80) which were waiting for me when I got back from a business trip. I would like to buy the G.D. Armour, *Hunting Alphabet*.

I have the other books listed in your letter.

I am quite interested in the three books you listed as coming from England, and will wait to hear from you as to their condition and price about a month from now, after they arrive.

With best regards,
John H. Daniels

* * *

Dear Mr. Daniels,

Some of the books I ordered from England have arrived. Following is the list.

Sincerely,
Helen Hennessey

February 21, 1980

Dear Mrs. Hennessey,

Thank you for sending me the list of some of the books you have received from England.

In checking this list against my file cards, I find I have four of them already but would like to purchase the other two.

Sincerely,
John H. Daniels

* * *

March 13, 1980

Dear Mrs. Hennessey,

I just got back from a trip to Minnesota and have your postcard.

My wife and I are making a quick trip to England starting on March 22nd. I have always wanted to see the Grand National Steeplechase at Aintree and we are going to do it this year. (Two American horses are running.) We get back here on March 31st.

With all best wishes,
John H. Daniels

April 12, 1980

Dear Mr. Daniels,

I am very pleased that you are satisfied with that appraisal and I thank you for your check.

Sincerely,
Helen Hennessey

[*During the winter of 1979-1980, Helen Hennessey did an appraisal of the books in the Mulberry Library. Gittman's Books in Columbia, S.C., had done an inventory and appraisal in the 1930s. Xerox copies of the index cards Gittman's had made were sent to Hennessey so that she could update the values almost fifty years after the original appraisal. Index cards were also created for books that had been added.]

April 16, 1980

Dear Mrs. Hennessey,

I was glad to receive your letter of April 12 and your additional billing for the appraisal of the Mulberry Library's sporting books.

I know that I had put you to a good deal of work as the reams and reams of indexed file card sheets went your way, and I was at a loss at how best to arrive at a figure that would adequately compensate you for the splendid job you were doing.

Your solution is fair and okay with me, and I am enclosing my check.

I feel that we have made great strides this winter with the Mulberry Library. We have a better card file system, many of the books are in much better condition after being cleaned and after applying a judicious amount of dressing to the leather-bound books, and we have an up-to-date inventory.

The area that still needs work is with the appraisal of "local" books of the nineteenth century having to do with South Carolina and the Civil War and post-Civil War period. This was not really your field and I am going to pursue this with some of the local universities. If you happen to know of any persons or institutions that might be able to throw some light on this field, I would appreciate getting your advice.

With all best wishes,
John Daniels

April 16, 1980

Dear Mr. Daniels,

Description:

J.W. Seigne, *Irish Bogs: Sport and Country Life in the Irish Free State*. N.Y. and London, 1928. 8vo. Illus, with 31 photos. Loosely laid in are two pamphlets, one from the Irish Sporting Estate Agency, offering to find accommodations for you, the other titled "Notes on Life and Sport in the Irish Free State." Also a signed letter from Seigne (long-hand) addressed to Connett. Green cloth. Fine condition.

I thought you would be heading north by now!

Sincerely,
Helen Hennessey

* * *

April 18, 1980

Dear Ms. Hennessey,

Enclosed is my check for J.W. Seigne, *Irish Bogs*. The mails take about a week for books to come down here.

Sincerely,
John H. Daniels

Dear Mr. Daniels,

Could you use a copy of Thomas Smith's *The Life of a Fox*, 1852?
I'm making plans to go to England in October, but I'm very
much afraid I won't be able to, as Mr. Hennessey objects to
being taken care of by what he calls strangers, but aren't really.
However, it doesn't hurt to dream.

Best regards,
Helen Hennessey

May 17, 1980

Dear Mrs. Hennessey,

One of the pleasures of getting home is to meld the books that came in during the winter with the books that are here. I'm pleased with the progress I've made over the past three years. It certainly is a learning experience.

I would be interested in having you price and describe the 1852 edition of Thomas Smith's *The Life of a Fox*. I have the 1843 first and two later editions—1896 and 1920.

You have been most patient about my delay in getting *Masters of Foxhounds* published. It is finally going to the binders after being held up for four weeks by the lady who did the index. I am hopeful that it will be in the mails by the end of June—or at least before cub-hunting begins. Quite a few more photographs have been added, and I believe that it is going to be a fine book. It is almost sold out.

One disappointment, however, is that Alexander Mackay-Smith, who wrote the original draft, has been very ill and cannot use his hands. We are therefore forced to print a facsimile of his autograph.

I hope that your plans to go to England in October work out. We are going to be in London for a few days at the end of October on our way to Denmark for a pheasant shoot.

I really appreciate your continuing efforts to find prices on the "unfound books at Mulberry." The inventory and appraisal have been a great success.

With all best wishes,
John H. Daniels

Dear Mr. Daniels,

Nice to hear from you and to learn of your pleasant trip home. I have a few items you may or may not have.

Thomas Smith, *The Life of a Fox Written by Himself*. London, 1852. 12mo. Five full pages of B&W plates. Half leather, dec. boards. Spine with five raised bands & gold tooling. 2nd ed. A very fine copy.

Colonel Marcellus Davis, *The Stranger, a Story of Foxhunting in the Southern Hills*. 1938. 8vo. DJ. First trade ed. Fine.

Your favorite friend, Snaffle (not to be confused with anyone except Charles Dunkeld), *Gun, Rifle, and Hound in the East and West*.

Would you be interested in an unusual book that I've never seen before titled *Every Horse Owner's Cyclopedia* by J.H. Walsh? The plates are of great thoroughbreds and trotters. Philadelpia, 1871. 8vo. Fine.

Eighty-nine in Saratoga today. I'm boxing it for November.

Best regards,
Helen Hennessey

Details for list B-80:

Anthony Trollope, *Hunting Sketches*. Chapman and Hall, London, 1865. 12mo. Red cloth, with title on cover in gold. First appeared in the *Pall Mall Gazette*. First edition. A nice tight copy with 32 pp of ads.

Do you have the following:
Gordon Grand, *A Horse for Christmas Morning and Other Stories*. North Carolina. Limited to 150 copies.

Another Anthony Trollope, *Hunting Sketches*. Published at the Sign of the Gosden Head, 1933. Small folio, 950 copies. Signed by Robert Ball.

June, 1980

Dear Mrs. Hennessey,

Thank you for your recent quotes on my list B-80.

I would like to get both Anthony Trollope *Hunting Sketches*, the London, 1865 first edition and the 1933 limited edition. My check is enclosed.

All best wishes,
John H. Daniels

P.S. I have the Gordon Grand *A Horse for Christmas Morning and Other Stories*. It's a lovely book and a fine collection. I have three of Grand's original Christmas books and am trying to find any others. (Ergo my listing on B-80.)

June 24, 1980

Dear Mr. Daniels,

May the 31st you wrote me about disposing of Louis Dupre's *Voyage to Athens and Constantinople.* Unfortunately, I phoned on the day you were not available for conversation. That was pure selfishness on my part, phoning like that. I didn't want to compose a letter.

The following has developed after talking to three print men in New York. These men handle material such as the Dupre, and they don't want to touch it because of the Arab situation. Also without your permission, I placed a price on it which was probably too high for them.

As I explained to you, in reference to the appraisal on Mulberry Library, I priced the value high due to replacement cost. And as you are a learned book man, I'm sure you realize that when you dispose of books, unfortunately, you cannot obtain their full value. However, this seems a fair price to me, if the plates are bright with no foxing. The book will bring more money abroad, either through an auction house or through a bookseller with the right clients. Early this month I phoned an English dealer who has a customer that may be interested, and yesterday I had a letter from him. He would like more information, essentially, price and condition (when I spoke to him on the phone I only mentioned that the book was available). What I need now is your permission to give him this information.

Should you decide to put it up for auction, I suggest Christie's or Phillips in London, and place a reserve on it.

Best regards,
Helen Hennessey

June 29, 1980

Dear Mrs. Hennessey,

Thank you so much for your most interesting and helpful letter about the possible disposal of Louis Dupre's *Vogage to Athens and Constantinople*. I realize that the appraised price you put on this book was as a replacement value and not necessarily what could be realized by making a sale. Time is on our side—at least as far as inflation and current effects of the recession are concerned—so there is a time gap which I believe will work to our advantage.

I think it would be best for the time being at least to withdraw your asking price on the book.

I have a hunch that eventually we might do better in finding the right buyer in Europe, but time will tell.

Thank you so much for your help and your interest.

Sincerely,
John Daniels

P.S. The two Trollope books arrived safely and are most attractive.

Dear Mr. Daniels,

It seems like a long time since we corresponded. I have found nothing exciting in the book field and I didn't want to bore you with the weather.

I bought a small library of gunning books recently and among them were a few horse books, one in an unusual fine binding, written by J.C. Curryer, MD, a native of your state:

> *Horse Sense, A Practical Treatise.* Minn., 1900. 8vo. Bound by Root and Son in half blue morocco, gilt top. First edition. Author is the founder of *Minnesota Horseman.* Fine.

And another book:

> T.F. Dale, *Foxhunting in the Shires.* London, 1903. 8vo. With 41 fine engravings & portraits. Finely bound by Riviere in full green morocco, Gilt top. Bookplate: Sir Jonathan Ed. Mound Backhouse.

I would be very interested to know what was your final decision in disposing of Louis Dupre's *Voyage to Athens.*

Christie's had a sale a couple of weeks ago, with fifteen deluxe Derrydale Press books that sold for $80,000 plus 10% premium.

Best regards,
Helen Hennessey

October 24, 1980

Dear Mrs. Hennessey,

It was good to hear from you again. I would like to get the book *Horse Sense* by J.C. Curryer, my fellow Minnesotan. My check is enclosed.

I have really just been sitting on the Louis Dupre book *Voyage to Athens*. It is really a beautiful and exceptional book, and I guess with the markets as they are, it is only going to appreciate with time.

The deluxe Derrydale sale at Christie's is amazing, but after the recent Meyer sale of paintings, nothing is surprising. I was interested in what one of the auctioneers said about "too much money chasing too few treasures."

We are going to make a quick two-week trip to England and Denmark starting on October 27th.

Sincerely,
John H. Daniels

Dear Mr. Daniels,

Welcome home, and in the same breath, a safe trip south.
If I don't behave myself, I will be grounded soon. I have, to
date, four citations for speeding. In N.Y. State you lose your
license after three tickets, but I made up a sad story.

I don't know what to advise you about the Louis Dupre. In my
old age I'm learning not to commit myself. If it were mine, I'd
use it for a tax break or send it to auction in Europe.

Best regards,
Helen Hennessey

November 19, 1980

Dear Mrs. Hennessey,

Thank you so much for your welcome home. Our trip to Denmark, via London, was marvelous. In London I had the time to look up some special sporting prints that I wanted for my new office.

I also spent part of an afternoon in Joe Allen's upstairs room at J.A. Allen* where I was really rather disappointed and only found four or five books that were of interest. Joe is still as active and garrulous as ever, but his "old book room" is a mess, and I suspect he doesn't know what is there and what is in his warehouse.

Your advice about the Dupre book is concise and good.

With all best wishes for the holidays,
John Daniels

[* "Joe" Allen is the owner and manager of J.A. Allen & Co.—The Horseman's Bookshop. It is widely known and patronized in England because J.A. Allen stocks "every title in print in Great Britain dealing in equine and equestrian activities, and also the leading books from abroad." J.A. Allen also carries a complete line of magazines and journals about equestrian sports. The bookshop has always been located at 1 Lower Grosvenor Place near Buckingham Palace. Joe is in his nineties but is still in charge and very active. On his own initiative he has had printed a large number of equestrian books that were out of print. Unknown to most of the walk-in trade, Joe has an upstairs room which is filled near to overflowing with hundreds of rare or scarce out-of-print sporting books. It's a wonderful place for the collector to spend a rainy day.]

Dear Mr. Daniels,

Enclosed is a description of Schwerdt's* book.

I forgot to ask you if you would like your list returned.
It's a very fine collection, as I said before, and I'm sure you
are proud of it.

I found *The Sporting Life of the Norwegian Fields,* 1878.
Does that thrill you?

Hurriedly,
Helen Hennessey

[* A complete description of C.F.G.R. Schwerdt's remarkable book appears
on page 72. Schwerdt was an insatiable sporting book collector who assembled the largest and most comprehensive collection that has ever been made.
With the help of his wife, he produced a masterpiece of a bibliography complete with superb full-page color reproductions of many of the rare books.
The first three volumes of his *Hunting, Hawking, Shooting* appeared in 1928
and the final volume followed in 1937. Schwerdt died at the beginning of
World War II (it is said of a broken heart because he was torn apart by his
German ancestry and his British citizenship). His entire collection was sold
at auction during the war years and was dispersed at prices which were greatly depressed by the wartime economy.]

January 19, 1981

Dear Mrs. Hennessey,

Two letters from you today. My cup runneth over!

First, in reply to your most interesting letter of January 13, I agree with you completely that the condition of a book is terribly important. And I haven't been paying close enough attention to this. Although I think that most of my books are in the category of "very good to fine," I want to spend some time this spring going over the books with *condition* in mind. I know that I will find some "clinkers" that should be upgraded.

Rather than take a broad swipe at all of the authors of fishing and hunting books that you listed, I would prefer to start with Haig-Brown because I like his work and have a feeling that his reputation is going to continue to go up.

I only have two of Haig-Brown's books right now. *Bright Waters, Bright Fish* and *Woods and River Tales*. Perhaps you could quote me on some of the other books by Haig-Brown.

I would like to buy the Henry Alken *A Panorama of the Progress of Human Life* with the text by Schwerdt. My check is enclosed.

Incidentally, I mailed you a new list of desiderata, A-81. In that list I included C.F.G.R. Schwerdt, *Hunting, Hawking, Shooting.* Since making out that list, I have looked at the Colonel's* List 80 L–Z and see that he has (or had) three to offer me at what seem to me to be outrageous prices. Do you think that I would have to go that high for a good to very fine set of the four volumes?

With all best wishes,
John Daniels

P.S. Please keep the list I sent you. It might help show you what I already have.

P.P.S. Please tell me more about *The Sporting Life of the Norwegian Fields*. Then I will know if it thrills me.

[* "The Colonel" was the nickname given to Colonel Henry Siegel, the owner of The Anglers and Shooters Bookshop, located in Goshen, Connecticut. Colonel Siegel mailed all of his customers two catalogues of rare sporting books each year. In the spring he would send out his A–K catalogue, and in the fall he would send out his L–Z catalogue, alphabetized by author. Each was filled with hundreds of attractive sporting books from his splendid inventory. In particular, the Colonel had developed a fine personal collection of outstanding fishing books, which he sold at a series of auctions in the early 1990s. Although his asking prices were generally on the high side of the market, his material was always of high quality and in great demand. Since his death his successors continue to send out his well-known catalogues.]

January 27, 1981

Dear Mr. Daniels,

I mailed Alken's *Panorama* off to you on Saturday.

My daughter and I went to N.J. and N.Y. on Friday, and I must say I'm speechless. My colleagues have delusions of grandeur. I could have come home and worn out three erasers changing prices. I saw a nice copy of Surtees *Horseman's Manual* for $3,000. That has an auction record of £220. I left it behind. The Colonel sets his prices on a guide that many dealers follow. I prefer to use my own mind.

Schwerdt sold to someone called Hay in 1979 for £920 or $2,208. I have a very fine set, but I enjoy knowing that I possess it. If you will give me some time, I'll try to find a set for you at a reasonable price.

I have a set of Haig-Brown's *Western Angler,* boxed, that I might part with. Cummins* has an unboxed set, not in the very best condition.

Description:

> L.A. Fries, *Sporting Life on the Norwegian Fields.* Woolwich, 1878. Translated from the Norwegian by W.G. Pock, with jottings on *Sport in Norway.* 375 pp, no illus other than map. Hard green cloth, gold lettering on spine. Fine cond.

It's a fine book if you're going to Norway someday. It's sort of a history, plus laws governing hunting and fishing. (Thrill you?) It leaves me cold, I'm not going to Norway. I've had a sample of cold weather here this past month.

Sorry I have nothing on your list, but I'll keep it on the desk and work on it.

Best regards,
Helen Hennessey

P.S. Do you need a book titled *Books from Chapel Hill?* A complete catalogue 1923–45, University of N.C. Press, 1946. Fine DJ.

[* James Cummins sold me more rare sporting books than anybody else. From the time I first met him in Brentano's rare book department until I finally stopped collecting books, Jim probably sold me 75% of my entire collection. He also taught me a great deal about sporting books and he represented me as my agent at all the important book auctions. I consider Jim Cummins as premier sporting book specialist.]

February 1, 1981

Dear Mrs. Hennessey,

Thank you for your letter of January 27th. I would appreciate it if you would be on the lookout for a set of Schwerdt "at a reasonable price." I think that I should have a copy in my collection and for reference work. (Incidentally, I have found that Higginson's *British and American Sporting Authors* is a most useful reference book even though Sydney Smith's *Bibliography* is full of errors.)

I would like to buy *Sporting Life on the Norwegian Fields* even though I share your feeling about cold, cold Norway. So I am enclosing a check.

Could you price your Haig-Brown *Western Angler* for me?

I, too, have just returned from New York. I didn't have time to do any book searching because the entire three days were taken up with meetings of the Masters of the Foxhounds Association. You will be pleased to know that the Board of the MFHA voted unanimously to raise the price on the few remaining unsold copies of *Masters of Foxhounds* from $40 to $50. The book has gone over very well and has had some good reviews.

With all best wishes,
Sincerely,
John Daniels

Dear Mr. Daniels,

I've been procrastinating, as I'm still a monument of indecision about *The Western Angler* (mine).

I have found one in nice condition, not boxed, for $550. However, the dealer won't hold it too long for me. Would you please phone me when you receive this letter?

Hurriedly,
Helen Hennessey

* * *

February 13, 1981

Dear Mrs. Hennessey,

Thank you for your help in locating a nice copy of Haig-Brown's *The Western Angler*.

I am enclosing my check, and will understand that it will take a couple of weeks for you to get it and to forward it on to me.

With all best regards,
Sincerely,
John H. Daniels

Dear Mr. Daniels,

I would be delighted to try to find you a Schwerdt. It may take
time. Two years ago you had trouble trying to sell a set, but it's
a different story today. Schwerdt has magnificent prints in color,
but it's not as easy to work with as Higginson. The word is
around that you are looking for it, so be patient, unless you
receive a reasonable quote.

Later . . . Nice to talk to you today—now you can have your
Western Angler and I can have mine, too.

Strange story about how I acquired my *Angler*. I bought it from
Isabell MacKenzie in Montreal, several years ago, who gave me
several hours of *tsouris* [Yiddish word for trouble]. I always felt
I earned the damn book. She is a strange woman who sometimes finds wonderful books in the very best condition. But she
really knows nothing about books. So, if you want to buy a
book, it must be extremely valuable or why would you want it,
then she doesn't know what to charge you for it. So every time
I look at the book, I think of my afternoon with Isabell, my
American dollar, which I got no credit for, plus the dealer's
discount. I hope I don't get stuck in the sticky wicket again.
End of saga. A book dealer by the name of John Hendsey is
going into the book auction field. He is having his first sale in
March. He tells me that he has some nice sporting books going.
I gave him your name and suggested he send you a catalogue.
It's to be held in Concord, N.H., and I will be going over.
If there is anything you'd like, let me know (price) and I will
bid for you.

Does a copy of Finch Mason's *Tit Bits of the Turf* interest you?

Best regards,
Helen Hennessey

Dear Mrs. Hennessey,

Many thanks for your letter about carrying on a search for
Schwerdt. I will be patient.

Thank you, too, for asking John Hendsey to send me his auction catalogue. When it comes, I'll go over it and let you know
if there are items of interest that you could help bid on for me.
I don't know Finch Mason's *Tit Bits of the Turf.* Please tell me
more about it.

All best,
John H. Daniels

February 25, 1981

Dear Mr. Daniels,

I received my catalogue from John Hendsey, and while I am a little disappointed in the material, I'll bid on a few items. Perhaps something else after I have time to study the catalogue more. Do you get a catalogue from Way? I had a friend, who has since died, who used to say that you could close up your business and open a year later and double the price of your books. After reading Way's catalogue, I'm beginning to believe her. Perhaps I should go to England for a year. I almost bought a house there last week. But my family had a fit.

I'm a little upset. I asked Hendsey a couple of weeks ago if he had a *Western Angler* and he told me no. Now I find it in his catalogue. I'll try to return your copy if you'd like me to.

Best regards,
Helen Hennessey

P.S. Description:

> Finch Mason, *Tit Bits of the Turf,* scattered about by Finch Mason and collected by Miss Fores. The Publishers, 41 Piccadilly, London, 1887. Obl folio 14 x 19½. 16 hand-colored plates, scarce colored copy. Original boards. Very good condition.

The reason I bought it was because I have the original watercolors of his. There are humorous drawings in the book, and you may prefer your horses serious. My cat is sitting in the middle of this letter, but because he is president of the firm, I can't very well move him.

March 4, 1981

Dear Mrs. Hennessey,

Here is an update to the A-81 want list. The University of South Carolina in Columbia has a comprehensive listing of Archibald Rutledge's works and I found some I didn't have.

I don't think I want the Finch Mason's *Tit Bits of the Turf,* but if you ever come across Mason's book *Heroes and Heroines of the Grand National,* please let me know.

Sorry John Hendsey was so disappointing.

All best wishes,
John Daniels

* * *

March 27, 1981

Dear Mr. Daniels,

Nothing important to write about from this end. I've had very little time for the book business as I have been doing a very complicated manuscript appraisal for the Adirondack Museum. Extremely tedious.

Now for books—any interest in:

W.C. Baldwin, *African Hunting.* 1863. 1st ed.
Alfred Ronald, *Fly-Fisher's Entomology.* 1849. 4th ed.
Paul Kendall, *Polo Ponies,* Derrydale.
Higginson, *An Old Sportsman's Memories*
Higginson & Chamberlain, *Hunting in United States and Canada..*
    Limited, signed.
Jean Delacour, *Waterfowl of the World.* 4 vols. illus. by Peter Scott. 1st ed.

Best regards,
Helen Hennessey

March 31, 1981

Dear Mrs. Hennessey,

Thank you for your recent letter (3/27/81). I would be interested in getting more information about your four-volume first edition of Jean Delacour's *Waterfowl of the World* (price, condition, no. of illus., etc.).

I'm still hopeful that you will succeed in finding me a reasonably priced edition of Schwerdt's four volumes. This and the Somerville and Ross first or second of *An Irish Cousin* are at the top of my want list.

I visited a strange rare book barn (literally a barn) in Newberry, S.C., yesterday and amidst the horrible news flashes of the attempted assassination of the President, I found some rare presentation copies of some of Archibald Rutledge's works.

Have you seen or read Frank Herrmann's new book, *Sotheby's: Portrait of an Auction House*? I finished reading it about a week ago and consider it a *must* for any collector.

Our great excitement down here is that Professor C. Vann Woodward's new book, *Mary Chesnut's Civil War*, is coming out in April, and Woodward is coming to Camden in mid-April to give a lecture and have a signing, and will be staying with us at Mulberry, which was Mary Boykin Chesnut's home. It promises to be the major literary event of the year.

I hope that your complicated manuscript appraisal has finally come to an end.

Best wishes,
John H. Daniels

p.s. Did you get anything at the Hendsey auction?

[Postcard]

> Joseph W. Brooks, Jr., edited by Connett, *A World of Fishing.*
> Princeton, N.J., 1964. Chapters on Ireland, Mexico, Africa, etc.
> 8vo. 375 pp. First edition. As new.

Regards,
HBH

* * *

April 4, 1981

Dear Mr. Daniels,

I didn't make a very big splash at Hendsey's auction. The man from Connecticut, who was at the December 11th sale that you and I attended, the one who bid $7,400 for Connett's *Magic Hours,* was there and that eliminated me quickly.

However, I bid and was successful on item eleven, Argent's *Tobacco,* a fine set in pristine condition. It was a nice holiday for me.

It must be fun to have such a large family. You ought to be able to get a good poker game together.

I haven't forgotten Schwerdt's, and I remember Somerville, too.

> Jean Delacour, *The Waterfowl of the World.* 4 vols, 4to. 66 colored plates
> by Peter Scott and numerous illus in B&W. 108 distribution maps. dec.
> cloth. Country Life, London, 1954-1964. Vol 2 lacks DJ. 1st eds, nearly
> new.

Are you interested in *The Sporting Magazine,* a monthly calendar, London, 1794? Six issues, bound under one cover.

Best regards,
Helen Hennessey

April 7, 1981

Dear Mrs. Hennessey,

Thank you for your card about Joseph Brooks and your letter of 4/4/81. Yes, I'd like to get:

> Joseph W. Brooks, Jr., *A World of Fishing*
> Jean Delacour, *The Waterfowl of the World.*

My check is enclosed.

Please tell me more about *The Sporting Magazine,* 1754. Is this the one that was later taken over by Apperley and Ackermann? Details, condition, etc.

Next excitement is when C. Vann Woodward and Betsy Muhlenfeld visit Mulberry on April fourteenth and fifteenth for the publication of Woodward's *Mary Chesnut's Civil War* and Muhlenfeld's *Biography of Mary Chesnut* (written up in the April 13th book section of *Newsweek,* etc.).

Best regards,
John H. Daniels

* * *

April 9, 1981

Dear Mr. Daniels,

I mailed you two packages today, *The Waterfowl* and *The World of Fishing.* Many thanks.

I included *The Sporting Magazine* for you to look at. If it is not your dish of tea, just send it back. You must be having a wonderful time at the Plantation. I'm envious.

Best regards,
Helen Hennessey

Dear Mrs. Hennessey,

The four Delacour books and the Brooks book on fishing arrived safely.

I am returning *The Sporting Magazine* bound volume to you by separate mail. According to Neville, *The Sporting Magazine* was published in three series, 1793 thru 1870, so that a fragment such as the one you sent would not be what I want.

All best wishes,
John H. Daniels

April 13, 1981

Dear Mr. Daniels,

I was looking over your fishing and hunting list that you sent me in January and then I looked over things on my shelf, and, if I haven't made a great mistake, here are a few books not on your shelves in January that might interest you.

John Phillips, *Wenham Great Pond.* Peabody Museum, Salem, 1938. Large 8vo. Slipcase as new. One of 100. Windsor White bookplate.

Frank Forester, *Trouting Along the Catasauqua.* Privately printed (at Derrydale) for Connett, for the Angler's Club, N.Y., 1927. Large 8vo. Limited to 423 copies, #46. Fine.

Philip B. Sharpe, *The Rifle in America.* N.Y., 1938. 4to. Imitation dark red leather. 3rd printing. Fine condition.

Col. Harold Sheldon, *Tranquility.* Derrydale, 1936. 8vo. Fair.

John Hightower, *Pheasant Hunting.* N.Y., 1946. 4to. In slipcase. 1st ed. Limited to 350 copies, #275. Fine condition.

Sir Herbert Maxwell, *Fishing at Home and Abroad.* London, 1913. Thick folio. 52 plain plus 7 colored plates. Full brown leather binding, gold lettering. Limited to 750 copies, #193. Bookplate of Olive Guthrie of Toropay. Fine condition.

Zane Grey, *Tales of the Angler's Colorado.* New Zealand. 4to. DJ. And *Tales of Fishing Virgin Seas.* 4to. Both firsts. Both fine.

You will be heading north soon. My brother returns on Wednesday. I think they expect to surprise me on my birthday. Little do they know.

Best regards,
Helen Hennessey

Dear Mrs. Hennessey,

Thank you for quoting me the books on fishing and shooting in your letter of April 13th. I have some of these and for the time being do not want or need the others.

Please keep me posted.

Sincerely,
John H. Daniels

* * *

May 16, 1981

Dear Mr. Daniels,

I sent off the four-volume set of Schwerdt yesterday, by United Parcel, to your home address, as they don't like delivery to box addresses because there is no one to sign for insured packages.

I think it's a superb set and I hope you will think so, too.

I hear the Col. sold his set last week at the New York Book Fair for $5,000.

Best regards,
Helen Hennessey

May 20, 1981

Dear Mrs. Hennessey,

The four-volume *Hunting, Hawking, Shooting* by Schwerdt arrived today, as I told you on the phone, and I am simply delighted with them. They are really the frosting on top the cake in my new office.

I'm enclosing some Polaroid shots. The four volumes of Schwerdt are in the bookcase directly behind my desk, where I can admire them. I enclose my check for the Schwerdt books. Our trip to Europe is nearing. We leave here for New York on the 10th and sail on the *QE2* on the 12th with two of our grandchildren.

Thank you for your great help in locating the Schwerdt.

With all best wishes,
Sincerely,
John H. Daniels

* * *

C.F.G.R. Schwerdt, *Hunting, Hawking, Shooting*. Privately printed for the author by Waterlow & Sons, Ltd., London. Large quartos. Illustrated in *A Catalogue of Books, Manuscripts, Prints, and Drawings Collected by C.F.G.R. Schwerdt*. Bound in 3/4 green morocco by Kelly and Sons, London. In four volumes, the first three published in 1928 and the fourth volume in 1937. Limited to 300 copies, of which this is #257 (and all plates have been destroyed). Together, a superb set.

A. Henry Higginson, in his book *British and American Sporting Authors,* quotes in turn Mr. Ernest R. Gee, not only a dealer in sporting books but a collector of note, who says, "The late C.F.G.R. Schwerdt's magnificent catalogue is undoubtedly the best bibliography of sporting books yet published."

Schwerdt was in his seventy-sixth year when he published Volume iv in 1937. He died in 1939, and his great collection of sporting books was auctioned off at Sotheby's in that season at a dreadfully low price because the war was raging. His dates would be b. 1861, d. 1939 (incorrectly stated by Higginson as circa 1872–circa 1945).

* * *

May 22, 1981

Dear Mr. Daniels,

I went down to the Buckley preview yesterday and I thought you might find the catalogue interesting.

There were miles of bookshelves, but not a book. I asked where they had gone, but either they didn't know or they didn't wish to tell me.

It seems a shame that they are going to turn it into condominium.

Best regards,
Helen Hennessey

May 29, 1981

Dear Mr. Daniels,

Thank you very much for your check for the Schwerdt. I feel lucky that it turned out to be such a nice set. I was told about it over the phone, and while I emphasized condition, no two people have the same interpretation of the word.

The pictures of the office are really charming, and it was very thoughtful of you to send them over. It looks like a super excellent place to sit and have great thoughts.

Best wishes to you and your family for a fun-filled holiday.

Best regards,
Helen Hennessey

May 30, 1981

Dear Helen Hennessey,

You were thoughtful to send me the catalogue of the auction at
Great Elm. Some day I'll find out what the Buckleys did with
their books. Maybe they divvied them up in a literary family.

When we get home in July, I want to spend some time on want
lists. I have a feeling that there are some holes in my Somerville
and Ross collection after going through Elizabeth Hudson's
Bibliography again. I also want to readdress myself to the shoot-
ing/fishing books.

In spite of a dreadful review in the Sunday *New York Times
Book Review*, C. Vann Woodward's *Mary Chesnut's Civil War*
has been very well received, and now *Mary Chesnut's Biography*
by Betsy Muhlenfeld has come out, L.S.U. Press, as a marvelous
companion piece.

Please stay in touch.

With all best wishes,
John Daniels

July 14, 1981

Dear Mr. Daniels,

Welcome home.

I think you told me you were going to stay a few days in Broadway. There used to be a wonderful bookshop there, so perhaps you found some treasures, and with the pound holding at $2.00 and below, if you had time you could find some bargains.

I found a nice copy of *Well Dressed Lines, Stripped from the Reels of Five New Englanders.* Privately printed by the Stinehour Press for the Angler's Club of New York, 1962. Limited to 500 copies.

The town is getting ready for August. Paint, paper, and flowers. The natives rent their homes so the houses are looking their best.

I bought a lot of inexpensive books, no fine bindings, but good, clean stock, modern material. I feel sad that it's so hard to find the fine old books.

Welcome again,
Helen Hennessey

Dear Mr. Daniels,

I'm enclosing a card with some sketchy information about the
Dodds book. It's a hard one to describe.

Have you any interest in Izaak Walton? I have the Nonesuch
Press *Complete Walton* and other limited fine editions, which I'd
be glad to describe.

Have you given up horses?

Hurriedly,
Helen Hennessey

July 30, 1981

Dear Mrs. Hennessey,

Thank you for your letter of July 24th. No, I don't think I want the Dodds book and am returning the descriptive card.

In answer to your question, "Have you any interest in Izaak Walton?" I guess I would say, "I'm terrified."

In front of me, as I write this, is a copy of Arnold Wood's *A Bibliography of "The Complete Angler" of Izaak Walton and Charles Cotton, Being a Chronologically Arranged List of the Several Editions and Reprints from the First Edition* MDMCLII *Until the Year* MCM. (Wood lists 110 editions through 1900.)

And I have the good Colonel from Connecticut's 1980 L–Z list in front of me, where he lists eighty-seven different editions (and some fairly horrible prices).

In other words, I guess I don't know what to do about Walton, as he seems to be a collection unto itself that is fairly open-ended. I notice that our friend Schwerdt copped out by having a "token" Walton—II, 289, 1882—that's not much help.

What would you advise?

All best regards,
John H. Daniels

Dear Mr. Daniels,

I want to thank you for a fine copy of *Sporting Classics Magazine*. I've almost completed reading it from cover to cover and thoroughly enjoyed all the articles. I shall certainly subscribe.

I am sorry I didn't make myself clear when I asked about your interest in horses. I meant horse books.

I think Walton should be represented in your extensive library. However, Walton is a collection unto itself and you can get bloody well lost. For reference, we use Horne and Oliver. Some Walton's have increased in value and others have not. But, the same thing applies to Walton as any other book—value is based on the number of copies printed. Limited editions are the most desirable, with the exception of some of the fine old editions. The first American edition, 1847, is very scarce. I have had only one and that had to be rebound.

I don't want to quote you any of the Waltons I have on hand. I feel self-conscious. But if you'd like me too, I could mention a few of the more important ones.

Best regards,
Helen Hennessey

August 11, 1981

Dear Mrs. Hennessey,

Thank you for your letter of August 7th. I'm glad you cleared up the horse business question. The answer is definitely "Yes," I am still interested in horse books. They are the basics of my collection.

The problem is that although the field is far from exhausted, it does get narrower once you have the important Beckfords, Apperleys, Grands, Higginsons, Surtees, etc.

This is why I am tentatively "branching out" into angling and shooting books. Both are gigantic fields, but I have a good start.

I would appreciate getting your advice on Izaak Walton, especially the few more important ones. I agree that I don't want to make a career of collecting Walton, but I should have a few good ones.

All best regards,
John Daniels

Dear Mrs. Hennessey,

Thank you so much for your letter of August 17 and the information about the Izaak Walton. I guess I'll get my feet wet in
a small way. I would like to buy the following editions that you
quoted me:

> Oliver 75—Second Nicholas Edition, 1860
> Oliver 92—First stock facsimile, 1876
> Oliver 268 (I think)—the 1929 Dr. Keynes's edition, limited to 1,100
>   copies, full rust-colored morocco
> Horne 314—The Heritage Press, 1938
> Oliver 19—Hawkins-2nd Bagster, 1815

I think that these five editions will at least provide me with a
representative set. My check is enclosed.

I was glad to hear that Babs Cocks and Louis Murdock had
stopped by. They are both good friends and we see them in
South Carolina in the winter months.

I'm off for England a week from today. Two days in London
and then a week in Northumberland where we will be grouse
shooting. It looks as though the air controllers' strike is under
control enough to make this trip on schedule.

I would hope that the Waltons will be waiting for me when I
get back.

With all best wishes,
John Daniels

P.S. The Colonel puts a very high price on the unusually fine
copy in your own library—the 1888 first Marston.

September 19, 1981

Dear Mr. Daniels,

I've been away on a short holiday and when I returned I found your want list. I'm sorry to say that I have nothing on the list, but I'll look for your titles when I'm off looking for stock.

I do have a book by Captain Mervyn Richardson, London, 1853, that might interest you, if you don't already have a copy. *Horsemanship or the Art of Riding and Managing a Horse*. A fine copy with five steel plates.

I also have Fred Shaw's *The Complete Science of Fly Fishing and Spinning*. London, 1920. 2nd edition, presentation copy. A fine copy of a rather important book. The part I enjoyed the most was the ten pages of advertisements.

The National Horse Carriage Association had a meeting in Saratoga this week and I have been conducting Cook's Tours in my old carriage house. Everyone was absolutely fascinated with all the old equipment around. I haven't been so popular in years!

Best regards,
Helen Hennessey

September 25, 1981

Dear Mrs. Hennessey,

Thank you for your recent (9/19) letter. I would like to buy both of the books you described.

> Capt. Mervyn Richardson, *Horsemanship.*
> Fred Shaw, *The Complete Science of Fly Fishing & Spinning.*

My check is enclosed.

All best regards,
John Daniels

      * * *

October 10, 1981

Dear Mr. Daniels,

Did you receive Sotheby's catalogue on sporting books, sale to be held the end of this month? I was rather disappointed over the condition. However, I think I will go down. Also, at the moment I'm planning on attending the Boston Book Fair. I'll take your list with me. Perhaps I'll find a treasure for you.

Have you any interest in Richard Salmon's *Trout Flies*?

Have a safe and pleasant trip south.

Best regards,
Helen Hennessey

P.S. Do you still need F.W. Millard's *Game & Foxes*? I think I know where there is one.

October 16, 1981

Dear Mrs. Hennessey,

I got a copy of the Sotheby's October 30th sporting book auction catalogue and I share your disappointment about the bad quality of the books being offered. Some of their price estimates are out of this world, too! The Michaux that they expect to get $2,000–$2,500 for I got last spring for $650!

I am not really interested in Richard Salmon's *Trout Flies* and have already got a copy of Millard's *Game & Foxes*.

I do wish you luck at the Boston Book Fair, and hope that you come across some of my desiderata while you are there.

With all best wishes,
John Daniels

* * *

Happy Birthday and Many, Many More

HBH

* * *

October 28, 1981

Dear Helen Hennessey,

Thank you so much for the beautiful print of a colt by SBH '81. Is that your daughter who did the work of art? It is charming!

Many many thanks for remembering me on my birthday.
(I claim that today is the 30th anniversary of my 30th birthday!)

Again—thank you so much . . .

Fondly,
John (Daniels)

Dear Mr. Daniels,

Have you any interest in *The American Farrier* or *N.Y. Horse Doctor?* Being a further improvement upon Adancourts's *Taplin Improved* (page 16 of Henderson's *Early American Sport,* Grolier Club, 1937). Troy, 1826. Small 8vo, old calf. 188 pp. Calls for 10 plates, but I can't find plate no. 2, so I assume it is missing. Some foxing.

I did not go to N.Y. for Sotheby's sporting book sale. I felt that the condition was too disappointing.

However, I'm off to Boston Friday. I've been offered the Duke of Newcastle's *General System of Horsemanship in All Its Branches* at a God-awful price. But at the moment I'm not tempted. He's bringing it to the fair.

Best regards,
Helen Hennessey

* * *

November 9, 1981

Dear Mr. Daniels,

I found one book at the Boston Book Fair that was on your list. David Randall's *Dukedom Large Enough,* 1969. First edition, as new, DJ. Later this week I'll send you a list of the books I purchased at the fair. Maybe there is something to strike your fancy.

Best regards,
Helen Hennessey

November 12, 1981

Dear Mrs. Hennessey,

This is in answer to your letters of November 4th and 9th.
Enclosed is my check for the two books you wrote about:
The American Farrier and *Dukedom Large Enough.*

I look forward to getting the list of books that you purchased at
the Boston Book Fair.

I am planning to go to New York next week for the Swann
Gallery sale of sporting books.

With all best regards,
John Daniels

* * *

November 16, 1981

Dear Mrs. Hennessey,

Many thanks for your letter and list on the Boston Book Fair.
I agree with you about the high prices for the British Sparrow.
I got my copy at a Swann Gallery auction for almost half the
price you mentioned.

From your list of hunting and fishing books etc., I would like to
get the following:

> Charles Grayson, *Sportsman's Horn Book.*
> Austin Haight, *Biography of a Sportsman.*
> Henry Mayhew & Cruikshank—1851 or . . .
> Alfred Prime, *The Arts and Crafts in Phila., MD., and S.C.*

My check is enclosed.

Had a marvelous week with a Mulberry cattle roundup.

All best regards,
John Daniels

November 19, 1981

Dear Mr. Daniels,

I'll send the books off today. Thank you very much for your
check and order.

I have a couple of treasures I'll write about after Thanksgiving.

I bid on items 66 and 126 in Swann's sale today. I hope you had
a great time and outbid the Colonel.

Best regards,
Helen Hennessey

November 23, 1981

Dear Mrs. Hennessey,

I had a great old time at the Swann Gallery sale last week. The quality of the books sold was very uneven and so I was glad to have had a chance to examine them the day before the sale.

I was able to buy some goodies, and in a few cases the Colonel, who was there in his loud, checked three-piece suit, may have been outbid. He was surprised, for example, when I bid on a couple of Izaak Waltons.

There were a couple of lots that went for surprisingly high figures. Lot 7 sold for $850 and Lot 176 for $450.

By and large, the Derrydale Books went for reasonably low prices except for Lot 176, which I have mentioned, and Lot 154 for $850, Lot 180 for $300, and Lot 181 for $375.

The two Lots you bid on went for (Lot 66) $175 and $150 (Lot 126). I don't know if you were the successful bidder.

I look forward to hearing from you after Thanksgiving about the "treasures" you mentioned in your letter.

With all best wishes,
Sincerely,
John Daniels

Dear Mr. Daniels,

Nice to have your letter. I enjoyed your description of our
Colonel.

Marguerite Kirmse always goes high, because they split her up.
I bid $225 on 66, and $200 on 126. I also got 249 for $125, which
has to go to the binders. I'm pleased with my efforts.

Did you bid on the Lea and Dove edition of Walton? It didn't
seem to be in the best condition.

I don't buy Derrydales the way I did years ago. I find that they
just move from one dealer to another and never find a home. As
a result, the price is redoubled over and over.

What I need is a machine that will spell for me—

Best regards,
Helen Hennessey

November 30, 1981

Dear Helen Hennessey,

I hope you survived Thanksgiving. I would love to get my hands on some bibliographies that I keep running into. I was able to buy the Peter Oliver *A New Chronicle of the Compleat Angler* at the Swann Gallery sale on November 19th.

Horne is the other authoritative book on Walton, I understand. How difficult is it to get Horne's book?

A couple of other bibliographies are:

> Joseph Sabin, *Directory of Books Relating to America*. Miniprint Corp., N.Y., 1961-1962.
> R.V. Tooley, *English Books with Colored Plates, 1790 to 1860*. Dawson, London, 1979. Revised edition.

Could you help me get a line on any of these?

Are there other good bibliographies that pertain to Sporting Books that I should be looking for? I have a number already, including Hudson's bibliography on Somerville & Ross; the Frank Forestor Bibliography, Higginson's *British and American Sporting Authors*, a number of Sparrow books, and, of course, the Schwerdt that you got for me.

All best regards,
John Daniels

December 11, 1981

Dear Mr. Daniels,

In *Sporting Classics Magazine* for September is a piece by
George Reiger on Decoys, page 31. He suggests some books and
I sent for four of the titles he mentioned. I don't know whether
you have any interest in this field. They are very fine books
printed on very fine paper, which is a joy in the book field
today. If you are interested, here is a list of the four:

> Henry Fleckenstein, *Shore Bird Decoys.*
> Henry Fleckenstein, *American Factory Decoys.*
> Wm. Mackey, *American Bird Decoys.*
> Shirley and John Delph, *New England Pond Decoys.*

I have a trade edition of Hugh Sheringham's *Book of the Fly
Rod,* fine. I have ordered from England a new book on Cecil
Aldin, *The Story of a Sporting Artist.* If you have any interest, I'll
try to get you one. I finally found Horne's first name is Bernard.
His book has also been reprinted in 1970. If you can give me
time, I can probably find one.

I just phoned the British Book Center and they informed me
that they had stopped importing in 1979. I had thought I might
find biographies on Apperley, Beckford, Edwards, and Mills.
I'm not defeated yet, though.

I think you have a very large and fine reference library. Do you
subscribe to *Antiquarian Book Monthly Review* from England?
If you don't, I think you might enjoy it.

Our letters seem to be crossing, perhaps this one won't.

Best regards,
Helen Hennesey

December 14, 1981

Dear Helen Hennessey,

Our letters *are* crossing in the mail. But I grabbed back the letter I wrote to you yesterday when I saw your letter of the 11th on the breakfast table and will now add to my original letter. *Sporting Classics* is an interesting new magazine. I was in on the beginning of it with John Culler, who is editor and publisher. At first, he had wanted to form a small corporation and I had told him that I would like to invest in it. Unfortunately—for me—he was unable to find other backers and so he decided to go it alone. In just a few short months he has done a fabulous job. I think he is well over halfway to his target of 100,000 subscribers and he is getting a lot of good advertisers. He lives here in Camden, S.C.

I will follow up on ordering some of the decoy books that are still in print. I have a lovely copy of Milton Weiler's *Classic Shorebird Decoys,* limited and signed.

Could you give me the address of *Antiquarian Book Monthly* and what a subscription costs? I'd like to get it.

I would also appreciate it if you could get me a copy of the book on Cecil Aldin, *The Story of a Sporting Artist.* I think I saw a copy of it for sale at J.A. Allen's bookstore in London, but was in such a rush at the time (looking at old books upstairs) that I didn't get a copy.

I'll be delighted to give you the time to locate a copy of Bernard Horne's 1970 reprint.

Thank you for sending me the old *Orvis* greeting card. I'd never seen one before.

I am enclosing my check for Sheringham's *Book of the Fly Rod.*

With all best wishes,
John Daniels

Dear Helen Hennessey,

I have learned about one bibliographical book that sounds interesting. It is by Stella Walker and is called *Lionel Edwards, Painter and Sportsman*. Do you know of it and could you help me locate it?

I was reading a Christmas book that my brother gave me, *American Stables* by Julius and Jacqueline Trousdale. On page 196 is a photograph and caption about your marvelous bookshop and office. I wonder if you have seen it?

Christmas still seems to be going on full pace here with children and grandchildren swarming around.

With all best wishes for 1982,
Sincerely,
John Daniels

January 7, 1982

Dear Mr. Daniels,

I knew about the Trousdale Sadler book *American Stables.* She is an old friend. They took the pictures a year ago and then when they had the coaching meeting in town this year, she brought a lot of people by to see the carriage house. I ordered the book in October, but as of now I haven't received it. I spoke to her on the phone last night and told her how pleased you were with the book.

Now I have everyone working on Stella Walker's *Lionel Edwards,* including the Library of Congress. When I find out where to order one, would you like me to get you one, too? Thank you for the extra check for the Besterman. Please let me know when you receive it. I was told that Rowman and Littlefield Publishers aren't very reliable.

By now you must have the Streeter. I hope it's a nice set.

Have you heard of an art gallery called The Artist Parlor at 341 Newberry, in Aiken, S.C.? Anything you can tell will be appreciated.

Best regards,
Helen Hennessey

Dear Helen Hennessey,

The Streeter collection books arrived and I'm delighted with them. They are most informative and, of course, my wife is very interested in the section about the Carolinas.

Yes, please keep up the search for Stella Walker's book about Lionel Edwards. I do have a copy of her book *Sporting Art England 1700–1900*—published by Clarkson N. Potter Inc., 1972, first edition—but if she did an entire book about Lionel Edwards I would love to get my hands on it.

I will keep my ears open about The Artist Parlor in Aiken, S.C. I don't know anything about it as of now.

With all best wishes,
Sincerely,
John H. Daniels

January 16, 1982

Dear Mr. Daniels,

With Streeter, Sabin and *U.S. Iana* on your shelves you have the tools of a real bookman. You will be a very fussy collector—

I think I missed my calling. I think I might have made a good detective. Stella Walker's book on Lionel Edwards isn't being published by Potter, who as you know did her other books. It seems to be a mystery who is or has published it. It's not in American or British Books in Print for 1982. Do you suppose your friend Allen in London has it on the fire?

Do you have a set of Appleton's *Cyclopaedia of American Biography,* edited by Wilson and Fiske. You might want that if you don't have it already.

Are you interested in the catalogue of Robert Hoe's auction, 1911? Also, I have William Orcutt's *In Quest of the Perfect Book,* limited, signed, 1926. And Smith and Benger's *The Oldest London Book Shop*, 1928.

I have a nice *Brookfield Stud of Old English Breeds of Horses,* by Burdett-Coutts MP. London, 1891. Published for the Brookfield Stud, Highgate Rd., N.W. Shenley Herts. Folio, limp gray hard finish cloth. Seven colored lith. plates plus B&W.

Hurriedly,
Helen Hennessey

* * *

January 19, 1982

Dear Mr. Daniels,

I put Cecil Aldin in the mail today. I enjoyed it very much, of course, he is one of my favorite artists. No artist can put an expression on a dog's face the way he did.

Best regards,
Helen Hennessey

Dear Helen Hennessey,

With many thanks to your help I seem to be getting all of the tools to be a real bookman.

The Streeter collection arrived, as I already wrote you, and is excellent. Horne's *Compleat Angler* is also here, and since I picked up Peter Oliver's *Compleat Angler* at the Swann Gallery sale in early December and had picked up Arnold Wood's *Bibliography of the Compleat Angler* at a Swann Gallery sale a year earlier, I seem to have more than enough about Walton and Cotton.

Sabin has arrived from Readex Microprint and I am waiting to get delivery of a Universal Micro Viewer to start work on that.

Tooley is on order from Dawson Book Service in Kent, England. (The Shoe String Press referred me to him because they are indefinitely out of stock.)

R.R. Bowker has my check for Howes Wright's *U.S. Iana* and I should be getting that fairly soon. You have placed an order for me for Theodore Besterman's *World Bibliography of Bibliographies*.

I have recently located and acquired a copy of the 1945 Parke Bernet Catalogue, *Five Centuries of Sport*—the Alfred B. Maclay collection.

When you put all of these alongside the Schwerdt and the other bibliographies about sporting books that I listed in early December, I think that I have just about all the reference books I need. (Now I have to get busy and get better acquainted with them and how to make use of them.)

My wife has Wilson and Fiske's *Cyclopaedia of American Biography*, which she has been using on other projects.

I am enclosing my check. This is for the Cecil Aldin book and for the *Brookfield Stud of Old English Breeds of Horses* by Burdett-Coutts, MP, that you wrote about at the end of your letter 1/16/82.

Thank you for your note about the Swann sale 1246. I had already picked on Lot 390 from the same catalogue, so will now try for Lot 51 as well.

Tell me more about Robert Hoe's auction, 1911 and Smith & Benger's *The Oldest London Bookshop*, 1928. (I have the Wm. Orcutt.)

I'm running out of space.

All best regards,
John Daniels

* * *

February 1, 1982

Dear Mr. Daniels,

I xeroxed the Hoe catalogue because I thought it might be clearer than if I tried to describe it—two volumes in one, black cloth, in fine condition.

> George Smith & Frank Benger, *The Oldest London Bookshop*. London, 1928. Folio, 12 plates. This is the story of John Brindley, who started a bookshop on old Bond Street in 1728 and it remained in the family until 1928. It tells of some of the books he published and the rare items that passed through his hands.

If you should be so lucky again to have Maclay's catalogue, *Five Centuries of Sport*, offered to you, would you purchase it for me?

Quote from Jerry Melton: "Locked within the heart of every bibliomaniac is the dream of discovery."

Best regards,
Helen Hennessey

Dear Helen Hennessey,

Thank you for your prompt reply of February 1st to my inquiry about the Hoe catalogue and Smith & Benger's book, *The Oldest London Bookshop.*

I think that the Hoe is a bit too far out of my field, but I would love to get the Smith & Benger book and am enclosing my check.

I located my Maclay catalogue, *Five Centuries of Sport,* from a bookseller I met at the Swann Gallery auction last December. His name is Edward Johnson, Telly Hill Books, 3004 North Calvert Street, Baltimore, MD. 21218. He is relatively new in the bookselling world, but has some nice things. He specializes in sporting books.

I have a hunch that he may have more copies of the Maclay catalogue up his sleeve. It's worth a try.

All best wishes,
John Daniels

February 8, 1982

Dear Mr. Daniels,

I just had a conversation with Biblio Distribution Center, who I ordered Besterman from on December 28th. For some unknown reason, I felt that they hadn't posted you the books yet, and I was right. After three phone calls and my blood pressure going through the roof, I found out they sent them out February 5th by UPS. So with any luck you must have them now.

Best regards,
Helen Hennessey

P.S. They had our money to play with since December 30th.

* * *

February 10, 1982

[Postcard]

Thank you for Mr. Johnson's address. I phoned him, but he didn't have another *Five Centuries of Sport*. (Don't you think that's a fine catalogue?) However, I found a bound copy. I'm going to corner the market on those catalogues.

HBH

February 15, 1982

Dear Helen Hennessey,

Thank you for your notes. Yes, the Besterman finally arrived. I'm sorry that they put you to so much trouble. I'm glad to have it (spent some time yesterday afternoon browsing through it).

Richard Hooper in Oregon called me about some other books last week, and when he said he had a copy of the Maclay catalogue I suggested that he get in touch with you.

The Swann Gallery sale 1246 worked out well for me. I was able to get both Lots #51 and #390. Mrs. Daniels was delighted! The prices were quite reasonable.

Best regards,
John Daniels

February 26, 1982

Dear Mr. Daniels,

I'm glad you finally received Besterman and that you are enjoying it. Mr. Hooper is sending me a bound copy of Maclay's *Five Centuries of Sport,* 1945. I hope that's the one you found, because there are two of them, another in 1956, which is not too important. I'm trying for a curb on the market of Maclays. I don't know what to quote you that would excite you. I've forgotten most of the titles I've quoted, and I don't know whether it's horses or fishing now.

I've been selling a lot of Paul Brown lately, mostly prints. I have a nice copy of Hon. Grantly Berkeley, *The English Sportsman in the Western Prairies.* London, 1861. Morocco with decorated boards. First, in fine. (Now's your chance.) Howes B374, Phillips, page 42.

Sherri, our daughter, is having a show in Aiken. I thought you might enjoy her invitation.

Best regards,
Helen Hennessey

Dear Helen Hennessey,

Thank you for the announcement of your daughter's show of watercolors and etchings at Aiken in April. I'm sorry that we will miss the Aiken show, especially because it coincides, as you know, with a centennial polo tournament in Aiken.

Thank you for your offer of the Grantly Berkeley, but I got a good copy at the Hendsey auction last March. Whatever happened to Hendsey? He seemed to be getting off to such a good start with interesting catalogues and good books, and he seems to have disappeared from sight.

One book that I'm looking for is an Apperley, *The Horse and the Hound*, Nimrod Press, Edinburgh, 1842. If you hear of it please let me know.

I'm glad you were able to get the 1945 Maclay from Hooper. I find it very useful, especially since I've been dickering for a couple of items that were in the sale.

I am going to hold off on a new want list until late spring. In the meantime, please keep me posted on any goodies, especially on horses, that you might come across.

All best regards,
Sincerely,
John Daniels

March 27, 1982

Dear Mr. Daniels,

I finally pulled myself up by my bootstraps and sent a catalogue off to the printers. Now that's behind me, I think I will go down to the New York Book Fair. I am very disappointed in the number of dealers that are showing this year, probably due to the country's finances.

I was going to Aiken for Sherri's show, but I've decided at this moment not to go. However, it is still open.

Have a safe trip north.

Best regards,
Helen Hennessey

* * *

March 30, 1982

Dear Helen Hennessey,

I look forward to getting your new catalogue.

If you decide to go to Aiken for Sherri's show, we would love to see you here if we haven't left for Minnesota by then.

Good luck at the N.Y. Book Fair.

All best regards,
John Daniels

Dear Mr. Daniels,

Do you need a copy of Daniel's *Rural Sport 1801–02 to 1813*, Maclay's catalogue item 182. I also have, in fine binding, G.E.M. Skues's *The Way of the Trout*, 1928, second edition, and companion volume, Minor, *Tactics of the Chalk Stream*, 1914.

The book fair didn't excite me. No sporting books and a great many dealers didn't participate.

Best regards,
Helen Hennessey

* * *

April 4, 1982

Dear Helen Hennessey,

Many thanks for your letter of March 31st. I already have Daniel's *Rural Sport*, but I would like to buy the two books by Skues. My check is enclosed.

All best,
John Daniels

May 15, 1982

Dear Mr. Daniels,

Nice to hear from you with your want list. I hope you had a pleasant trip north. The country around here is suddenly beautiful. Maybe it is because the winter seemed so long and unpleasant.

Sherri had a wonderful time in Aiken, lots of parties, and she thought the city was beautiful. Sorry I couldn't make it myself. The polo boys have started to open their houses here and next week Fasig-Tipton is having a sale of thoroughbreds, the first this early in the season.

As to your list, I can quote you F.G. Griswold, *The Gourmet.* Dutton, N.Y., 1933. 8vo. Signed, limited to 200 copies. Gray boards, vellum back strips. As new.

F.G. Griswold, *French Wines and Havana Cigars.* 1929. Limited to 300 copies, signed. Companion volume to above. As new.

One you didn't ask for, but bound the same, *Old Madeiras,* Dutton, 1929. Signed, limited to 200 copies. As new.

Nice to hear from you.

HBH

P.S. Nice that you had your trip on the *QE2* last year.

June 5, 1982

Dear Mr. Daniels,

Between the weather and lack of business and the hungry bugs,
I have very little of interest to write about. With Brentano's and
Braniff folding, I have nothing to complain about. However,
I am cleaning my muskets in preparation to help the British
in Argentina.

I bought a small library of one hundred sporting books—
horses, bullfighting, and cockfighting. Does George Scott's
limited *History of Cockfighting* thrill you, or John Masefield and
Edward Seago's *The Country Scene*? *Animal Portraiture* by R.
Lydekker?

I've been flying lately in a small plane that one of my colleagues
owns. It's so noisy that we can't even argue over the price of
books.

However, we enjoy each other.

Best regards,
Helen Hennessey

June 8, 1982

Dear Helen Hennessey,

Good to hear from you, but it sounds as though you have the early summer blahs. I'll join you with the British in the Falklands although I hope they have it all wrapped up by the time you get this letter. (Was glad to hear the *QE2* got out of there safely.)

I haven't entered bullfighting or cockfighting yet. How much is the Masefield book with Seago's illustrations? I see from my little Masefield bibliography that there was a "regular" edition of 2,250 copies and fifty copies signed by himself and the artist.

Be careful in those little planes—especially if they only have one motor. (I had my quota of close ones in that kind about twenty-five years ago.)

All best regards,
John Daniels

Dear Mr. Daniels,

Your descriptive phrase "summer blahs" is absolutely correct and today is doing nothing for my disposition. Don't put your musket away yet, the Argentines are an obstinate and determined race of people.

> John Masefield, *The Country Scene.* Published by Collins, Pall Mall, London, 1937. 4to. With 42 colored plates by Edward Seago. Original cloth in DJ, uncut paper, TEG. In fine condition

I think it's nice that you and Mrs. Daniels are book collectors, even if your fields cross. Before Mr. Hennessey became ill, we thoroughly enjoyed ourselves. His field was literature and he had a wonderful brain and memory. I have a Winnie-the-Pooh brain.

Yes, the plane has only one motor, but I'm a fatalist. Many years ago, I used to fly in a Piper Cub with no doors on it. This young man's plane is a Cadillac compared to the old Cub.

Best regards,
Helen Hennessey

* * *

July 12, 1982

Dear Mr. Daniels,

Do you happen to have a spare copy of Henry Davis's *Wild Turkey Shooting*? If you do, would you sell it to me?

It's quite busy in Saratoga. I'm having the trim on the house painted. Plus summer company. Business is very slow, so I'm doing things I postponed for a long time.

Hurriedly,
Helen Hennessey

[No Date]

Dear Helen Hennessey,

I'm sorry, I don't even have a single copy of Henry Davis's *Wild Turkey Shooting.*

My "Wild Turkey Book" inventory consists of:

> * James F. Brady, *Modern Turkey Hunting.* Crown, N.Y., 1973.
> Tom Turpin, *Hunting the Wild Turkey* (first reprint with intro. by Roger Latham). Penn's Woods Call Co., Delmont, PA., 1966.
> John M. McDaniel, *The Turkey Hunter's Book.* Amwell Press, Clinton, N.J., 1980.
> J. Wayne Fears (editor), *The Wild Turkey Book, An Anthology*, Amwell Press, Clinton, N.J., 1981.

> *Brady's book has a Bibliography that includes:
> H.E. Davis, *The American Wild Turkey.* Small Arms Technical Publishing Co., 1949.

Doing a lot of work on a catalogue of my collection,
starting with the oldest books where I'm still bogged down.

All best,
John Daniels

July 29, 1982

Dear Mrs. Hennessey,

I really think it takes a knowledge of the occult to come up with any kind of a guess as to what some of the books will go for at the F. Ambrose Clark auction on August 11th. I have listed the following five lots as ones that interest me, and put a top price on them that does not include the Christie ten percent commission that I would pay now.

Lot 801	Alken	$250
Lot 819	Blew	$300
Lot 847	Fairfax	$280
Lot 874	Mills	$300
Lot 894	Sidney	$300

I decided not to bid on Lot 907 or 914. I probably will strike out, but it's worth a try.

I will leave it completely up to you as to judging the condition of the books. If any of them appear to be in poor condition, I'm sure you will rule them out.

I get back from the U. of Denver Seminar on Friday, August 13th, and will either call you from Denver before I get home or call you after the thirteenth.

I really appreciate your help, and wish you luck.

With best wishes,
Sincerely,
John H. Daniels

P.S. I have the Henry Custance book *Riding Recollections and Turf Stories* (which I purchased from Joe Allen in London in 1979) and enclose a copy of the title page & frontis., as well as an interesting account of Custance by Higginson.

July 30, 1982

Dear Mr. Daniels,

Nice to talk to you yesterday. However, I am afraid we are going to be working against each other. We both have the same interests.

I find it unusual that Christie's hasn't advertised the books and also that they've put such low estimates on almost everything, but especially the books. But Mr. Clark didn't collect first editions, so perhaps that controlled Christie's value. Again, the leather bindings are probably dry and may not stand up through the preview.

I have all the books in 894. 874 should go lower than the estimate, and I'll try for you. I have most of 847 and most of 819. *American Turf Register* has a high auction record and I'll go high on that and 877, and on 900, if the condition is all right. I may have a ball and again I may come home empty-handed.

Good luck to us both,
Helen Hennessey

Dear Mrs. Hennessey,

I was delighted to hear that you had been able to buy in Lot 874 for me at the Christie's sale at Iroquois Mansion. The horror stories that you had to tell about the sale itself are really incredible. What is this world coming to?

I am enclosing my check, which is for the hammer price of Lot 874, buyer's premium, and your commission. I have not included anything yet for sales tax and shipping and handling, so please bill me for those items.

I look forward to seeing the Mills books, which from your description sound most attractive.

The week-long seminar in Denver was extremely worthwhile. It will take me a while to digest it all, but really the most important thing is that I realize after it is all over that I'm not as much of a dummy as I could be in this collecting world. I'm going to be in England for about ten days (August 25th to September 4th), mainly grouse shooting, but also some time allotted to books in London.

If I'm not in the doghouse from too much traveling, I hope to get to New York for the Swann sale of sporting books on September 23rd. George Lowry, who was one of our "profs" at D.U. says that there are a *lot* of Derrydales in the sale, and some other good stuff. I look forward to seeing the catalogue.

Thank you so much for your help in Cooperstown. I hope to see you in N.Y. in September.

Sincerely,
John H. Daniels

September 28, 1982

Dear Mr. Daniels,

Thank you for your check. I'm glad you are not upset that I didn't bid on the fore-edge angling painting, but I felt that it would add nothing to your fine library. I've been offered a fore-edge in Gosden binding with a painting of anglers, but they want $500. With patience, we will find something less expensive.

Would you be interested in three bound copies of *Forest and Stream, Rod and Gun, The American Sportsman's Journal*? Weekly, for the full year of 1879, 1895, and half year for 1878. They are in fine condition, even for their age, and it will take you a year to read one.

I also have a bound copy of Porter's *Spirit of the Times, a Chronicle of the Turf,* March 1858 to August 1858, bound in buckram, a duplicate from Yale Library.

Good hunting—I had a black lab once.

Best regards,
Helen Hennessey

* * *

October 15, 1982

Dear Helen Hennessey,

I don't think I will buy either the *Forest and Stream* or *Spirit of the Times,* but thank you very much for bringing them to my attention.

I got the Swann prices for the Derrydales and they certainly were on the high side in my opinion.

All best,
John Daniels

Dear Helen Hennessey,

Many thanks for bidding for me at the Swann sale yesterday. I was particularly glad that you did not bid in the fore-edge painting (Lot 14) because it sounds terrible.

I was glad that you were able to buy the Chifney and the Markham and especially glad that you were able to get the Markham for such a low price.

If you come across any good fore-edge books with sporting scenes, please let me know. So far I have collected four nice ones that include John Gilpin's *Ride*—a fox hunt in full cry with one rider thrown from his horse, a coach and four rattling down a country road, and some partridge shooters. I have averaged a bit under $300 per fore-edge book so far.

Best regards and many thanks,
Sincerely,
John H. Daniels

* * *

I was fascinated that Lowry knew I was bidding for you.

I'm not sure he knew what items tho'.

Many thanks,
HBH

September 27, 1982

Dear Helen Hennessey,

My guess is that George Lowry knew that you had bid for me at the Cooperstown sale and put two & two together. My check is enclosed.

All best regards,
John H. Daniels

* * *

November 19, 1982

Dear Mr. Daniels,

For a month now, I have been busy with a large appraisal. At last it's finished.

Did you get John Hendsey's auction catalogue? I am going down to the sale, more as a holiday than anything else. I have a large stock of hunting and fishing books so I don't need anymore, but he did have a few horse books.

You and your family have a nice Thanksgiving.

Best regards,
Helen Hennessey

Dear Mr. Daniels,

It seems a long time since I have heard from you. I hope that nothing uneventful has kept you from your typewriter.

I went to John Hendsey's sale last Saturday. There were more transactions in the parking lot than in the auction room. I bought a few items, but nothing unusual.

I saw the Col., who was charming. Also, Judith Bowman and Don Frazier, so it was sort of a social event.

I found a book a couple of months ago and I thought of you, as I found it a good reference book. It's Roger Longrigg's *The History of Horse Racing,* with a foreword by Paul Mellon. Macmillan, London, 1972. Folio. DJ. As new.

Best regards,
Helen Hennessey

December 17, 1982

Dear Helen Hennessey,

I have been "out-of-touch" for the last five weeks on a simply fabulous trip to South America. Starting in Lima, with a side trip to Machu Picchu, the main thrust of the trip was a three-week voyage of 4,550 miles on the *MS World Discoverer* which started in Iquitos, Peru, and went 2,300 miles down the Amazon River to the river's mouth, and then on down to Rio de Janeiro with stops on the way.

I'm really out of touch with the book market. Do you know what the Schwerdt *Hunting, Hawking, & Shooting* sold for at the Phillips auction on December 15th?

All best holiday greetings,
Sincerely,
John H. Daniels

P.S. The John Hendsey auction came and went during our absence and I only knew about it after we got home last Tuesday.

Dear Mr. Daniels,

I was very glad to hear from you, because in my childish way I was concerned perhaps I'd done something wrong—you must have had a fabulous trip. Now I'll have to interest you in some South American material.

I'm so mad at myself—I did not go to the Phillips sale because I thought everything would go very high. Instead, no interest was shown on the horse books.

Schwerdt	$3,000
Roland Clark	$4,500
William Robertson	$20
Somerville and Ross	$250
Williams	$1,100

That's all of the figures I have. But everyone tells me I should have been there—

Have a nice holiday,
Best regards,
Helen Hennessey

* * *

December 27, 1982

Dear Helen Hennessey,

Thank you for your letter of recent date, which arrived here in Camden today. I'm so glad we have reestablished communications. (I should have sent you a postcard from the Amazon.)

The news of the bargains at the Phillips sale is most interesting. The prices, especially the Schwerdt, are mighty low.

With all best wishes and holiday greetings,
John H. Daniels

January 21, 1983

Dear Mr. Daniels,

I was reading *Sporting Classics* at breakfast and I thought what fun can be had in S.C., all the sporting places to visit, not too many bookstores, but lots of print, gun, decoy shops to visit.

We are in a cold wave here, 15° below this morning.

I have a nice book on and about Peter Scott, titled *Peter Scott, Observations of Wildlife*, foreword by the Duke of Edinburgh. Printed at the Phæton Press in England, 1980. DJ, folio. As new. Also:

> *The Modern Traveler, a popular description, geographical, and historical and topographical of various countries of the globe, Brazil and Buenos Aires.* London, 1825. 12mo. Two volumes, folding map plates, contemporary calf, rebacked. Sabin 49816. (Picture of Brazilian hunters is worth the whole book.)

> *Exploration of the Valley of the Amazon,* made by the Navy Dept., Wm. Lewis's Herndon and Pardner Gibbon, Wash., 1853. Three volumes, foxed maps plus plates, lg, eight volumes.

Best regards,
Helen Hennessey

Dear Mr. Daniels,

If no unforeseen drama occurs, I expect to go to England the first of May.

I saw a Somerville and Ross item in an English catalogue and I thought of you. *Happy Days,* a first edition with an A.L.S. Of course, I have no idea if it's still available.

Have you any interest in *Muybridge: Man in Motion,* by Robert Hass? University of California, 1976. Small folio, DJ. As new.

Best regards,
Helen Hennessey

P.S. Did you find all of the Will James books?

March 7, 1983

Dear Helen Hennessey,

It was good to hear from you. Your trip to England in May
should be in a lovely time of year. Warmed with spring
but not overheated with tourists. If you see any A.L.S. of Edith
Somerville's, I would be interested. I have all of their first editions except for the rare first of *An Irish Cousin,* which has been
eluding me for a decade.

I was able to locate a first and a first American of *Black Beauty.*
For some reason, the Will James first editions have been very
slow in turning up. As I understand it from various conversa-
tions, they are not particularly rare or expensive, but they haven't
been knocking down my door. Of at least twelve books that
Will James wrote, I only have four of his first editions. I think
that searching for them by title may be more successful. I'll try
that next.

I don't know a thing about *Muybridge: Man in Motion* by
Robert Hass, but my curiosity is piqued and I am enclosing
my check.

Best wishes,
John Daniels

March 11, 1983

Dear Mr. Daniels,

Muybridge is famous for his animals in motion. There is some
horse material in this book. I ordered a half dozen and only
have one left. That's the reason I mentioned it to you.

In an English catalogue I saw a Somerville and Ross titled
Happy Days: Essays of Sorts. 1946, first, with a one-page A.L.S.
If you are interested, I'll find out. I think it is £30.

I'm reading a book that I know you would like if you don't have
it. O.F. Snelling's *Rare Books and Rarer People.* He worked for
Hodgson's Auction Rooms in London from 1949 for almost
thirty years. It's a very entertaining book. (I've been there.)
I have ordered some copies for stock. Let me know if you'd
like one.

Also give me a couple of Will James's titles that you are hunting. I just don't want to stock him.

Best regards,
Helen Hennessey

March 18, 1983

Dear Mr. Daniels,

What was the name of that five vol. set of books that cost you around $500? I've forgotten the title, but it should tell you if a bibliography of Will James was written.

I'll put Snelling's book in the mail for you.

I called England this morning and the Somerville was sold. If you wanted me to, I could look for a Somerville A.L.S. while I'm over there, if you would give me a suggested figure to pay.

I'm going to a sporting book auction a week from Sunday. Ninety-seven Derrydales and a couple hundred other sporting books. One item caught my eye: La Guernière's *École de Cavalerie Connoissance, L'Instruction,* a first, with nice plates. The auctioneer expects to get $1,250. However, I won't go that high. I just bought two Derrydale Voss hunting prints, which are very nice and hard to come by.

I phoned a couple of dealers in sporting prints and they had no Will James prints. But I should think there would be loads of them around. He loved to draw.

Hope you enjoy the Snelling. I did—I sent you my copy. It will be months before I get the others.

Best regards,
Helen Hennessey

March 30, 1983

Dear Mr. Daniels,

Have you any interest in the Rt. Hon. Lord Woolavington's
Sporting Pictures at Lavington Park, plus the Supplementary
Catalogue of his Sporting Pictures? 1927. Two volumes in full
gilt, lettered vellum, 4to. All illustrated by sporting artists in
B&W. Privately printed. While it doesn't say limited, I feel cer-
tain it was. Fine copies.

Also, do you have Wm. Woodward's *Cherished Portraits of
Thoroughbred Horses?*—and Rives's *The Coaching Club?*

Have a happy Easter.

Best regards,
Helen Hennessey

        * * *

April 4, 1983

Dear Helen Hennessey,

I am enclosing my check for the two volumes of Rt. Hon. Lord
Woolavington's books. They sound very attractive.

I do have Woodward's *Cherished Portraits*—a presentation copy.
And I have Rives's *The Coaching Club.*

Spring is finally here.

All best wishes,
John Daniels

April 4, 1983

Dear Mr. Daniels,

I'm a monument of indecision about the Swann sale, because last Sunday I went to a sale in MA. that had sixty-four Derrydales that Swann has going, plus dozens of other books that are in his sale. So it would be like sitting through the same thing over again. However, when the moment comes, I'll probably be there—*Magic Hours* went for $5,100—still not worth that price.

I just got a copy of *Who's Who of American Women* and found my name listed—they left me out for a couple of years and now I'm back. They must have had an empty space.

Best regards,
Helen Hennessey

* * *

April 20, 1983

Dear Mr. Daniels,

Have you any interest in obtaining any of the prints from William Woodward's *Cherished Portraits*? The prints were done by the Derrydale Press, measuring 26 x 20 inches, on heavy handmade paper. Some of them are proofs before printing and unsigned, B&W. I have probably five in color (not a complete set). I've never been able to find out how many of the horses in the book were printed.

Do you have a set of Alexander Pope's *Upland Game Birds*?

Best regards,
HBH

Dear Helen Hennessey,

Thank you for your letter of April 20th about the prints from *Cherished Portraits* and the Pope *Upland Game Birds*. I have a nice copy of the Woodward book and I don't think I'll get the extra prints.

I'd be interested in getting a description and price of Pope's *Upland Game Birds*. (I don't know it.)

I do hope that your trip to England in May is pleasant and worthwhile. Be sure to let me know what goodies you find.

All best regards,
John H. Daniels

May 15, 1983

Dear Mr. Daniels,

I returned from England yesterday, literally mildewed—buying books over there isn't the treat it used to be. I found two Somerville and Ross's *An Irish Cousin*, 1903, one volume and J.K. Stanford's *And Some in Horses*.

You will find the Pope I mentioned in Whitman Bennett's *American Nineteenth Century Color Plate Books*, p. 90.

> Alexander Pope Jr., *Upland Game Birds and Waterfowl of United States*. Charles Scribner, 1877. Oblong folio 22 x 27. Twenty chromo lithographs. Bright and in fine condition, except for edges of mats chipped. Plate 15, "The Upland Plover," foxed. A brief account of each species by Ingersoll. Folio in poor condition. Apart from the slight defects mentioned, a fine copy of a scarce work. Last sold at auction at Am. Book Prices. Current for 1979–1980.

I have one item of Walton's coming that I had never seen before. I'll quote you when the books come in from England.

Best regards,
Helen Hennessey

May 27, 1983

Dear Helen Hennessey,

I'm so glad that you got home safely from your trip to England.
From what I have heard, they have been suffering from endless
rains over there for the last six weeks!

Please be sure to quote me on the Somerville and Ross *An Irish
Cousin*, 1903, one volume. I have been looking for it for years.
I have a first of Stanford's *And Some in Horses*. It's a great
humorous sequel to *The Twelfth*. I have quite a few of
Stanford's books (see list), but am also searching for others of
his (also see list).

When the books arrive from England, please be sure to quote
me, especially on the Walton you had never seen before.

Welcome home,
John Daniels

July 7, 1983

Dear Mr. Daniels,

Descriptions:

> Somerville and Ross, *An Irish Cousin*. Longmans Green & Co., 1903. 8vo. Green cloth, gilt dec. First edition. Nice condition.
>
> *The Sportsman's Dictionary, or the Country Gentleman's Companion*. London, 1735. Two volumes, 8vo. Near 30 copper plates. Full morocco, back strips laid down. Fine set.
>
> Walton's *Angler*. Folio. 54 India proof engravings. All plates tied in. The plates are mounted on tissue and all are fine. Some foxing to a couple of pages. These seem to be from the Pickering edition for 1836. Full green morocco, TEG, bound by Holloway, no title page.

I'm sorry about my description of the last book, but it is difficult to describe. I feel that it's one of a kind because of the proof plates and no auction records. Bookplate of Forrester Colvin.

Dr. Coigney wanted me to send it down to him, but I had told you about the book so I thought you should have first say.

Best regards,
Helen Hennessey

Dear Helen Hennessey,

Many thanks for your letter of July 7th with the descriptions.
I would like to get the Somerville and Ross, *An Irish Cousin,*
1903, and also the Walton *Angler,* 1836, which I believe is in
Horne 43 or at least part of it.

My check for these two books is enclosed.

I find that I already have a nice copy of *The Sportsman's
Dictionary* which I believe is Schwerdt II, 220 pp, DJ.

Best regards,
John Daniels

July 20, 1983

Dear Mr. Daniels,

Have you any interest in the following:

> Walter Sparrow, *George Stubbs and Ben Marshall*. London, 1929. Folio. Handmade paper, bound in full vellum (white). #68 of 100 copies for sale in America. *The Sport of Our Fathers*. Beautiful copy.

Also, I have:

> Sparrow's *Henry Alken & George Stubbs & Ben Marshall*. London, 1927, Marshall, 1929. Folio. Matched set in quarter red morocco, bound by Baytom. Limited to 100 copies. Alken signed, by Theodore Cook, who introduced the book. Bookplate of R.N.H. Moore Stevens. Again a beautiful set.

I will be interested to know what you think of the Walton. Dr. Coigney is hurt that I sold it to you.

Best regards,
HBH

P.S. The mention of raspberries reminds me of a dear friend, Samuel Hopkins Adams, who put crushed raspberries in his martinis. I've never been able to enjoy a martini since then . . .

Dear Helen Hennessey,

I have begun to worry about you. You have been such a constant correspondent in the past and now more than two months
have gone by without receiving a single one of your always
interesting letters. I do hope that everything is all right.

We are planning our routine move to South Carolina next
Saturday. We will be at Mulberry Plantation for the winter by
Monday, October 31st.

I look forward to hearing from you.

With all best wishes,
Sincerely,
John Daniels

November 4, 1983

Dear Mr. Daniels,

It was nice to hear from you. I'll admit I have been a bit neglectful. Please accept my apology. I felt with the Current Company in your front yard and all the catalogues you must be receiving that a letter from me would hardly be missed.

I bought very little sporting material in England—too many people are in the business now. So I concentrated on Americana, and that was very scarce.

We had a wonderful month of August here—I'm a member of the Polo Club and it was just one long month of parties. We saw our first snow this morning, but it didn't stay.

I'm still playing with the idea of moving to S.C., but a wonderful lady by the name of Mrs. Hopewell, from Aiken, tells me it's not the place to live year-round.

Best regards,
Helen Hennessey

Dear Mr. Daniels,

You must be jumping for joy after reading the Colonel's catalogue—the value of your books has increased by 100 percent.

If my memory serves me (and it hasn't lately), didn't Mrs.
Daniels like officers of the Civil War? Forgive me if I'm wrong.
I have a copy of *The Life of a Lieutenant—General Nathan
Bedford Forrest,* by John Allan Wyeth. N.Y. & London, 1899.
First edition, fine condition.

Best regards,
HBH

* * *

November 14, 1983

Dear Helen Hennessey,

Yes, the Colonel's prices keep going up and up. I really hate to
buy from him, and only do so as a last resort.

I don't actually think that the Colonel's prices reflect the real
world. I guess he uses some kind of inflation factor and auto-
matically raises his prices five to ten percent each time he puts
out a catalogue.

All best wishes,
John H. Daniels

December 4, 1983

Descriptions from a list:

> R.C. Lyle, *Brown Jack.* London, 1934. 4to. Quarter vellum, green cloth, TEG. Limited to 250 copies, signed, Lyle, Lionel Edwards, and the owner of Brown Jack. Fine.

> Peter Lewis, *Fox Hunters' Anthology.* Printed in G.B., but distributed by Macmillan, 1935. 8vo, red cloth. Fair condition.

Do you need Rives's *Coaching Club,* Derrydale?

* * *

December 9, 1983

Dear Helen Hennessey,

Thank you for your prompt reply. I would like to get the R.C. Lyle *Brown Jack,* but I think that I will hold out for a better copy of Peter Lewis's *Fox Hunters.* Yes, I do have a very fine copy of Rives's *Coaching Club.*

I would like to get both of the books with reference to Generals D.H. Hill and Pettigrew: Fuller's *Decisive Battles* and Thompson's *The Fiery Epoch.* Mrs. Daniels will like them both for Christmas.

My check is enclosed.

With all best wishes,
Sincerely,
John H. Daniels

Descriptions from your want list:

Will James, all firsts:

> *The American Cowboy*, fine
> *All in a Day's Riding*, fair
> *Scorpion*, spine faded
> *Flint Spears*, fine
> *Uncle Bill*, fine
> *Horses I Have Known*, soiled cover

All together I have nine other titles, five of which are firsts. However, they are not on your list. I have a nice copy of James's first book, *Cowboys North and South*, which I believe was first printed in a magazine in 1924. My copy is dated 1925 on the title page, but the copyright reads "Curtis Publishing Co., 1924," which makes me believe it's *Curtis Magazine*.

Helen Hennessey

* * *

December 22, 1983

Dear Helen Hennessey,

Thank you for your letter about books by Will James. I would like to buy the following:

> *An American Cowboy*, 1942, first edition, fine
> *Flint Spears*, 1938, first edition, fine
> *Uncle Bill*, 1932, first edition, fine

I'm basing my first edition dates on a bibliography that is in the biography of Will James, *The Last Cowboy Legend*, by Anthony Amaral, University of Nevada Press, 1980. An interesting account of James, who led a sort of double life.

With all best Christmas wishes,
John H. Daniels

May 12, 1984

Dear Mrs. Hennessey,

I haven't heard from you for so long that I wanted to write you to see how you were doing and how things are going.

We have returned to Minnesota after a busy winter in South Carolina. Seeing a second spring now.

With all best wishes,
Sincerely,
John H. Daniels

Dear Mr. Daniels,

Thank you for your note. I've wanted to write to you and, as a matter of fact, I did, but then I destroyed the letter as my news was so depressing and I'm not big on sharing my problems.

My daughter has terminal cancer. The fast-moving variety. It started in a lung and when they operated, it had spread to her lymph glands, around the heart, esophagus, and stomach, and then went to the brain. She has been in the hospital fourteen weeks. Now that the radiation therapy is over, we are in hopes she will feel better, and will be able to rest. The doctors in the beginning gave her a year, now they say six months and she knows this.

We had more than a daughter-and-mother relationship, we were friends—we made our twenty-fifth trip to Europe together last May. No sympathy please, I've done my crying.

I still buy a book or two, but I'm very selective. I have no one to leave this collection of oddments to.

Best regards as always,
H

May 23, 1984

Dear Helen Hennessey,

I knew that something was wrong when I wrote to you recently because we have had such a good exchange of correspondence over the last six years. I am simply appalled by your most recent letter and the dreadful news about your daughter, Sherri. You write, "No sympathy please, I've done my crying—." So be it.

I would like to take this opportunity to thank you for all of the help you have been to me in the past six years. Some special highlights:

The deluxe edition of Sabretache's *More Shires & Provinces,* and our five dollar bet that the Munnings counterpart would go for over a thousand dollars. Thanks to our bet, I upped my bid and got it for less, just a thousand—but got it.

You helped me get my feet wet on Izaak Walton, and in spite of losing out to Judith Bowman on the first edition, I have developed a nice, controlled collection of the old fisherman.

You helped me locate a magnificent edition of Schwerdt, which I treasure.

Your appraisal of the Mulberry Library was terribly useful and timely. Incidentally, we had to sell the Dupre to paint the exterior & make repairs to Mulberry last summer. I got it sold for $17,500, which paid for the Mulberry job even though it should have brought more money.

You were a great help at the Christie's auction of Mrs. Ambrose Clark's books—& got me the John Mills *The Flyers of the Hunt* in an otherwise crazy sale. And you steered me through a Swann sale with great acuity.

Besides all of that, you have really helped to educate me about books—not just sporting books—and have helped to find many, many of the good books in my collection.

I am most grateful to you for all of this, and especially for the
friendship that has developed over our years of correspondence,
which I hope will continue through thick and thin.

I admire you and send you my love.
John

* * *

May 30, 1984

Dear Mr. Daniels,

Your letter is a hard one to answer—I've sat at my desk for half
an hour, trying to think of something intelligent to write—my
mind is a blank.

I don't deserve, nor have I earned your fine opinion of me.
It was just good old New England common sense that steered
me to your treasures.

I am glad you didn't get the first edition Walton that Judith
Bowman got that time. It wasn't a fine copy—internally it was
an outlaw. If you haven't found a first, and if you still would like
one, I'd be glad to go on a treasure hunt. It might keep me out
of trouble, which I seem to be in with the doctors—they prefer
parents ignorant of medicine.

However, we had two doctors in the family and I spent fifteen
years at Belleview in Radiation.

Medicine has changed in America. The doctors are afraid of
being prosecuted.

Many thanks again for your kind words.
H

June 10, 1984

Dear Helen Hennessey,

After giving a lot of thought to your interesting offer to go on a treasure hunt for a Walton first, I have decided that it would be out of scale with my collection. For the same reasons that I was relieved to have been outbid by Bowman at Swann—notwith-standing the state of that particular Walton first—I would rather keep on adding fine things of good quality to a uniform collection of fine sporting books than throw money at the idea of acquiring one or two books that really belong in an institution.

To put it another way, I am infinitely happier with the representative collection of the thirty Waltons which I have acquired— at about half the cost of the Swann/Bowman/First—than to own the latter.

I hope that I have made myself clear on the most troublesome idea that you suggested. In my opinion, it is all a matter of degree and balance. I'm not at all sure that you agree.

With all best wishes,
Sincerely,
John Daniels

July 5, 1984

Dear Mr. Daniels,

If I remember correctly, I told you once that Walton should be represented in your fine library, and thirty seems like a generous amount.

Everything is at sixes and sevens here at our house, and I'm in a foul frame of mind. However, with me it doesn't last long.

Sherri came home for twenty days, but is back in the hospital again. Some days she is fine, but we never know what the next day will be like.

Have you any extra polo material, not Dale or Bent? It is about that season here—the part of the summer I enjoy the most—I lock the door on the books and go to the matches in the evening.

Best regards,
H

* * *

July 21, 1984

Dear Mrs. Hennessey,

Barbara Walzer was out here for a visit this week and told me the terribly sad news about Sherri's death. After all of her suffering, it must have been a relief in many ways, but it is a loss so great for you that there is no real consolation.

In one of your letters, you stoically said, "No sympathy please, I've done my crying," and that says it all in so many ways.

I send you my love and admiration—and will be thinking of you often.

As ever,
John

August 2, 1984

Dear Mr. Daniels,

Thank you for your nice letter. Everyone has been more than kind to me, but as you wrote, while it's a loss, Sherri couldn't get better and she really suffered a great deal.

Barbara tells me that you are buying fore-edge paintings. That worries me. There are too many deceptions. I remember, in England ten years ago, Maggs Brothers showing me some fakes that had been beautifully done on eighteenth-century books by an expert, which they considered worthless. So be careful, friend.

I'm thinking of going to England with Barbara in September. She's going to do a book show and I ought to be able to find some trouble to get into.

Best regards,
Helen

Dear Helen,

I had a nice visit with Barbara Walzer and Rob Rulon-Miller out here just before my wife and I took off on a sixteen-day junket to the Olympic Games in Los Angeles and a week's fishing in the wilds of Alaska. I had the opportunity of showing them some of my collection.

I appreciate your admonition about fore-edge paintings. I have tried to concentrate on sporting themes and have fore-edge paintings of about twenty different sports, from coursing and hawking to baseball, golf, and football. Some of the latter are most certainly modern, but I'm really not getting carried away. As a matter of fact, as I have collected the fore-edge paintings, it has been an education on what is really fine and old and what is obviously modern and often rather simplistic. I have reached the saturation point of fore-edge paintings now, and unless something of rare interest turns up, I'm no longer riding that hobby horse.

Your possible trip to England with Barbara sounds most worthwhile. When and where is the book show that Barbara is doing in England? I'm going to be over there rather briefly (twelve days) in late August and early September—mainly for some grouse shooting—but will be in London for four days en route.

While I'm in London, I'm trying to arrange things through a friend to spend a couple of days in the reading room of the British Museum. I want to do some research on Cuthbert Bradley and on John Corlett (publisher of *The Sporting Times*). There is almost nothing about them biographically that I have been able to find, and since I have a lot of their original material, I'd like to find out more about these two rather unimportant but interesting men.

With all best wishes,
John H. Daniels

August 22, 1984

Dear Mr. Daniels,

Nice to hear from you. I thought of you last Saturday. I went to a sale in Shelburne, Vermont, and Holbrook's *Ichthyologia of South Carolina* was up for sale. I thought I remembered you having a copy, but this was such a fine copy that I sort of wanted it, but Cummins bid it in for $2,000. That eliminated me. Have you any interest in an Elephant Folio of *Traité de Fauconniere*, by H. Schlegel and A.H. Verster van Walverhorst, a reprint of the original that was published 1844–1853? This is the portfolio with 17 plates only, no text, limited to 550 sets. In sturdy red canvas folder. Published in London, 1979. Bound in Edinburgh. As new. First edition sold to Quaritch for £5,200. I'm asking $750 for this reprint. The English Book Fair is September 18th, 19th, and 20th at the Hotel Russell.

Best regards,
Helen

* * *

August 23, 1983

Dear Helen,

Thank you for your recent letter. I am enclosing my check for the *Traité de Fauconniere* portfolio. It sounds like a magnificent reprint of a very rare and beautiful book.

I'm off for London next Tuesday. I'm looking forward to my three or four days in the British Library. I get back home the 8th of September, so will miss the English Book Fair, which doesn't start until the 18th.

With all best regards,
John

Dear Mr. Daniels,

I just bought an original drawing on board of Finch Mason's
and I thought I remembered you liking him. In color, signed,
and I think it's great. Down in the corner in Mason's handwrit-
ing, it says, "Don't be alarmed, ladies: the mare isn't dead. It's
only Senor Smitherini (whose circus is in the neighborhood)
giving himself a cheap advertisement. Dick Turpin's ride to
York terminating with the death of Black Bess is a prominent
feature of the entertainment." Measurement 10 x 14 inches.
Sorry about the Polaroid. I'm not good at it.

Best regards,
H

            * * *

September 11, 1984

Dear Helen,

I am enclosing my check for the original Finch Mason drawing.

My trip to England was unsuccessful. Found a few nice books
at Henry Sotheran's and a modestly priced Lionel Edwards
original at Tryon Galleries. (With the pound at under $1.30, it
makes for some attractive buys.)

With all best wishes,
John H. Daniels

September 23, 1984

Dear Mr. Daniels,

Did you like the print? I have something you might want to give to one of your grandchildren.

> Maurice Sendak, *Pictures by Maurice Sendak*. N.Y., 1971. Elephant folio. 20 drawings in 9 wrappers, laid loose in a cloth-backed patterned box. Limited to 500 copies. A previously unpublished drawing of Jennie, the Sealyham terrier who posed for the heroine of *Higglety Pigglety*, signed in pencil.

Sendak is considered today's leading American illustrator of children's books. He won the Caldecott Medal. The folio is mint.

Best regards,
H

* * *

September 27, 1984

Dear Helen,

Many thanks, but I don't think I'll buy the Sendak although it sounds charming.

All best wishes,
John

P.S. Did you get to London?

Dear Mr. Daniels

I didn't make the English trip, mostly because I am the executrix of Sherri's estate (a word used loosely). Something came up that I had to be here for. I was disappointed, but I'm a fatalist.

I've had a great week. Sunday, a dog bit me that hadn't had his rabies shots, then on Monday I fell off the ladder. Today is Saturday, so one more thing has to happen and then everything will be settled into its dull routine.

I'm going to the Boston Book Fair November 9th. Any treasure you'd like me to run down?

Did you get Frazier's green postcard from Calderwood's Books, with 214 Derrydales for sale? Hickok and I have a bet on that he wants $98,000.

Best as always,
H

November 15, 1984

Dear Mr. Daniels,

Welcome to S.C. I was disappointed at the material at the
Boston Book Fair. However, I enjoyed myself, saw a lot of our
old colleagues. I was dusting the stock today, and I found a few
things you may or may not be interested in:

Racing in France. 1950. Folio. Printed in color by DuPuy, translated by
Atkins. Imitation vellum. Fine.

A reprint of *The S.C. Jockey Club.* Spartanburg, 1975. As new.

E.M. Humphries, *The Life of Fred Archer.* N.Y., 1923. 8vo. Colored
frontispiece, 24 illus. First edition. Fair.

Captain R.N. Marryat, *The Pirate and the Cutters.* London, 1836.
20 splendid engravings from drawings by R.A. Clarkson Stanfield,
Esq. Full contemporary morocco, blue, gold dec, a fine binding (bound
at Sotheran), TEG.

William Bartram's Botanical and Zoological Drawings, 1756–1788. Edited
with an introduction & commentary by Joseph Ewan. Philadelphia,
1968. Large folio. Plates in color and B&W. DJ. As new.

Best regards as always,
H

P.S. Happy holidays to you and your family.

Dear Helen,

A belated thank-you for your Christmas greetings and the lovely watercolor by Sherri of "The Start." It was so thoughtful of you to send me such a special gift, especially with all of its memories. It is so heartbreaking for you to have endured the terrible loss of your beloved daughter.

I grieve for you, and send you my love.
John

* * *

January 22, 1985

Dear John Daniels,

I was so pleased to have your letter today. I had heard that you were ill and I wanted to write to Mrs. Daniels to find out if it was correct. But with my small art of letter-writing, I didn't know how to really approach the subject. Now, have you really been ill, and how are you?

I'm glad that you liked Sherri's print. I know that she would be pleased at your enjoyment. She was a great gal—naughty, but I wouldn't have had her any other way.

Affectionately,
H

January 26, 1985

Dear Helen,

To answer your compassionate questions—yes, I have been really ill, and yes, I am fine. I am a recovering alcoholic.

When I went up to Minnesota in early December, my four grown children showed their love and concern by intervening and persuading me that I was an alcoholic and that I needed help. As a result, I entered St. Mary's Rehabilitation Center in Minneapolis where I spent thirty-one days undergoing treatment.

Now I am committed to a lifetime of sobriety and I have never felt better. My children have literally saved my life, and I can now look forward to living a whole life, day by day.

It is a very traumatic experience, and I appreciate the fact that I risk anybody's love or friendship when I tell them that I am a recovering alcoholic, because many people don't understand the disease.

I hope that you do, and I send my love.
John

February 5, 1985

Dear John Daniels,

You are a very courageous gentleman, and your children must be very proud of you. I'd send you a medal if I could find an appropriate one. Also, I feel very honored that you wrote me.

I went to N.Y. last Thursday with the family jewels. I'm trying to put my house in order, before I leave this vale of tears. I had planned on going to Swann's sale, but time wouldn't permit it. Anyway, it seemed to be the same sporting books over again. Please remember that I am very proud to know you, and you can't do anything wrong as far as I am concerned.

Affectionately,
H

    * * *

February 10, 1985

Dear Helen,

Your letter made me feel very good! Thank you for those heart-warming thoughts which I will cherish. Your encouragement helps me on a continuing basis.

We've had some fun together. I'll never forget our five dollar bet on the Munnings book. Nor the way you went to bat for me at Mrs. Clark's sale. I look forward to more good times with you.

The sale of the family jewels sounds painful. I hope it went successfully and wasn't too drawn out. Jim Cummins got in a couple of goodies for me at his Swann sale. You're right in that there wasn't too much that was worthwhile. He did get the Lee Sturgis *Salmon Fishing at Cain River* which was rare & very nice. Jim said that the Colonel was there & Judith and a "lot of people."

I hope you are well, and send you my love.
John

February 18, 1985

Dear John Daniels,

I'm toying with the idea of buying a v-12 Jaguar . . . I only have fifteen speeding tickets now and I thought I could stimulate myself and the police almost as soon as I'd get out of the driveway. They told me that the next time I get caught they are going to ground me.

It's time I got in trouble!
H

    * * *

March 2, 1985

Dear Helen,

Instead of bombing around in a v-12 Jaguar, why don't you invest in a moped? I worry about you.

I'm enclosing my check for the Finch Mason *Tit Bits of the Turf*. I'm happy to find another one of his books, which for some reason are always difficult to locate. I now have ten of his titles plus all of the things he contributed to *Fore's*.

Yes, I do have copies of the four-volume Mellon collection. The one on books is extremely well done & useful.

John

Page forty-eight is where I used to live. I thought you might get a kick out of the piece.

H

"Alexander Woollcott and the members of the 'Neshobe Club,' who acquired Neshobe Island and began visiting here regularly in the 1920s. Through the 1930s the Buddha-shaped Woollcott included among his occasional hand-picked disciples not only Groucho Marx, but his brother Harpo, Noel Coward, Helen Hayes, Ruth Gordon, Moss Hart, George and Beatrice Kaufman, Dorothy Parker, Alfred Lunt and Lynn Fontanne, Laurence Olivier, and Vivien Leigh.

". . . a few natives even became part of the crowd over at Neshobe. Helen Burt was one of these favored few. Raised in Hydeville, she worked in several of Bomoseen's hotels, and became acquainted with her future husband, Joseph Hennessey, manager of the Neshobe Club and Woollcott's close friend. Mrs. Hennessey, now a sturdy, silver-haired, energetic bookseller who lives and has a shop in Saratoga Springs, N.Y., testifies to the fascination people on the mainland had for Neshobe, and to the added allure the island gave Bomoseen. Woollcott's guests were driven to a highly conspicuous spot on the east shore between Cedar Grove and Trakenseen hotels, known as 'Bull's Landing.' William Bull, or his son, Howard, native Vermonters who operated an inn along the lake, would then take the guests in a launch over to Neshobe. Mrs. Hennessey recalls with a laugh that, "Everybody [on the mainland] would watch to see who it was—they wanted to see if there was a celebrity." *

* Terrence Petty, "Bomoseen, The Lay of the Lake," *Vermont Life*, Vol xxxviii, Summer 1984, No. 4, pp 48-49.

March 12, 1985

Dear "sturdy, silver-haired, energetic bookseller" Helen,

Life at the Neshobe Club on Lake Bomoseen in the thirties and early forties must have been stimulating and quite special. Thank you for sending me the most interesting article in the summer edition of *Vermont Life*.

We're getting primed for a big Mulberry house-party over the Carolina Cup Race weekend at the end of March. Ten Yale classmates & their wives are descending on us!

Love,
John

* * *

March 15, 1985

Dear John,

Sherri would have gotten a kick our of her little old gray-haired mother flying around on a moped. (She was the one who wanted me to have the Jaguar.) The car is here and has more buttons than a computer, which I haven't figured out yet.

You will be leaving for the north country soon?

Nice to have you worry about me. I appreciate the compliment. I have three original watercolors of Finch Mason's, under glass, signed. I'll have Polaroids made and send them along to you. I've enjoyed them for a long time. I bought them at Lady Isabel Throckmorton's in Alcester, England. You've got to meet her sometime, she's funnier than I am.

I hope you liked *Tit Bits of the Turf.*

Affectionately,
H

Dear Helen,

I thought that Finch Mason's *Tit Bits of the Turf* was grand!
He gets so much color and action (and gossip!) into his pictures. I think he is one of the most durable and best of his
era—certainly one of the most prolific with his many, many
contributions to *Fore's*. Too bad Higginson did such a poor
write-up of him. Are there any other biographical sources about
Finch Mason? I'd love to know more about him.

I would like to see the Polaroids of the three original watercolors of Finch Mason's under glass. Remember, you sold me
his original of *Señor Smitherini* last September which has been
suitably framed and now hangs in my "rogues gallery" along
with the four Edith Somerville Derrydale prints and a good
polo print by Cuthbert Bradley.

Love,
John

* * *

March 22, 1985

Dear John,

I took the three Finch Mason original watercolors to a professional photographer and because they are under glass, he couldn't
or won't take any pictures. So if it's all right by you, I'll send them
over by UPS. If you don't like them—just pop them back.

Have fun with your Yale companions.

Hurriedly,
H

P.S. I'm asking a hideous price.

March 28, 1985

Dear Helen,

Thanks for the note about the three Finch Masons. I think it is a splendid idea to send them on approval via UPS. I look forward to seeing them.

The Yalies & spouses are arriving today and tomorrow. It should be a great reunion. Very interesting guys and special old friends.

Love,
John

* * *

April 11, 1985

Dear Helen,

The three Finch Mason original watercolors arrived safely while we were away in the Bahamas for a week of R&R, so I only just opened them up. They are charming! So nicely matted and framed. I like the story the two tell of one poor little jockey going into—and then coming out of the water. He certainly isn't happy. And the picture of the gigantic owner/trainer bending in half to talk to his diminutive jockey is nicely funny. The jockey is so dapper.

My check is enclosed with my thanks for selling me such a good set of Finch Mason originals.

Our Yale reunion was a great success. Thanks again for the Finch Mason watercolors.

Love,
John

April 21, 1985

Dear John,

I'm very pleased that you are happy with the Finch Masons. There is a great satisfaction when I sell something that people enjoy.

I was worried when I didn't hear from you. I thought that temptation might have visited you when the Yale Boys were there.

Don't give me and the Jaguar a second thought—it looks like an old lady's limousine and I drive it that way—however, the neighbors are fascinated.

Affectionately,
H

* * *

May 7, 1985

Dear John,

So you are back in the north country. Hope you had a pleasant trip.

I think I'll take off for Ottawa next week for a few days—as the not so brilliant people I used to live with on the dear old Neshobe would say, I need to blow the stink off—I've just become interested in beavers and otters—if you have any interest, I have Lewis H. Morgan's *American Beaver,* 1868, and James Lamas's *Otter Hunting Diary,* 1910. I'll look for a Canadian treasure for you.

Affectionately,
H

[No Date]

Dear Helen,

I hope your Canadian caper helps to "blow the stink off" (a picturesque phrase!), and that you see some otters in their natural habitat. We have had two pairs of otters in our little lake near the house in South Carolina. They are terribly wild and shy and they dive the minute they see you. We love having them around.

I don't mind the English hunting foxes—varmints—but I hate the idea of them hunting otter. Richard Clapman's *Book of the Otter* is fierce about the subject.

Love,
John

* * *

May 26, 1985

Dear John,

My holiday to Ottawa was a disaster—for two reasons. One, I couldn't find any treasures. Two, I got two speeding tickets ten minutes apart. The Officer of the Day was very arrogant and gave me my second ticket as I was coming back on the highway. I think he was bucking for the Cop of the Year award. The first ticket I deserved, the second one I didn't—however, my lawyer is trying to get the bloody tickets reduced and some good comes from everything. If I lose my license, I'll move to S.C.

Have you any interest in *The Spirit of the Times* for 1876 and 1877? Both half years.

Affectionately,
H

Dear Helen,

I'm so sorry to learn that your holiday to Ottawa was so lousy.
Two speeding tickets inside of ten minutes from the same cop
should go into the *Guinness Book of World Records.* For a gal who
already had fifteen speeding tickets, you really are showing the
flag! I still think you ought to consider a moped. Anyway, I
will be happy if you move to S.C.—at least half of the year I'm
down there.

Jim Cummins really hit the jackpot for me at the May 22 Sotheby
PB sale. Although we didn't exactly steal them, we had the good
fortune to bid in Lots 3, 7, and 16 at very decent prices. When you
think that it probably took Lindley Eberstad a lifetime to collect
*The American Turf Register & Sporting Magazine, The Cabinet of
Natural History,* and *The New York Sporting Magazine*—all in
original parts—it was quite a coup to land all three in one day at a
single auction.

I have a very competent bookbinder who lives up in the boon-
docks along the Gunflint Trail in northern Minnesota. I've been
working with him for the last five years and his work is superb.
He has been invited by the Library of Congress to be one of
the two interns in advanced conservation study in the Rare
Book Restoration Section for a year, beginning this September,
and the Bush Foundation here in Minnesota (3M money) has
also given him a fellowship to cover his expenses for the year.
What a happy guy!

I am looking forward to having this bookbinder visit me next
Saturday. He is interested in seeing my collection and I'm planning an exhibit for him of some of my most outstanding bindings. It should be a nice get-together.

The truck drivers who drive around in those big eighteen-
wheelers love to "keep the hammer down" whenever they can,
yet have an uncanny ability to outwit or avoid the smokies.

Better you should buy one of them a cup of coffee and find out how they do it. With seventeen (+ or -) speeding tickets, you'd better do something.

Love,
John

P.S. I'd be interested in hearing more about your *Spirit of the Times* for 1876 and 1877.

* * *

June 9, 1985

Dear John

You won't believe this, but I've been out of trouble for ten days— I bought myself a radar detector which takes two and a half hours to install, so I'm in hopes it's worth the effort. Also, I only travel on secondary roads.

I found myself having too much time on my hands, so I'm making up a catalogue—probably my swan song—very few sporting books. However, I'll send you one. I must say cataloguing is a bibliographer's nightmare.

As you suggested, I usually follow eighteen-wheelers, but there were none on the road when I was moving along. They might have known there was a speed trap on the North Way at that location and moved over to a side road.

Are you going to take up bookbinding now?

> *The Spirit of the Times*, Jan.– Jun. 1877, nicely bound in fine condition
> *The Spirit of the Times*, misc. issues, 1875-1876, most for 1876
> Altogether 20 issues in a custom-made box with ties

Affectionately,
H

June 20, 1985

Dear Helen,

Enclosed is my check for *The Spirit of the Times* for Jan.– June 1877 & misc. issues, 1875–1876.

Do you know where I could locate more old copies of *Polo*? I have two, beautifully bound, vol. v, Dec. 1930 to May 1931, and vol. vi, June to November 1951, and I'd love to get all of the back issues.

Do you know how long *Polo* was published? I rather think it was a casualty of World War ii.

Instead of a *radar* you, maybe, should be thinking of a *governor.*

John

June 24, 1985

Dear John,

I sent *The Spirit of the Times* off by UPS this morning. Many thanks.

When you asked for *Polo* magazines, I remember when you bought the two that you have. It was at Swann's, and I bid against you until I discovered that you were bidding.

I started reading Bent's book on American polo, and was surprised to discover it started here in our country as early as 1877. I'm on the trail of some magazines for you and I'll let you know how I make out.

Pete Vischer was one of the editors of *Polo,* some forty or more years ago, but when it started, I don't know. Vischer was an old friend from my checkered career. You have to be my age to remember people of that vintage.

Never mind a governor on my car, everyone is delighted that I'm flying around the country. You have to experiment with everything before you die and as yet I haven't had the excitement of jail.

Best,
H

P.S. Do you have T.B. Drybraugh's book on polo?

Dear Helen,

Spirit of the Times arrived here, safely, yesterday. My, but it is grand fun to read & browse through.

I'm delighted that you are on the trail of some magazines for me. I'd love to get hold of all of the old *Polo* magazines. They cover an era when I was very active in the game.

I was interested in learning that you knew Vischer.

No, I don't have Drybraugh's book on polo. Please tell me about it.

Keep out of jail—please!

Love,
John

      * * *

July 8, 1985

Dear Helen,

Thank you for your notes. I have been a member of the U.S. Polo Association since 1933, so I have their yearbooks going all the way back. Used to be a 4-goal player, but that was a while back. Also have a number of books on polo—but thanks.

I'm delighted to know that you are working on *Polo* magazines. As I wrote, I only have a run from December 1930 thru November 1931 and would dearly love to have a complete run of that wonderful publication. So see what you can do.

Love,
John

[No Date]

Dear John,

If you don't have it, I have a book for you—it says that *Polo* was first published in 1927.

> Peter Vischer, editor, *Horse and Horseman*. N.J., 1967. 4to. An anthology of articles and pictures from America's most celebrated horse magazine. DJ. Small mark on the spine, otherwise as new.

Do you want me to return your *Sporting Magazine* material? I think it's a very fine piece of research and should be made available to the public.

Hurriedly,
H

Dear Helen,

I'm so glad that you located *Horse and Horseman*, edited by Peter Vischer. My check for it is enclosed.

Please keep the copy of *200 Years of Sporting Magazines* catalogue. I wanted you to have a copy and I'm happy that you liked it. I am sending a copy to Peter Winants, editor of *The Chronicle of the Horse* to see if he would like to publish a cut-down version in his magazine.

I have started work on a new "catalogue." It dawned on me recently that 1985 was the 200th anniversary not only of James Audubon, but also Henry Alken. I don't think anybody has yet done a study of Henry Alken in recent times and it would be appropriate to celebrate his 200th birthday along with Audubon's and Bach's. I have about thirty original Alken books and lots of supporting stuff and have just started on the project. What do you think?

Love,
John

July 18, 1985

Dear John,

I received a catalogue from Thomas Thorp the other day, and I was fascinated to see that he had a set of the *Annals of Sporting & Fancy Gazette* for £3200. I hope Cummins did better for you.

I should think that a catalogue of Henry Alken would be interesting to put together and perhaps has a sale value.

A great deal has been written about Audubon lately, some of it repeated.

I'm still hunting for *Polo Magazine*.

I like to pick raspberries, but it's not time here.

Affectionately,
H

* * *

July 22, 1985

Dear Helen,

Nice to get your letter and the encouragement about writing an essay about Henry Alken, Sr. Also glad to know you are searching for *Polo Magazine*.

Jim Cummins apparently did all right by me on the *Annals of Sporting*. I paid $2,000 in February 1984. The set I purchased contained the rare June number. The thirteen volumes were nicely bound in matching red morocco slipcases and boxes. The set was complete.

Love,
John

Dear John,

If you don't have item 9, it's a beautiful set and has been one of my treasures for a long time. Item 32 is very unusual. The misspelling is not my fault . . . blame the typist.

9. Thomas Cross, *The Autobiography of a Stage Coachman.* London, 1904. Two volumes, folio. Illustrated, 45 plates by James Pollard, Robert Havell, C. Cooper Henderson, C.B. Newhouse, Thomas Rowlandson, H. Alken, and others. The plates in duplicate, one hand-colored and one plain. Half brown morocco, buckram sides, gilt tops, other edges uncut. Deluxe edition, limited to 50 numbered copies. A superb set. Bookplate of R.N.H. Moore Stevens. Bound by Bantum Riviere.

19. Sir Walter Gilbey and E.D. Cumming, *George Morland, His Life and Works.* London, 1907. 8vo., 288 pp., 50 colored plates. Green decorated cloth. First edition. Fine.

32. C.M. Moseman & Bros., *Moseman's Illustrated Guide for Purchasers of Horse Furnishing Goods, Novelties, and Stable Appointments, Imported and Domestic.* I can't find a date but I'm guessing 1900. If you could purchase some of the items in this catalogue, your horse would be the best dressed at Madison Square Garden. Large folio. 7 colored plates, numerous full pages, black and white illustrations. Reddish brown cloth. No foxing. 304 pp of absolute enjoyment.

August 8, 1985

Dear Helen,

This will confirm my telephone call this morning about your new catalogue. I would like to purchase the following:

9. Thomas Cross, *The Autobiography of a Stage Coachman*
19. Gilbey and Cumming, *George Morland, His Life and Works*
32. C.M. Moseman & Bros., *Moseman's Illustrated Guide*

My check is enclosed.

I enjoyed talking with you. I hope the young couple from New Jersey will be successful in finding copies of *Polo Magazine*.

Love,
John

* * *

Thank you for your order. The Cross has been my pride and joy for many years. I'm glad it's going to your house. I sent the books to the Parkview address because the UPS doesn't like box numbers.

Dear John,

I think your piece on Alken is great. I hope you are going to have it published.

Barbara Walzer tells me she visited you a week or so ago and had a wonderful time. She's a damn good-looking woman.

Lillian Bostwick Phipps visited me the other day—perhaps you played polo with her brother. She's a lovely lady and lives her life in a wheelchair. Josy used to play croquet down on Sands Point at the Swope house with that crowd.

Do you need a limited edition of George Henry Mackay's *Shooting Journal*?

In John Howell's reference library sale by Swann, Item 724 has some works of Somerville that might interest you if you don't have them. I could use the Gee if you bid on it.

We have our tickets for England, September 27th for two weeks. We have to take Josy in a wheelchair, so you'd better say a prayer for me.

Best regards,
H

September 16, 1985

Dear Helen,

Just got home from a week's grouse shooting in Northumberland. Great time, birds not as plentiful as last year. We enjoyed the best week of weather England has had since February! This time I flew in & out without getting into London.

I'm glad you liked the Henry Alken article. *The Chronicle of the Horse* has accepted the thing & will publish it.

Barbara Walzer came out & we had a good visit. I agree with you about her book knowledge.

I'm not going to bid on Swann's Lot 724 as I have two copies of the Hudson bibliography of Edith Somerville. I didn't see much else of interest in the catalogue.

I don't know anything about George Henry Mackay's *Shooting Journal.* Tell me more.

I hope your two-week trip to England starting September 27th is successful. Take lots of warm clothes! They are having the coldest, wettest year in history.

Love,
John

October 17, 1985

Dear John,

The trip was partly a success. The weather was fine and the nurse I had to have along for Josy worked out fine. However, the book hunting was a waste of good talent. I found some polo books at Grant's in Edinburgh. When they come, I'll write you. I found an original pencil drawing by G.D. Armour, signed, that might interest you. If so, I will describe it.

I also got some fine Cecil Aldin's at Quaritch's. I know you don't care for him, but he happens to be a favorite of mine. Do you need a signed presentation copy of Captain James J. Pearce's *Everybody's Polo,* London, 1949?

What does it mean when you see the geese flying south in England the first of October, and where were they going?

Affectionately,
H

October 24, 1985

Dear John,

I sent the book, *Everybody's Polo,* off to you by UPS yesterday in hopes you receive it before you leave for Camden. Descriptions:

> The G.D. Armour pencil drawing is matted and framed in an attractive hardwood frame. Frame measures 13½ x 16½ inches, drawing measures 11 x 8½ inches. Title, printed in ink on mat reads, "Hunter with Whip—'Stopping Them (3 hounds) from an Old Fox.'" Signed in pencil, but not dated. I would guess 1900, as the glass is old with bubbles in it.

> The Cecil Aldin again is an original pencil drawing. Frame measures 14½ x 21½ inches (bird's-eye maple), drawing measures 6 x 13¾ inches. Three hunters going over a fence with hounds in front. Signed, dated 1898. Black mat.

I have four other colored limited hunting prints. They are foxed in the margin and I'm going to leave them as is.

If you don't have Roy Heron's book on Aldin, *The Story of a Sporting Artist,* you'd enjoy it. I dearly love the expressions on dogs' faces in his drawings. The book is out of print now and I had a hard time finding two copies in England. The price of Aldins is very high in England. American's haven't realized his merit yet.

Barbara Walzer and I are dreaming of a trip south this winter—if I can find someone to take care of my responsibilities. Camden must have a country club, and if we make it, we will take you and Mrs. Daniels to lunch.

Have a good trip south.

Affectionately,
H

P.S. I envy you and Mrs. Daniels hunting together. I have fond memories of my days in the fields—I sold my deer rifle, but keep my twenty-gauge.

Dear Helen,

I'm enclosing my check for the G.D. Armour *and* the Cecil
Aldin pencil drawings. Please send them to me in Camden,
as we plan to get there for the winter by November 2nd & I'd
love to have them down there to enjoy.

The Roy Heron book on Aldin *is* good. Excellent illustrations.
Please keep me posted on the southern expedition plans that
you and Barbara Walzer are cooking up. Martha and I would
love to have you come to Mulberry. You are already familiar
with most of the good books, having done that great & useful
appraisal a few years back, but there are other goodies.

We'd not only like to show you the library but also expose you
to the old house, the plantation, and Camden, too.

Please bear in mind that Martha & I are going to be out of the
country from January 4th thru February 10th. We have recklessly
signed up for a Yale-Harvard alumni "excursion" on the *Illiria,*
which sails down the Red Sea and across the Indian Ocean and
ends up in Singapore. A zillion exotic countries en route. We are
getting very excited about this adventure to a part of the world
which we have never seen. Halley's Comet is thrown in.

If you and Barbara can work us into your southern itinerary any
time after mid-February, we would really love to see you both.
Your pal, and ours, Babs Cocks, lives nearby and we'd like to get
her and a few of our more literate friends in to join us for an
evening. So please keep us in mind.

Love,
John

October 24, 1985

Dear John,

I hope the pictures arrived safely—I had trouble with UPS. I had to tell them a lie. They don't like glass so I said there wasn't any. I've been concerned about them.

I think your piece on Alken is fine. You'll soon be famous with your writing appearing in print.

About your boat excursion, I'm delighted for you, but it's not my dish of tea. I'm an extremely restless person and I drive everyone crazy when I'm confined to shipboard. I'll play poker, but no bridge. Have a wonderful voyage. I hope I'll see you when you get back.

Do you need a copy of Armour's *Bridle & Brush*?

Affectionately,
H

Dear John,

Some of the books have started to arrive from England, and while I'll send you a complete list, I thought I'd mention three. You may already have them.

British Sports and Sportsmen, Polo and Coaching, edited by the Sportsman. No date, probably 1910. Folio. Full red morocco, all edges gilt, fine binding. Covers 500 years of polo. 291 pp on polo, 129 pp on coaching by J.A. Brindon. Limited to 1,000 copies, #550.

John Hinds, *The Grooms Oracle and Pocket Stable Directory.* London, 1829. Dialogue between two grooms engaged in training horses. 12mo, original boards, paper label, uncut. An unusual folding frontispiece by Alken, hand-colored. A fine copy of this book, seldom found.

British Hunts and Huntsmen. Compiled in conjunction with *Sporting Life.* London, 1908–11. Four volumes, folio. Half red morocco, raised bands, bound by Kelly & Son. Consists of s.w. England, n.e. England, West Midlands & Wales, s.e. England, Eastern England & East Midlands, North England, Scotland, and Ireland.

I think you are to be complimented on your research for your Buffalo piece, it must have been time-consuming. I have nothing of great worth on my bookshelves that would add to your already collected notes.

Have a nice holiday.

Affectionately,
H

December 29, 1985

Dear John,

The fourth of January is approaching and you'll be off on your holiday. Have a wonderful time.

There used to be a wonderful bookstore in Singapore. Perhaps it is still there and you'll find it.

Best regards,
Helen

* * *

Welcome home! We have snow up to a tall Indian's ass (if you'll excuse an old Vermont expression). Also no heat in the house for two days as a result.

Affectionately,
H

February 25, 1986

See how stupid I am.*
H

[*Envelope addressed to Camden, New Jersey! The post office returned it to Helen one month later.]

Dear John,

Thank you for the pictures. I especially got a kick out of Mrs. Daniels in the rickshaw. (She is a beautiful woman.) We had a rickshaw on the island. Alex must have weighed 200 pounds and we'd pull him around—down the hill to the dock was fine, but God help us getting him back up the hill. I left the bloody thing behind.

Did you like Barbara's piece in the *A.B. Weekly*? She's busy all this week with the women's literature program.

Business is very slow. I've almost forgotten what I have in stock. Thank God I'm a Democrat so the Republicans can't blame me for the economy.

The snow is still here. Not talking to the Indians anymore, but not left yet either.

Best regards,
Helen

March 20, 1986

Dear Helen,

Thank God you are persistent. If Camden, New Jersey, doesn't get to me for some strange reason, then try Camden, South Carolina—and I finally get your nice letter. Many thanks for the comments about Martha in her rickshaw & your experiences with a fat man in one.

Not too much exciting in the book collection, although I just found a book by Gordon Grand which I'd never heard about— *A Hunting Holiday in the County Cork.* P.P., Milbrook, 1936.

The Colonel up in Goshen was offering everything for forty percent off the other day, so I suckered into some Waltons I'd been lusting for.

Hope you're getting a spring thaw and the Indian is warming up.

Love,
John

April 3, 1986

Dear John,

Last week I went down to East Dennis on the Cape to Eldred's book sale. It was a disaster from my point of view. He falsified his descriptions in his catalogue of books. I wanted Alexander's *Costumes of China*, that he said had an original set of plates that turned out to be photo offset. However, I had a holiday away from home and I enjoyed myself—do you still need any more Waltons? I have a few special ones.

I didn't get to S.C. this year. But maybe next year. I'm still looking for your *Polo Magazine*.

If anyone ever offers you *British Sports and Sportsmen, Polo and Coaching*, like the one you bought from me, I'd dearly love to buy another copy.

Affectionately,
H

* * *

April 16, 1986

Dear John,

Welcome to the North. I thought you might enjoy this flyer on the Admiral Markey & Calumet Sale. I appraised the books several years ago and they weren't exciting, more a working-man's library, and were given to Skidmore.

I'm going to bid on the silver horseshoes. I'd like to get Alydar. I had one that Herbert Bayard Swope gave me that the Jockey Club gave him, now I'd like another.

Affectionately,
H

May 4, 1986

Dear Helen,

In your letter of April 3rd, you asked if I still "need" any more Waltons. What special ones do you have? Please let me know so I can compare with the fifty I have. I would like to selectively add without ever trying to pig my way into a lot more.

I hope you got your silver horseshoes from the Markey estate sale.

Keep me posted.

Love,
John

* * *

May 28, 1986

Dear John,

I have no news, either good or bad. My book business is at a standstill, so I'm bored.

I have a feeling that the racing season is going to be different this year. They have already closed the exercise track and barns because of the cost of insurance. So-o-o!

You and Mrs. Daniels must be having a lot of fun with your new additions. Have you ever counted your library?

Affectionately,
H

Dear John,

Writing about your colored slides and home movies reminded me of twelve large cans of home movies taken in the thirties. We have people in them like Henry Fonda when he was nineteen years old. We looked at them a couple of weeks ago, and didn't know half the old theater people. Sherri used to know, when she was around to help us. CBS wanted me to give the film to them, but I was a miserable old lady and wouldn't do it.

I like your piece on a "decade of sporting books." Have you thought of sending it to *Sporting Classics?*

Sorry about your hand. Increase your golf handicap and play for fun.

Everybody on the East Coast knows I'm looking for *Polo* magazines. So far, nothing. I haven't given up tho.

Affectionately,
H

P.S. My life is rather dull—I haven't even had a speeding ticket lately.

June, 1986

Dear Helen,

My thirteen-year-old grandson in Boulder, Colorado, called me last week. He is collecting out-of-print comic books and was going to an auction. He wanted my advice. I suggested three things:

1) Look at the books ahead of time
2) Be ready to drop out if the bidding exceeds your limit
3) Get somebody who knows what they are doing to buy for you

What would you add?

The most expensive words in the English language are: "While the builders (workmen) are here, why don't they . . ." I keep relearning this the hard way!

Have you thought of buying a fuzz buster for your car? Radio Shack sells them. It might save you some money.

Love,
John

Dear John,

I have a radar detector in my car, part of it is mounted under the hood and the other part on the steering wheel. It's a K40 and called the Rolls Royce of detectors. It is rightly named, it cost $450 and it works even on the eighteen-wheelers behind me. So far, it has kept me out of trouble.

Have you any use for twenty-nine volumes of Fore's *Sporting Notes & Sketches*?

I know next to nothing about comic books. I think you gave your grandson good advice.

Best regards,
Helen

* * *

July 3, 1986

Dear Helen,

Glad to know you've got a fuzz buster.

Thank you, but I already have a nicely bound set of twenty-nine volumes of Fore's *Sporting Notes*. Lovely on the outside, tacky on the inside.

I hope you have a safe and sane 4th of July.

Love,
John

July 23, 1986

Dear John,

Saratoga is beginning to look like the tourist town it is. I'm here playing with the idea of finding a house with one floor. It's getting more difficult every day for Mr. H to do stairs. My biggest trouble is I procrastinate.

Now for the bad news: a young man in a truck hit my Jaguar and demolished it, almost finished me off also. However, I only have a broken shoulder and a hurt back. Now I'm a monument of indecision. Do I want another Jaguar?

I started this letter a week ago—I think I better send it off to you. I'm getting better, because my disposition is foul.

Affection,
H

Dear Helen,

What a terrible happening! I can't tell you how sorry I was to get your letter about your accident. A broken shoulder and a hurt back are a dreadful, painful combination—especially in the hot summer. Thank God the young trucker didn't finish you off.

You are indeed a wonderful person. To go through an ordeal like that and have the courage and good grace to be asking whether or not you should get another Jaguar—and then brag about your foul disposition! In spite of all that life has dealt you, you are a superb survivor and a very game lady. Hang in there and please mend quickly. I will be thinking about you and in my own way, praying for you. What can I send you to recuperate faster?

Jim Cummins "stole" a few books for me at the recent Swann Gallery auction of sporting books. Apparently it was a typical midsummer sale with very few buyers. Although the quantity & quality of the lots wasn't particularly exciting, I did spot & buy the four books on cockfighting, which are quite scarce.
In casting around for the next major area in my collection to work on, it dawned on me that I have accumulated a lot of very old sporting books. I mean 16th, 17th & 18th century books.
I hadn't paid much attention to them over the years, but when I put them all together in chronological order I was really impressed, so I'm going to try to catalogue & describe them as a category of very old sporting books. What do you think?
You probably should get another Jaguar. In the horse game they always urge a fallen rider to remount as soon as possible. This might be the best medicine for a fractured Jaguar driver too.

Love,
John

August 2, 1986

Dear John,

That was a lovely letter you wrote me.

Everyone has been so nice to me. I didn't realize I had so many friends.

After deliberating for a week I went and got another Jaguar. But the thrill is gone. I was like a kid with a new toy with the first one.

I still hurt in various places, but I'll make it.

I'm a member of the Polo Club and I went to the game yesterday. I was pleased that I didn't get uncomfortable standing around.

Mrs. Daniels's office will be very colorful when she places her books on the shelves.

Affectionately,
H

P.S. So you are into cockfighting now. Why didn't you tell me? I used to have some wonderful things, but all I have left is the following:

> George Ryley Scott, *The History of Cockfighting*. 1957. Limited. First.
> Jerome Vogeler, editor, *Fights to the Death*. 1967. Original colored drawing. Signed. First.
> *Histories of Game Strains*. Gaffney, S.C., 1955.
> Willeford Charles, *Cockfighter*. N.Y., 1972. DJ.
> Capt. L. Fitz-Barnard, *Fighting Sports*. London, no date.

Dear Helen,

I'm glad to hear your are well enough to go to polo games and gritty enough to buy a new Jag. What a great spirit!

Thanks for the info on cockfighting books. Two of the books you listed were ones in the lot that I got at the Swann Gallery sale, but I'd like to buy the other three:

Vogeler, *Fights to the Death*
Histories of Game Strains
Willeford Charles, *Cockfighter*

My check is enclosed.

Love,
John

September 3, 1986

Dear John,

You have a very fine collection of books and it's specially wonderful of you to share them with the public. Maybe you will make some collectors out of our young people. Eddie Lazare, who owned *Book Prices Current* at one time, used to say there were no more collectors left in the world. I'll tell him about you.

I'm not ready for winter, but the furnace has been working for three days, so I guess it's on its way. I was up in the Adirondacks last week and the trees have a lot of color.

Have you any interest in Federico Grisone's *Ordini di Cavalcare*? Heredi de L. Valvassori & G.D. Micheli, Venice, 1584. 4to, vellum, with 50 woodcuts of bridles. Ties missing.

Business is very slow, but if the Hunt brothers with six billion dollars can declare bankruptcy, what am I complaining about? Besides that, it never did feed me.

Affectionately,
H

Dear John,

So now you are a member of the Grolier Club, do you need any of their books on their transactions? I have volumes II and IV, 1921 and 1894, limited editions; a small book report of the officers for 1948; bibliographical notes on 100 books famous in English literature; probably something else if I looked around.

Maine must have been lovely this time of year. I have some friends in Camden I thought I'd visit in October.

You haven't mentioned raspberries, I've been having fun picking at a friend's house.

Affectionately,
H

Description:

Federico Grisone, *Ordini di Cavalcare*. Heredi di L. Valvassori and G.D. Micheli, Venice, 1584. 4to. Contemp. vellum, with 50 woodcuts. Piece cut from the center of the title page. Ties lost from age. It's the same book as in Maclays Auction Catalogue #263, except for binding and date, watermarked paper. I have been unable to trace a first edition. This copy has very little foxing, considering its age. I bought it at an auction in N.Y. years ago.

Sept. 25, 1986

Dear Helen,

I'm enclosing my check for the Federico Grisone. It looks most attractive.

We are going back to Maine the first week in October for a family wedding. This one will be on Drake's Island near Wells, Maine. The autumn leaves will be at their peak—the same way they are here in Minnesota right now.

I hope that your back and shoulder are all healed by now—

Love,
John

P.S. Thanks for your offer of Grolier Club material, but they have absolutely swamped us with stuff.

　　　* * *

Friday

Dear John,

A friend of mine brought me back a doz. of these cards from the London Museum only because I'm so fond of Cecil Aldin, and I thought you'd enjoy one. I hope the wedding was held in better weather than we are having. Also, it spoiled the eclipse. I hope you are happy with the Grisone.

Hurriedly,
H

October 12, 1986

Dear Helen,

The Federico Grisone book is impressive. I was so pleased to be able to add it as an important sixteenth-century sporting book. It's amazing to me how something as fragile and perishable as a book can last for 400 years.

Thank you for the Cecil Aldin card. I share your fondness for the artist.

Love,
John

* * *

October 13, 1986

Dear John,

I found these two items at the Shaker Museum yesterday and I thought of you—perhaps Mrs. Daniels will make you a spice cake!

What did you think of Swann's Catalogue of sporting books? I've lost confidence in Mr. Lowry, he isn't quite honest about conditions of books.

Could you use a nice copy of H. von Michaile's *Birds of the Gauntlet*? London, 1952. 4to. 8 colored plates, numerous fine line drawings (sepia). First edition.

Affectionately,
H

October 17, 1986

Dear John,

I'm glad you were pleased with your book. I have another old book that you might be interested in if you don't have it. Not as old, but interesting.

> Niccolo Rosselmini, *Dell'Ubbedienza del Cavallo* (obedience training of the horse). Written in Italian, published in Livorno (sea portion, the west coast of Italy), 1764. 8vo. Steel engraved title page of a horse and gentleman, watermarked paper. Two folding plates of the horse & equipment. ½ vellum, marbleized paper boards (not bright). No record of auction sale. (This, also, was among my upstairs treasures. It's taken me an hour to translate.)

You must have forgotten to tell me about building a house. Where?

Affectionately,
H

October 18, 1986

Dear Helen,

Loved the spice cake recipe from the Shaker Museum. Thank you for your thoughtfulness.

The Chas. B. Wood III collection at Swann doesn't have much for me, except for a couple of Waltons I'd like to get if they don't cost an arm and a leg. The price estimate for Lot 487 (Joseph Seccombe's *First American Angling Book*) of $8,000–$12,000 is amazing. I'll be most interested in what it sells for because I got a copy for half of the low estimate some time ago.

I'd like to buy your copy of H. von Michaile's *Birds of the Gauntlet* and enclose my check.

Love,
John

* * *

October 23, 1986

Dear Helen,

Enclosed is my check for the nice-sounding, old Italian book by Niccolo Rosselmini, *Dell'Ubbedienza del Cavallo.*

Love,
John

October 25, 1986

Dear John,

So you are going to have a birthday—many more. I'm not certain at what age one becomes a senior citizen—but I think I've been one for eleven years and I'm not sure it's made any difference in my life.

People are polite to me due to the wrinkles on my face, so there must be an advantage to age.

Have a happy birthday.

Affectionately,
H

* * *

November 2, 1986

Dear John,

Welcome to S.C. Your letter made me envious—you won't have a moment to get bored and will be the busiest people in town this winter. I especially enjoyed the "no guest room." I once lived in a house with fourteen bedrooms that were occupied all the time. At that time it was fine, as we had three on the staff and I was younger and enjoyed conversation and having to entertain—now peace is pleasant.

Have a window facing the pond where you can sit and have breakfast and watch the ducks. Also you haven't had any fun until you have a pair of peacocks (who scream "help" when they are mating). We had a pair that joined us for cocktails on the terrace.

I'll run through the prints to see what's in keeping for your new home as a housewarming gift. Cockfighting or horses?

Affectionately,
H

November 9, 1986

Dear Helen,

No peacocks! Our farm manager's wife—who collects all kinds of birds & animals—had four peacocks and they drove us crazy—especially with their cries for "help."

A local sporting magazine is going to publish my article on General Davies's book *Ten Days on the Plains* in their Jan./Feb. issue. I titled it "The Millionaire's Hunting Party," which is what Buffalo Bill Cody called it. I'll send you a copy.

Love,
John

November 22, 1986

Dear John,

Jo Hennessey had his ninetieth birthday this week and we gave him a party, which I'm sure he didn't enjoy. However, we didn't let that spoil our fun. I'm not sure I want to live that long.

I mentioned that we had fun with our peacocks. . . . We lived on the island, and when the peacocks screamed "help," it carried across the water. People on the mainland thought we were in trouble, and would get in their boats and come over to help us. That called for an open bar and lots of uninvited company.

Affectionately,
H

P.s Could you use a copy of Don Juan Segundo's *A Treatise on the Suitable Bitting of Horses*, with a description of a new system of bridle bits? Translated from the original Spanish manuscript. London, 1832. 8vo, 40 pp. Engraved advertising leaf. Ed. Patchford, bridle bit maker; folding engraved plate. Marbled wrappers. Front wrapper rubbed, worn. Otherwise, a good copy of an unusual pamphlet.

Do you have a complete set of the Jockey Club's *American Stud Books*? I saw these in my travels recently, nicely bound.

Dear Helen,

I loved your description of the way your peacocks' screams for help summoned the people on the mainland and led to an open bar and lots of parties. On your uninhibited island of yore you must have had lots of fun and games.

Suitable Bitting of Horses sounds unusual. My check is enclosed.

Tell me more about the complete set of Jockey Club's *American Stud Books*, please. I'm not sure whether I want them because thoroughbred racing is on the periphery of my collection, but I'd like to know more about them (i.e., How many volumes? What kind & condition of the bindings? Price?) before I make up my mind. With all of those new and beckoning bookshelves in our new house, I'm being lured by the temptation of putting lovely-looking volumes on the shelves. This is basically a lousy idea, I know, but I want to look at all the possibilities.

Martha and I are nearing the point when the last of our Thanksgiving guests—sixteen family members—are about to leave, and we are savoring the thought of peace and quiet being restored.

Your spouse's ninetieth sounds bittersweet.

Love,
John

December 7, 1986

Dear John,

Before you jump off the deep end, in having fine bindings on the bookshelves in your new house, let me give you a word of advice (I'm older than you are, so I can do this.) Make sure the contents of the book is more important than the binding.

Now I hate quoting books, which you probably have guessed (because of the poor way I do it), but I have a dozen or two of fine bindings that I brought back from England on hunting. I could be tempted to part with some. At the moment I'm looking at fifteen volumes of Theodore Roosevelt. Putnam, 1900. Preface by Roosevelt dated Sagamore Hill, 1889. Small 8vo. Each vol. with a frontispiece plate. ¼ mor., TEG, red leather labels. Bookplate of Richard Rexsamer Baker. Near mint.

Now about the Jockey Club, *The American Stud Books:* a complete set from vols 1 through 27. (I'm not sure 28 has been published yet and it will contain several years.) First published in 1869, is that correct? Only two volumes would be described as other than fine or mint. Bound in calf as issued, leather labels. These books don't belong to me—I saw them in my travels. He is asking $8,000 and will give me ten percent. (Should satisfy me.)

It's snowing and Jaguars don't like snow. The back comes around to the front going down the street, so I'll be housebound for a few days.

Affectionately,
H

Dear Helen,

I hasten to take your advice—not because you are older than I am but because you are much wiser. Are the contents of Theodore Roosevelt's fifteen volumes more important than the lovely ¼ morocco bindings? Did Teddy have fifteen volumes worth of hunting lore to describe? It sounds very interesting and I'm greatly tempted. Please tell a bit more.

Thank you for the information about the *American Stud Books*. I'm not going to buy them—nice as they sound—because I really am not anxious to get that much involved in thorough-bred racing.

Love,
John

December 25, 1986

Dear John,

If the prices in *Book Prices Current* are any indication of Roosevelt's value, I'd have to say the public has found them important. He is very readable, you decide the value to you.

It's Christmas day and the fog is thick and it's raining. Also, the streetlights are on. No Sherri to buy a gift for, so I sent some money off to her college. I think she'd be pleased about that. Don't I sound depressed? I'm not tho.

James Cummins's catalogue #18 should excite you if you are going in for fine bindings. The prices astonished me.

I'm looking for a gun catalogue on Fox Sterlingworths, for myself. I kept the Fox and the twenty-two octagon barrel, I learned to hunt with them. The older you get, the more you depend on memories. So if you come across a Fox catalogue, I'd like to buy it.

Have a happy holiday and a wonderful New Year. Have you laid the cornerstone yet?

Affectionately,
H

Theodore Roosevelt, 15 Volumes
Titles: *Rough Riders*
             Wilderness Hunter
             Naval War of 1812 (2 vols)
             Administration, Civil Service
             American Ideals
             Hunting Trips on the Prairie
             Hunting Trips of a Ranchman
             Hunting the Grizzly
             Winning the West (6 vols)

December 29, 1986

Dear Helen,

Thank you for the information about the titles of the Teddy Roosevelt fifteen volumes. It looks very inviting. I'm enclosing my check for the set.

I'll keep my eyes peeled for a Fox gun catalogue and let you know if I can spot it. Are you interested in prices for your Fox? Orvis has a very extensive used shotgun (and some rifles) department and could be helpful. I found a lovely reconditioned Parker twenty-gauge side-by-side for Martha at Orvis a year ago.

I hope that the New Year will bring you happiness, good health, and all good things. It certainly will have my love—

John

January 8, 1987

Dear John,

I sent the Roosevelt off to you Saturday—I hope we did the right thing and that you didn't buy them to make me happy. If you will let me know what you'd like to make your library beautiful, I will look around. It will keep me out of trouble . . .

I took all the guns over to Orvis and had them appraised, and to make sure they were also in fine working condition before I sold them. Orvis has changed, and unfortunately not for the better. The gun department is still good, but the rest is junk—fast turnover merchandise.

Don't you think we should go to Monaco for the Jeanson sale in February? I sent for a catalogue. They expect to make three million pounds. I don't think we should miss it. The trouble is, I've forgotten how to read French.

I like your piece that you wrote for *The Chronicle of the Horse*. You are becoming so famous I won't be allowed to correspond with you.

Affectionately,
H

Dear Helen,

I loved your sparky letter. The Roosevelt books made me happy.
If my buying them made you happy too, I'm glad. So we are
both happy.

I'm not sure if you would be happy if I kept you out of trouble
by having you look for more lovely sporting books, but I'll take
the chance and encourage you to do some looking if it doesn't
cramp your propensity for trouble too much. Seriously, I'd be
delighted if you could find some nicely bound sets. I ran a
rough calculation of the bookshelf space that's going to be
available in our new living room and there is going to be plenty
of room for extra books, which is good. I mean plenty.

Before coming south in October I did an inventory of the
books that I'd like to bring down here when the new house is
finished. I'm thinking of bringing all the shooting and fishing
books down (the "hook & bullet" books). I'd leave the horse and
hound, foxhunting books in Minnesota. This somewhat arbi-
trary division would roughly split my collection in half and
might be a good solution. In any event, I'll have some much
needed space for my collection at both locations.

I'm glad you liked my article for *The Chronicle of the Horse.* I've
got another article in a different type of magazine that is just
about to be published. I'll send you a copy quite soon and hope
you enjoy it, provided you promise to continue to correspond
with me.

Glad you got your guns checked out at Orvis. They are good in
that department. They also have some first-class fishing (fly)
equipment.

Jim Cummins is sending me a set of the Sotheby catalogues for
the Jeanson sale in Monaco. He called me and said that some of
the items were "staggering." Apparently, Jeanson got a lot of
books at the Schwerdt sales in 1939. Jim says he may go to

Monaco for the sale. Even though my French is still pretty good, I'd rather view the sale from South Carolina. I'm scared.

Love,
John

* * *

March 3, 1987

Dear John,

Hope you and Mrs. Daniels had a nice holiday. Spring has finally arrived, and in the middle of April I expect to go off to Canada for a few days.

Have you any use for Westwood & Satchell, *Considerations upon the White Herring & Cod Fisheries*, 253 pp?

Also, I thought Mrs. Daniels might like *The Narrative of Lieut. Gen. Sir William Howe*, USiana 729.

I'm busy trying to make the yard presentable.

Affectionately,
H

Dear Helen,

I hope that you had a safe & jolly trip to Canada and that your spring yard cleanup is behind you.

Martha and I had a delightful trip to the South Pacific. After I have sorted through the thousand-odd color photographs we took—including a number of spectacular shots of tropical fish with an underwater camera while snorkeling—I'll try to send you a few evocative shots.

We got back here in time to participate in a week-long marathon of annual family meetings about the plantation, and the other rite of spring, the Carolina Cup steeplechase meeting. We are now slowly catching up on our sleep.

The desk top has finally been cleared, too! While we were away, they finally started building our new house. Given a gestation period of nine months, I think we will be able to move in after Christmas, three months later than we'd hoped, but still something good to look forward to.

Thank you for suggesting them, but I don't want *Considerations upon the White Herring & Cod Fisheries,* but could you describe, briefly, the book by Sir William Howe? If included is mention of Lord Cornwallis's southern campaign, it could be of interest.

I'm still waiting to get a complete report on the Monaco/Sotheby sale from Jim Cummins.

Love,
John

April 10, 1987

Dear John,

I'm glad you had such a nice holiday. The weather here is delightful, everybody's disposition has improved. Now for Lieut. Gen. Sir William Howe's book.

> *The Narrative of Gen. Howe. In a committee of the House of Commons, on the 29th of April, 1779. Relative to his conduct, during his late command of the King's Troops in North America: To which are added, some observations upon a pamphlet entitled, 'Letters to a Nobleman.'* Baldwin, London, 1780. First edition. USiana H. 729. Sabin 33342. Large watermarked paper. ½ red morocco. Decorated boards and endpapers, AEG. Page 63—Examination of Earl Cornwallis; Bookplate of B. Franklin Barger, and another Frederick J. Bradlee; page 103—Lord Cornwallis mentioned with his troops at German Town.

I bought the book because I am particularly fond of Burgoyne, but Howe was a naughty boy and didn't get any further north than Albany—nice copy.

You and Mrs. Daniels will have a wonderful time watching your house grow. I envy you.

Affectionately,
H

Joseph Hennessey on Neshobe Island, VT (circa 1940)

"I was thirty-three when Alex died. Josy and I
were married when I was thirty-four (1944)."
[Joseph was born in 1896 in New York City.
He was 14 years older than Helen.]

Helen Hennessey adrift on Lake Bomoseen, VT (1940's)

"I took a frigate years ago from California to New York
with a standard French poodle and three paying guests—
made a lot of money playing poker."

Neshobe Island on Lake Bomoseen, VT

"About five years after Sherri was born (1951), I was seriously ill, with no insurance, and I owed the doctors $135,000 so we had to sell the island. I never regretted it. If you needed a toothpick you had to get in a boat and go to the mainland, and that could be a bloody bore."

Joseph Hennessey (circa 1975)

"Josy celebrated 95 last week—
we only let him have
one drink though"

Helen Hennessey, April 13, 1994

"I let all the hired help go.
I'm living alone with a Siamese cat ("Gin")
who loves my company."

Helen Hennessey, May 24, 1979

"I thought you might enjoy the enclosed pictures of the book shop and the carriage house. 'The Shadow' is my Abyssina cat, who is a very good companion. We once had eleven dogs, one belonged to Moss Hart, one to Dorothy Parker, but we lived on an island then, and all you had to do was to open a door."

Alexander Wollcott

"Alex and I didn't like each other. I told him once that he couldn't write
worth a damn and that fixed me." (Helen Hennessey)

"Going To a Fight"

A fourteen-foot long panorama by Robert Cruikshank, London, 1819.
Two years later, discovered Pierce Egan's 36-page pamphlet which describes
each scene in the panorama. Bought from Helen Hennessey.

hand-colored print by Sherri Hennessey (1980)

Sherri Hennessey: Born in 1946 when Helen was thirty-six. Sherri and her mother were very close. They made more than twenty-five trips together to England on book buying expeditions. Sherri was a professional artist and was living in Aiken, S.C. when she developed terminal cancer. She died in 1984.

"Treatsie on Horse Equipage," Tokio. 1857

Bought from Helen Hennessey.

Hunting, Hawking, Shooting

The 4-volume sporting bibliography by Schwerdt, bought from Helen Hennessey.

Dear Helen,

Thank you for describing the Lt. Gen. Sir Wm. Howe's book so thoroughly. I have decided not to buy the book because it is too remote from the main areas of interest in my collection.

I got a printout of the prices from the Jeanson sale in Monaco. Total prices ran to eight million dollars. I only purchased a few trifles.

I'm still confused by the implications of the Jeanson sale. If, as I've been told, the main group of buyers were the French, then it doesn't really say much about the real world of sporting book collecting. The Sotheby catalogue is a valuable addition to bibliography. Aside from that, the whole thing may simply be an aberration similar to the thirty-nine million dollar Van Gogh and the Wallace Windsor jewelry sales, both of which were hyped out of all proportion. Only time will tell.

Our new house is "a building" at a painfully slow rate, but it is finally progressing. I love to hear from you. Your letters are always interesting and saucy.

Love,
John

[No date]

Dear John,

I enjoyed the pictures of your holiday. You may not believe this, but I'm so restless that I'd have all the people aboard ready to throw me overboard. I spent my honeymoon on an ocean liner and need I say more.

About the Jeanson sale—they tell me that the French Ring or Pool (as we call it) is stronger than the British, so I expected the Jeanson sale would be covered strongly by the French. You may find the reason our young people are not collectors of rare sporting books is because of the reprint world. In Canada the rare sporting dealers had nothing but reprint material and were having a brisk business. I, on the other hand, am a snob about books and have no interest in learning that field.

Have a happy voyage north.

Affectionately,
H

* * *

May 31, 1987

Dear John,

You must be settled in the north country, but I must say that the weather has not been all that I desired.

I bought the enclosed book the other day. I've tried to get it away from its owner for five years. I finally was successful.

I thought it might interest you, as you hunted that country often.

Affectionately,
Helen

390. Fielding and Walton, *A Picturesque Tour of the English Lakes, containing a description of the most romantic scenery of Cumberland, Westmoreland, Lancashire, with accounts of Ancient and Modern Customs, and Elucidations of the History and Antiquities of that part of the Country, etc., etc.* Printed for R. Ackermann, London, 1821. 4to. Illustrated with 48 beautifully colored views drawn by Messrs. T.H. Fielding and J. Walton during a two-year residence among the lakes. Handsomely bound by Riviere in full dark green levant, gilt extra, gilt edges. A magnificent copy. Very scarce.

* * *

June 2, 1987

Dear Helen,

If you don't mind parting so quickly with a book that you have been stalking for five years, I'd love to buy Fielding and Walton's *A Picturesque Tour of the English Lakes.*

I looked it up in *Tooley* (219), where it is carefully described—all forty-eight plates. Although it is somewhat beyond the scope or description of the sporting book, it certainly has the association of depicting views of country that has been hunted over. (In 1978 Martha and I went beagling in the Lake Country with a bookseller friend—and of course visited John Peel's grave.)

My check is enclosed. Our part of the north country has turned hot, but this is good for the bass fishing which I am going to resume on my favorite St. Croix River this coming weekend.

I hope you are off to a good summer.

Love,
John

August 14, 1987

Dear John,

It's been a powerful long time since I have heard from you—I hope it only means you are busy with your new home.

Affectionately,
H

* * *

September 8, 1987

Dear Helen,

Thanks for your sassy note—a good & timely reminder that I haven't written you lately.

I've been working on several projects. I did an exhibit of manuscripts & autographs in my collection—part of the work I try to do each summer when I get a chance to single out some aspect of the collection for study. It turned out okay. I was surprised at how many MS and ALS had accumulated over the years. About twenty-five local friends and bibliophiles stopped by to see it during July & August, which led to some enjoyable book talks.

I belong to a men's dinner club in Camden, S.C. During the winter months, we meet (October thru April) once a month for a black-tie soup-to-nuts dinner and one of the members reads a paper he has written on any subject of his choice for about forty-five minutes before we dine. Topics in the past have ranged from the effects of altitude on mountain climbers to apartheid, the America's Cup Races, and a chapter of Reid Buckley's new book.

I am scheduled to give my paper in November and I've been having a ball doing the research. The title is "A Faker's Dozen" and it is about thirteen notorious literary fakers and forgers.

I start with Chatterton, Ireland, Spring, and Wise as warm-ups, then get into more interesting, current stuff such as Clifford Irving, the Hitler Diaries, the Vineland Map, and Mark Hofmann. I've just about finished writing and I'm rather excited with the way it's turning out. (I'll send you a copy of the finished draft for your comments and criticism.)

Our house is going along very well. We just got back on Sunday from an inspection trip. The workmanship is excellent, but it's slow! Hopefully, we'll move in by late December. I hope you are having a good summer. Do write soon!

Love,
John

* * *

October 8, 1987

Dear John,

Nice to hear from you, and that all is well. . . . Nothing new or exciting around here, except we had a snowstorm on Sunday and half the world here didn't have heat or lights. That stirred us up for a while.

I lost my outside man and so I've been compelled to get ready for winter on my own, and I must say that I'm not the kid I used to be. A little mentally disturbing to my independence. You once sent me a list of duplicate books and among the list was Cecil Aldin's *Time I Was Dead*. If you still have a spare copy, I'd like to buy one.

Maggs Brothers has a new publication titled *Bookbinding in the British Isles*. Two volumes, folio, paper, 524 pages (why they didn't use a fine binding is a mystery to me).

When do you go south?

Affectionately,
H

October 13, 1987

Dear Helen,

It was so nice to hear from you again after a long hiatus. I'm sorry you lost your handyman—it's no fun to have to put on your own storm windows.

In answer to your questions, I no longer have a duplicate of Aldin's *Time I Was Dead.* I'm quite sure I gave it to the James Ford Bell Library for their fund-raising auction last year.

I'd love to get a copy of Maggs Brothers' new publication, *Bookbinding in the British Isles,* and am enclosing my check.

Did you see the PBS television program *The Ten Year Luncheon*? It was an hour-long program about all of your old pals—Woollcott, Parker, etc.—at the Algonquin and up at your lake in New England. Lovely & nostalgic and quite saucy when Parker was quoted.

I have a grandson who is a freshman at Skidmore this year. He loves it! Says the ratio of girls to boys is superb! He is a handsome young devil, six-foot two-inch, lean, blond, and striking. Maybe you can get him to help put on your storm windows.

Love,
John

Dear John,

Yes, I saw *The Ten Year Luncheon*. It got very bad reviews not
only in the newspapers but also from me. But I'm glad you
enjoyed it.

So you are going to have a birthday. You're only a kid. I have
ten years on you. Have a happy day.

I hope you won't be disappointed in Maggs Brothers' two-
volume set on bindings. Someday, I'll quote you from my own
treasures, *The Facsimiles of Choice Examples of the Art of Book
Illumination,* large Quaritch, 1889, in color, fine binding. So
much better than Maggs. I was very disappointed in theirs.

You will have a wonderful time this winter. A new house stimu-
lates your mind and body. I could do with some stimulation like
that.

Skidmore wants to buy the Carriage House—perhaps because
the new president lives next door and he doesn't think too
highly of this old lady next door.

Affectionately,
H

October 25, 1987

Dear Helen,

I enjoyed your most recent letter, which was feisty as usual. What did you do to stir up the new president of Skidmore— race your sports car down his driveway?

The Maggs Bros. *Volumes of British Bookbinders* is beautifully illustrated. It makes an interesting reference book.

I suppose that any one-hour television show about the Algonquin gang would be a disappointment to someone like you who had known them all so intimately. From my point of view it was both informative and rather poignant. My parents hauled us around Europe in the 1920s and '30s when Dad was in the Diplomatic Corps, and I have fond memories of their gifted and artistic and attractive expatriate friends in Rome, Brussels, and Paris. It was a very special era!

This town has gone baseball crazy! Tonight is the rubber match for the World Series and "our" glorious Twins will go down in history for their fantastic comeback in the sixth game, no matter what happens tonight.

Affectionately,
John
(In S.C. I go by "Jack.")

Dear John,

I hope you had a pleasant trip south. I also hope the fires aren't near you.

Winter is on its way and I haven't finished the leaves. However, I think they will wait for me next spring.

Did I tell you that Skidmore wants to buy the Carriage House? I can't imagine why. They offered to buy it and let me live here until I die and they will take care of the house. So far it hasn't excited me.

You must have had a wonderful youth, traveling around Europe. My memories of the people from the island, what they taught me, have stayed with me for fifty years. Things that happen today don't seem very important.

Affectionately,
H

[No date]

Dear Helen,

It's still very dry down here, but I think we're over the worst of our forest fire scares after last week's very helpful rains.

The new house is getting more & more exciting to see as everybody pitches in for the last major effort. Carpenters, painters, electricians, plumbers, well and water treatment, landscapers, tile and plaster people, on and on and on!

All our new furnishings, including paintings, pictures, and 1500 rare books—plus beds, tables, sofas, etc., etc., etc.—are sitting in a nearby warehouse waiting for D-Day, which should be January 4th!

I'm going to try to get some new photographs and will send you a few if they are any good.

We are getting out of here for a week next Wednesday. While our daughter descends on Mulberry for five days with a dozen galloping housewives we will be frisking in New York and New Haven—Christmas shopping in the former and forty-fifth Yale reunion in the latter.

It sounds as if Skidmore is in love with your carriage house. Be *very firm* and *tough* with them and ask for the moon!

Love,
John

November 25, 1987

Dear John,

I'm glad all those lovely people are coming to your house tomorrow. That used to be fun in the olden days. We'd have a running poker game all day.

I've been sick and I'm off to the hospital Friday to see what's wrong with me. Probably nothing—except a bad disposition. So, I haven't read your piece. However, I'm honored that you sent me a copy and I'll report later.

Affectionately,
H

  * * *

December 7, 1987

Dear John,

I know that there was a reason I never went to any of my class reunions. The gals must have had a thrilling afternoon. It reminds me of the man who wanted a transplant on his hip, because he enjoyed sex in that position. If Sherri was here she'd tell you how I enlarged on the subject at a dinner party and nearly lost the whole party. Having had two doctors in the family and wanting to be one myself, some of my stories are a little rough.

The doctors—after several tests that were negative—have decided I had the flu. However, I'm healthy again.

I hear that you bought a lousy copy of Mrs. Sterling Clarke's *The Ladies' Equestrian Guide*. I thought I taught you that condition and contents were the most important value of a book?

Why don't you send your piece "A Faker's Dozen" to *Sporting Classics*? I think the public would enjoy it. I did.

I have a new speeding ticket—my own fault, I was daydreaming.

Affectionately,
H

December 13, 1987

Dear Helen,

I'm so glad to hear that you are healthy again. Now if you can just cut down on those speeding tickets you should be off to a great '88 (1988 that is).

I don't know where or how you got the idea that I bought a lousy copy of Mrs. Clarke's *The Ladies' Equestrian Guide*. I'm enclosing copies of the index cards on the three copies of Mrs. Clarke's books in my collection, and as you can see, they are in very good condition.

You most certainly did teach me that condition and contents are the most important values of a book and I have always tried to practice what you so eloquently preached.

So, where did you get this "lousy copy" stuff?

I just celebrated my third year of sobriety with a cup of black coffee!

Love,
John

December 21, 1987

Dear John,

Barbara Walzer told me about you buying the Clarke book in poor condition from Cummins and Blue Rider—owned jointly. I never buy from Blue Rider because his books are generally in very poor condition. Hooper on the other hand frequently has some very fine books.

So you've been a good boy and haven't had a drink in three years. You have my compliments. I, on the other hand, look forward to four o'clock when I have my liquid refreshment, sometimes two. Have a happy holiday.

Affectionately,
H

January 1, 1988, New Year's Day

Dear Helen,

Happy New Year! I hope that 1988 brings you a full measure of happiness, good health, prosperity, and love

Thank you so much for the fascinating Teichmann book,* *Smart Aleck*! I have been dipping into it ever since it arrived just before Christmas. When I dip into a book to read, it is a sure sign that I'm thoroughly hooked and that the book will merit eventual reading from cover to cover.

Of course what interests me even more than Teichmann's masterful study in depth of Alexander Woollcott is the story it tells about your life and your husband's and the relationships with Woollcott and his crowd. Although you only get a walk-on part in the book, Joseph Hennessey is well fleshed out, including that very handsome photograph. I can begin to see what an incredible era it must have been for you to have lived through. As they say, you were living in the fast lane. It must have been exciting and stimulating and so very easy to hold in your memory.

After Woollcott died, was it a "hard landing" or was there still enough time to build a good life for yourselves? How old were you? What did you do for an encore, as they say? My guess is that Woollcott had such a gigantic ego that everybody close to him was held completely hostage during his lifetime. Which of the "beautiful people" did you like the most? The least? Which were most friendly to you? Which were most aloof? I would love to get some of your insights and impressions. Did you or your husband ever write about any of this?

Thank you for sharing this with me. In your cute note you say that Teichmann's book "might explain why I'm a little strange." I love it! Especially the kind of way that you are a "little strange"—don't ever change!

Yes, I've been cold sober without a drop of booze for over three years now. I'm really pleased about it and the quality of my life is 100 percent better. I'd be lying to say that I don't miss it, but it isn't a big deal anymore as long as I don't get complacent and as long as I keep reminding myself that as an alcoholic I have an incurable disease. I wish I could join you in some "liquid refreshment" around four o'clock each afternoon—except for the fact that it would soon kill me. Being a "good boy" doesn't have anything to do with it. It's a matter of life or death for an alcoholic.

Did I tell you that I've also given up smoking? Wow! I haven't had a cigarette since early October. Three months now! I quit "cold turkey" and I really don't miss it very much except that I'm chewing a lot of gum these days.

Our good news is that we will be able to start moving into our new house in about two weeks! I'll send you a lot of photographs after we are all moved in.

Thank you, Helen, for all of your sprightly letters. You are a good writer and I look forward to opening each of your letters and am never disappointed with what I find inside.

Affectionately,
John

P.S. You *and* Barbara Walzer seem to both be screwed up about some book that I bought from Blue Rider that was in "poor condition." I haven't bought anything from Blue Rider in years! What is Barbara talking about?

*Howard Teichmann, *Smart Aleck—The Wit, World, and Life of Alexander Woollcott.* William Morrow & Co., N.Y., 1976.

January 12, 1988

Dear John,

I'll try to answer some of your questions—however, remember, I'm the gal that can't spell.

I was thirty-three when Alex* died (1943). Josy and I were married when I was thirty-four (1944) and Sherri was born when I was thirty-six (1946).

Alex and I didn't like each other. I told him once that he couldn't write worth a damn and that fixed me. Also, the dogs liked me and he didn't like sharing people or animals. Once he said, "Give them to her."

Alex was very strange about married people. He loved them, but never had them visit together. He dearly loved Bea Kaufman and George, but not together. (He knew he'd receive more attention from them when they stayed without their mates—p 170, mid-page, Teichmann's book.)

Everyone loved Alice Duer Miller. She was a great person and a member of the club. (She also, like me, wanted her drink at four o'clock.) Moss Hart was another favorite. He was so pleased when he got married and had twins, as many people thought he was gay.

About five years after Sherri was born (1951), I was seriously ill, with no insurance, and I owed the doctors $135,000 so we had to sell the island. I never regretted it. If you needed a toothpick you had to get in a boat and go to the mainland and that could be a bloody bore.

I learned a great deal in those days.

If the story of Alex at the White House is in the book, you'll get a kick out of it.

Hurriedly,
H

*Alexander Woollcott

January 16, 1988

Dear Helen,

Thank you for sharing those intimate glimpses of Alex. Although forty-five years have gone by since his death, he must still seem very vivid to you—especially because you continue to feel such a real sense of dislike for the man. What has happened to Neshobe Island since you sold it in 1951? Have you ever been back? The whole mystique of Woollcott continues to be of interest—especially for all of us who are old enough to remember his radio broadcasts. I was twenty-two when he died.

Our new house? The suspense is almost killing us. We had a horrible snow and ice storm here on January 7th and it's been very cold in South Carolina ever since. The storm has thrown everything off schedule. The carpeting being flown from Ireland on January 7th was lost for a week. The hard floor painter & finisher and the wallpaper expert, both of whom I suspect are victims of their own fumes, disappeared for several days, so that everything is now running late. My best guess—which I can't confirm with our nice building contractor because he's too wise or too shell-shocked, or both, to make a prediction—is that we will be able to start moving our new furniture into our new house by January 25th! I hope I'm right or close. I'd better be. Gr-r-r.

After we start moving in I'm sure that you won't hear from me for a month. Every day in February will be like Christmas morning. You see, every stick of furniture, every rug, every curtain, every pot and pan—the works—is brand-new! After forty-five years of marriage we are giving each other a whole new trousseau!

I'll try to get some good photographs after we are more or less settled. Meanwhile—take care of yourself and hold down the speedometer.

Love,
John

Needless to say, I didn't write this piece.
H

THE GHOSTS FROM HENNESSEYS' PAST
Rare Books Remain Ageless
By Doug McKnight, Staff Writer

'Few people read now, especially the young. Especially since television came along. It's up to the new generation to come back to the written word. How can people exist without books to read? I just don't know.'
—Helen Hennessey

There are ghosts in the barn. They've been there for twenty-four years now, all writers of old searching for new bindings, a good cleaning, and a set of eyes to wonder at their written word.

They came here because two lovers, Joseph and Helen Hennessey, called and promised them a new life. Or the lovers went to them, searching in England and at auctions throughout New York State to bring them to the Hennesseys' old and rare bookshop, an 1899 carriage house on Fourth Street in Saratoga Springs.

But while the ghosts they collect remain ageless, Helen and Joseph grow old.

Joseph, in his nineties, suffered a stroke and is paralyzed. The seventy-seven-year-old Helen waits for another browser or buyer to ring the doorbell and enter her world. When they do, at first her ghosts sleep while the room casts its spell.

The bare floor is cold but warmed by the several weaved oriental rugs pushed together. Sketches and paintings of horses and yellowed photographs of Dorothy Parker, Lawrence Olivier, and Ruth Gordon hang in every open spot and are even taped onto windows near the ceilings. The Hennesseys were friends with the movie stars when they lived on Long Island during the 1940s.

Limbs slap against the window pane, drawing attention to the heavy fall of the snow. A wiry Siamese cat called Gin makes a sporadic burst in all directions, leaping from to shelf to shelf and then straight up in the air like a Mexican jumping bean, teasing the ghosts and using them as mini-scratching posts.

Smoke from Helen's constant companion, a Pall Mall cigarette, creates a white haze that tumbles and crawls from book to book, then up to the ceiling to commingle with the older haze, its residue engulfing a small half-century-old handmade wooden sulky nailed to the wall.

"It was probably made by some grandfather for his grandson because it has that kind of handmade look," Helen says.

In the middle is a table and chair for those who just want to sit and rest or read, with small islands of books on portable shelves set nearby. And in the back, hidden by a partition, is the Hennesseys' office, staffed with a clutter of rare-book listings, a desk buried beneath tattered letters from old friends, decade-old newspaper articles, and even an original picture of Teddy Roosevelt holding a nephew, from an old family album the Hennesseys were given.

A Japanese samurai sword secured in a warped wooden sheath hangs by a purple tassel on the partition, supposedly used by one of the late emperors. In the middle of all this past, a bit hunched over and head cocked in thought, is Helen.

She pokes around the room trying to remember which rows of old books are alphabetized and which aren't. When she speaks, more often than not it is with a favorite phrase, "In the olden days . . . ," and with a hint of gruffness.

"She doesn't suffer fools lightly," says friend Edith Brown, who with her husband owns a bookstore in Greenwich.

"She's direct and can be a bit crusty at times. I adore her," Brown says, who met Helen through her husband, Hank Howard. Howard used to teach at Skidmore College and would frequent the Hennesseys' shop.

Helen stops sharply and pulls out a fragile leather-bound book of illustrations from the 1800s and delicately leafs through it. There is a name scratched on a page, but she can't make it out. As she squints hard at the illegible signature, a change takes place. Spirits in slumber awake.

Like the morning fog they come on little cat feet, hiding on their haunches behind Gin and watching their visitor with silent interest. They begin to beckon through Gin's call, a throaty meow.

Great and minor authors are all here, waiting for a cycle of fashion to return them to the favor of the literary world. They mourn their own passing, yet chirp excitedly about their return. Two old favorites will be mourning for awhile, it seems.

"Hemingway and Steinbeck (she has first editions of both) are out, so are a lot of the poets. They have had their day," she says matter-of-factly, not sad because with cycles you come to understand that nothing is good or bad, just is.

People are less interested in the contents than in what type of binding the book has, what type of dust cover protects the book (that's big now) and who illustrated the cover, if it has any, she says. Thomas Jefferson frowns and the others follow, arrogant that people will always want ideas and words before anything else.

The Hennesseys' oldest book dates back to the early 1600s, a time of great social rebellion in Europe, when ironclad governments were melted and the church was struggling to maintain its dominance, while man was just getting past the plague.

"In the olden days books were mostly written by the ministry, so they are dull as dishwater, but valuable just because they have existed for more than 300 years," Helen says, smoke escaping from her mouth with each syllable and curling around Gin's shadow.

Imagine a man leaning over his book with ink and feathered pen to scribble Christian beliefs onto a large blank page. He could have never believed his work would find a momentary resting place in a small brick barn in America, a name that would be as alien to him as some of his ideas are to modern man.

The costs of the Hennesseys' books range from $1 for some 1940s Modern Language editions of English classics to a couple thousand dollars for a hand-scripted Spanish music manuscript dating to sometime in the 1600s. It is locked away with the rest of her most valuable books, many at least 200 years old, she says.

Along the walls in the main room, voices of Blake, Keats, Twain, and Joyce mix into a choral bickering of why they have been forgotten and ignored for so long by readers, why they are only known by a small cluster of college literature classes. Authors are impatient with historical cycles.

Helen isn't, usually. But there is one cycle with which she is not pleased.

"Few people read now, especially the young," she says, "Especially since television came along. I mean, I was forty years old before I owned a television. It's up to the new generation to come back to the written word. How can people exist without books to read? I just don't know."

Helen and her husband's love affair with rare books began when they both worked in the book business in Manhattan in the 1930s and '40s. Joseph (she calls him Josy) worked in the old book business and in the new.

"It was so different in the 1940s," she says. "People made good money, but they never had any."

Joseph's later job as assistant director for the state's civil defense brought them to the Albany area in 1963. They settled in Saratoga Springs. They saw the rundown carriage house and bought it, making the bottom floor a rare book store and the top their home.

Within three weeks, the two had built all the shelves that stack up ceiling high and create a second wall of paper and ideas. Then Helen went to England.

"They have good books over there, well-made bindings," she says. "For most of the good old books, that is where they were printed."

She just returned from her twenty-fifth trip to England in November, scurrying from auction to auction to pick up rare books.

"It is getting more and more difficult to buy good books over there. It has gotten expensive because the dollar is not doing well," she says, combing through a row of books in search of a title that has popped into her mind.

To open for business they put an ad in the yellow pages and joined an antique book association, which publishes a trade magazine.

"It's not that difficult to get into the business. You sort of learn as you go along, learn what to pay for a book and what to sell it for," she says.

"Josy was good at English literature and I'm good at sporting books because I grew up poor in Vermont and hunting was our fun," she says, pausing for a moment at the short thud of a sound. Another ghost selling his ideas? No, just Gin doing flip-flops on the floor before leaping up onto the table. The cat throws its lean body against Helen and purrs loudly.

The store doesn't have any set hours. It has been that way since Joseph suffered his stroke a few years back. Now, she sits upstairs and waits for the sound of a doorbell or telephone. People know she is there, she says.

The height of the rare book business was five years ago, she says, but it has tailed off since then, another cycle to while away. While the August tourist deluge is good for business and happily awaited by her ghosts, it is bad for Helen.

"I want to run away," she says. "You make money during the time, but a lot of people come in here and mistreat the books. I don't like people who mistreat a book."

She takes care of her ghosts, cleaning the covers and brushing off the marks on the pages. She thinks hers are the best.

"I'm a snob about my books." And every merry ghost who finds a new owner, Helen replaces, though not as often nowadays, with another pouting author. Her books treat her well in return, she says. She is comfortable with her ghosts.

But one day she must pass from solid to spirit and her ghosts will leave this rustic old barn for another lover who will fawn over them, make them feel needed, and find a clear pair of young eyes to wonder at their words.

Memory of Helen and Joseph Hennessey will fade with the years, but ideas will and must survive, as Franklin Roosevelt once said. It's just the cycle of things.

Picture captions:

NO CHILLS INSIDE—Icicles that form outside the Hennesseys' bookstore on Fourth Street in Saratoga Springs are no indication of the warmth felt inside among the rare volumes.

SAYS IT ALL—Gin, a permanent fixture in the Hennesseys' bookshop, transmits an eerie feeling in this double-exposed picture.

RARE SELECTIONS—Avid readers can find about any book to their liking that fill these handmade shelves in the Hennesseys' bookstore.

—from *The Saratogian*—Sunday, January 17, 1988

Dear Helen,

What a nice newspaper article. I thoroughly enjoyed reading Doug McKnight's feature article, "The Ghosts from Hennesseys' Past," in the Sunday supplement of the January 17th *The Saratogian.*

You must have had fun with the reporter. It sounds to me as though you had him in the palm of your hand and got a lot off your mind.

Thank you so much for sending me a copy.

Love,
John

* * *

February 19, 1988

Dear John,

The house must be all settled by now, and you have found six things to change—no house is ever really completed.

It seems to me that it's been a long, dull winter—however, it's time for spring. Have you any use for *The Englishman's Guide Book to United States and Canada,* with an appendix to shooting and fishing resorts of N.A. London, 1883. Small 8vo, brown leather, 21 maps on tissue. Fine condition. Wonderful illus. for hotels, etc.

Welcome to your new home. May you have many happy years ahead of you.

Affectionately,
H

February 22, 1988

Dear Helen,

Enclosed is my check for *The Englishman's Guide Book to United States and Canada*—it sounds like a gem!

I'm sorry you have the "dull winter blahs." Hang in there because March is just around the corner after Leap Year's Day. Speaking of which, I had dinner the other evening with a chap who will be seventy-six but will only be celebrating his nineteenth birthday on February 29th!

I am enclosing a copy of the *The Three Wishes*, which I hope will ease you over the midwinter blahs. It is a "true" fairy story that I wrote based on the situation which obviously developed here in connection with our new house. Just as it has been for all fairy stories in the past, this one is based on real people.

I had fun writing it & I hope you enjoy it as a belated valentine.

Love,
John

* * *

February 28, 1988

Dear John,

The pictures of the house are great. I especially like the overhang and the color of your house. Suppose I could have one like that up here?

Three Wishes was fun to read. You needed me down there to drive the workmen with my holly whip. I sent *The Englishman's Guide Book* off yesterday. I thought it was great and sort of hated to see it go.

Affectionately,
H

Dear John,

Is the roof on your new house called a Ludovici roof?

Have you any use for Edward Spencer's *The King's Race Horses*, 1902? I seem to be full of questions today.

I'm in hopes of going to England the second week of May. That depends on if I find someone to take care of Josy. But it's time I went somewhere to blow the stink off me. I'm having trouble living with myself right now.

Affectionately,
H

[No date]

Dear Helen,

What is a Ludovici roof? It sounds like everybody should have one. Answer to question #2: Please tell me more about Spencer's *The King's Race Horses*. (This isn't my day.)

It sounds to me as though you have a bad case of cabin fever. Yes, it would be a good idea for you to take a trip to England the second week in May. Sounds like fun. (Find some nice books for me while you're at it.)

I'm enclosing a book that I just put together to send to about sixty people who are going on a trip with us to Europe in mid-May. The whole thing got started in October, when I sent a questionnaire to about 200+ of my old World War II pals who were in the same Field Artillery Battalion. I asked them if they'd be interested in a tour of our battle route across Europe. I was swamped with enthusiastic answers to the questionnaire saying it was a great idea & to include them in.

So since then I've found a great couple in New Jersey who specialize in organizing these kinds of tours. They have put together a sixteen-day tour—New York to Paris to the Normandy beaches & then all the way to Czechoslovakia along our battle route, which was Patton's. We end up in Munich & fly back on June 3rd. Martha and I are taking two grandchildren and it should be a ball!

I prepared the enclosed book and describe it in the introduction. I'm getting ready to mail it out to everybody who has signed up for the tour so that they'll have about a month or so to read up.

Love,
John

March 23, 1988

Dear John,

Thanks for your itinerary for May. I haven't finished reading all
of it yet. Should be an interesting trip.

Josy fought in the First World War, and I tried for officer's
training in the Second War, passed all the requirements, but
then flunked the physical. So I went to Hartford, Conn., to
work for Pratt and Whitney, making airplane motors. No unions
in those days, so I made so much money I didn't know what to
do with it.

A Ludovici roof looks like the overhang on your new home.
That's all I know about it.

> Edward Spencer, *The King's Race Horses*. London, 1902. Large 4to.
> A history of the connections of His Majesty Edward VII with the
> national sport. 21 photographic plates with tissue guards. Half paper-
> parchment, some wear, TEG. Printed on heavy paper, edges uncut.

Affectionately,
H

* * *

April 15, 1988

Dear John,

We will both be off on our holiday soon. Have a wonderful time.

I'll be glad to look for a book for you in England. But you have
so many, you'd better give me a title—don't forget the bloody
American dollar is only worth fifty cents. I'm going to shop
very carefully.

Affectionately,
H.B.H.

April 22, 1988

Dear Helen,

I'm glad that you are already thinking about your trip to England and are making plans about your search for books.

In giving you a hunting license for some rare sporting books, I would like to aim you at locating more illustrated books by Henry Alken. As you know, he is a favorite of mine and I have been able to get a number of his works. I'm enclosing a list of the Henry Alken books that I have already acquired so that if you find any new Alken goodies for me you will be able to spot them more accurately. *Good hunting!*

Please keep in touch.

Love,
John

* * *

[No date]

Dear John,

I don't see this book on your list.

> Robert T. Vyner, *Notitia Venatica.* Routledge, London, 1910. Large 8vo, 2 vols. A treatise on foxhunting. A new edition revised by Wm. Blew. 12 illus. by Alken and others, colored by hand. Fine binding features red leather, decorated boards, TEG. Bookplate of Thomas Leiter.

Hurriedly,
H

[No date]

Dear Helen,

In answer to your question, I do have about six different copies of Robert Vyner's *Notitia Venatica*—a lovely book with those very nice & unusual illustrations by Henry Alken.

When do you leave for England?

* * *

May 7, 1988

Dear John,

I leave Thursday May 12th from Montreal. Just about when you will be on your way. Have a wonderful trip.

I'm afraid I won't find many books because of the rate of exchange. However, I'm open to being pleasantly surprised.

Affectionately,
H

June 6, 1988

Dear John,

You couldn't possibly exaggerate when you describe the cost of Europe today. Being a thrifty New Englander, it curbed my appetite. A figure of speech.

Here's a list of books I brought back. I don't think any will be your dish of tea except the limited, deluxe edition of the Lonsdale Library.

> Geoffrey Brooks, *The Way of a Man with a Horse.* Signed by Brooke and Lionel Edwards. Full red leather.
> Sir Charles Frederick, *Foxhunting.* Signed by Frederick and Lionel Edwards. Full blue morocco.
> E.C. Stuart Baker, *Indian Pigeon & Doves.* 1913. ¼ morocco.
> Lionel Dawson, *Sport in War.* Illus by Edwards. First edition.
> Robert Elmer, *The Book of the Long Bow.* 1929.
> Watson, *Lionel Edwards, Master of the Sporting Scene.*
> Patrick Chalmers, *40 Fine Ladies.* Illus by Cecil Aldin.
> Wirth & Young, *Ballooning.*
> Sewell, *Black Beauty.* Illus by Lionel Edwards.
> E.T. Macdermot, *The Devon and Somerset Staghounds.* 1936. Illus by Lionel Edwards. Limited edition, signed by artist and author.
> *King Albert's Book.*
> Owen Jones, *The Grammar of Ornament.* 112 colored plates.
> British Sports and Sportsmen, *Polo and Coaching.* Full red morocco. Limited to 1,000 copies.
> British Sports and Sportsmen, *Sportsmen of the Past.* 2 vols. Full red morocco. Limited to 1,000 copies.
> Brand new set of bagpipes. A dueling pistol. A wooden clarinet.

I found no Alken.

I had trouble getting the pistol through customs, but they took one look at a wrinkled old lady and decided I wouldn't even know how to load the damn thing.

Welcome home,
H

Dear Helen,

I was so glad to hear from you after your return from England. I agree with you about the prices in Europe! Fortunately, our sixteen-day trip through four countries following our war route from the Normandy beaches to western Czechoslovakia was a package tour so most of our expenses were covered. But even so we got "sticker shock" over the extras.

You sent me an interesting preliminary list of the books you brought back. I pricked up my ears over the "limited, deluxe editon of the Lonsdale Library." Tell me more! How many volumes? What kind of bindings & how are the contents and condition?

I'm also interested in Watson's *Lionel Edwards, Master of the Sporting Scene.* Is this a new biography about Edwards? What is *King Albert's Book*?

I'm going to send you a few photographs of our World War II trip. It was really fabulous. How is your French? I'm enclosing a clipping about our group after a typical day in France.

Love,
John

June 21, 1988

Dear John,

I have just received an unusual (in French) book on ballooning, 1903. The last of the shipments. If you have any interest, let me know. It's a hot subject today.

Nice to hear from you. I'm glad you had a wonderful time. I'm spoiled, because the trips with Sherri were full of fun.

Affectionately,
H

Sir Charles Frederick and others, *Foxhunting*. The Lonsdale Library, London, 1930. Vol III, royal 8vo. Color frontispiece signed by Lionel Edwards, 4 other plates in color, plus 45 illus. Handmade paper, publisher's full blue morocco, gilt top, other edges untrimmed. Limited edition of 375 numbered copies, #157, signed by the editor. Fine.

Lieut. Col. Geoffrey Brooke, *The Way of a Man with a Horse*. The Lonsdale Library. Royal 8vo. Colored frontispiece signed by Lionel Edwards, plus over ninety illus. Limited to 360 copies for sale, signed by Brooke. On handmade paper, TEG, other edges untrimmed, full red morocco. Fine cond.

J.N.P. Watson, *Lionel Edwards, Master of the Sporting Scene*. Sportsman's Press, London, 1986. Folio, colored plates. DJ. New.

Hall Crane, editor, *King Albert's Book*. The Daily Telegraph, Glasgow, 1914. A tribute to the Belgian king and people from representative men and women throughout the world. Folio. Illus in color and B&W. Tan cloth. Fair condition.

June 23, 1988

Dear Helen,

The two Lonsdale Library books seem like special volumes
with their special bindings. Although I have both of the books
in their standard form, I would like to buy the two fancy copies
that you described in your recent reply to my inquiry.

My check, which is enclosed, is for the two Lonsdale books and
the new J.N.P Watson book, *Lionel Edwards, Master of the
Sporting Scene*. I have two other new books by this fellow J.N.P.
Watson who seems to be producing some original & worthwhile
books having to do with foxhunting.

I decided not to get *King Albert's Book*. It wasn't in my field.

I'm not sure about the French, 1903 book on Ballooning. I've
been up in a hot-air balloon in Kenya—looking at lions and
elephants in the Masai Mara—but I'm not sure about your
book. Can you describe it in more detail? Thanks.

Love,
John

July 1, 1988

Dear John,

I hope you noticed the boxes that I sent your books in: "Baked by the Nuns of New Skete." They make wonderful cheesecake, also love with some Russian preachers who have migrated here.

> J. Precornu, *The Balloone Book*. La Navigation Aérienne, Paris, 1903. 4to, 484 pages. Heavily illustrated. This copy is beautifully bound for Sotherans of London in contemporary half-red morocco. I can find no auction record. However, I think it is my best find of my trip. (As you read French, I am envious.)

As you can see from the pictures, I'm no photographer.
The book weighs 6½ lb. I'm almost afraid to tell you the price.
Fine cond.

I've been strawberrying, but the blackberries aren't ready yet.
We have had dry cold weather, the furnace on most mornings.
Have a fun holiday.

Affectionately,
H

* * *

July 8, 1988

Dear Helen,

The Balloone Book sounds marvelous. I'm sure that it's the best find of your trip—and I have to have it! My check is enclosed.

Love, John

P.S. Yes, I noticed the nuns' boxes.

July 16, 1988

Dear John,

I sent the book off to you yesterday. If you aren't happy with Precornu, you know that you are welcome to send it back. The weather is defeating me, it's affecting my brain, it was small to start with and now it's smaller.

Affectionately,
H

* * *

August 3, 1988

Dear John,

I hope the weather was cooler in Canada than it has been around here. Today is the start of the races—I feel sorry for the horses. It's ten o'clock and it's eighty outdoors.

I thought all you needed was money (in this world). I tried to have some air-conditioning put in the house and it was more complicated than it was worth. Besides that, I didn't want to fall over workmen for two weeks. End of dissertation.

Affectionately,
H

P.S. I bought some books from the Whitneys. However, they are not in pristine condition. Here are some of the books. You may have them all.

> Henry Herbert, *Frank Forester's Horse and Horsemanship.* 1857. Two
> vols. 4to. Green cloth.
> Reginald Rives, *The Coaching Club.* Derrydale.
> John Lawrence, *The History and Delineation of the Horse.* 1809.
> British Sports & Sportsmen, *Racing & Coursing & Steeplechasing.* Vol 1 only.
> Sir Humphrey De Trafford, *The Horses of the British Empire.* 1907. 2 vols.
> *The British Turf and the Men Who Made It.* 1906.

August 10, 1988

Dear Helen,

I hope your weather improves now that the racing season has started. We are getting the same furnace blasts and it isn't helping my golf game, although it has done wonders for my fishing! I have a number of the books that you listed but don't think I have the John Lawrence, *The History & Delineation of the Horse,* 1809. Can you tell me more about it? Also, *The British Turf,* 1906?

I have just completed editing a batch of rave letters about the tour that fifty-eight of us made in May when we retraced our World War II battle route from the Normandy beaches to rural Czech-oslovakia. I'll send you a copy when I get it back from the printers and I'd welcome your comments.

Affectionately,
John

Dear John,

That must have been great fun having a fish that size and weight on your line.

Your war voyage that you made in May just arrived. I haven't had time to read it yet, but will do so, perhaps this evening. Saratoga is a bit of a mess, from my point of view. The good old social register isn't here any more. Sidewalk sales and a lot of ugly people. When it gets cool I think I will house hunt, maybe back to Vermont.

I'm enclosing two cards on the books that you were interested in. Cheers!

Affectionately,
H

The British Turf and the Men Who Made It. The Biographical Press, London, 1906. Large folio, 10¾ x 14¾ inches, 501 pages, weight 12 lbs. Historical and contemporary work on racing. Containing articles on racing in all parts of the world. Numerous engravings & halftone illus. Full black morocco, all edges gilt. Only slight foxing on the back of plates. Very good condition.

John Lawrence, *History and Delineation of the Horse, in All His Varieties.* Albion Press, London, 1809. 4to. 15 illus, numerous devices and tail pieces. Anecdotes and biographical notices by distinguished sportsmen. Second title page reads "For His Royal Highness George Prince of Wales." The work is inscribed. Full calf. Outside back strap needing replacing. Apparently a first edition. A good copy.

August 22, 1988

Dear Helen,

Here's my check for *The British Turf*. It sounds very good & will fit into my other large books in that category. I decided not to get the John Lawrence.

I can imagine the fat ladies in their polyester leisure suits taking over Saratoga. They have done the same to Lake Louise and to most of the rest of the world.

I'm so mad at George Bush for picking Quayle as a running mate that I could spit!

* * *

August 27, 1988

Dear John,

I sent off *The British Turf* yesterday. Hope it is satisfactory. *Impressions of the 738th Field Artillery* is great. I have been thinking of giving it to our local library. A piece like that should be where the public can read it.

On elections, I have no feelings one way or another. However, if Jesse Jackson made the ticket I was going to leave the country. Years ago when I was in my twenties, I asked a learned statesman the definition of a Republican and Democrat, and he said a Republican had a bank balance and a Democrat could change his mind. I choose to be a Democrat. Josy was a Vermont Republican Senator, but we never had any disagreement. So you see, November doesn't really mean much to me.

Affectionately,
H

Dear John,

Nice picture. You are lucky that you can take off when the spirit moves. I'm planted.

I need help. What do you know about Theodore A. Cook, *The History of the English Turf.* London, 1901 (the only vol with a date). In 6 vols: Vol 1, Division 1; Vol 2, Division 2; Vol 3, Division 3. I can only find a record for three vols. Nowhere can I find anything about 6 volumes, folio, uniformly bound. They belong together.

Affectionately,
H

September 29, 1988

Dear Helen,

Theodore Andrea Cook was editor of *The Field* magazine beginning in 1910. He was knighted in 1916. His major work was the six-volume *A History of the English Turf*, London, 1901. The six volumes are numbered in a screwy way—typically British. There are three volumes in six parts. Each of the three volumes has two "divisions"—i and ii. There are hundreds of plates and text illustrations. My copy is a 4to, gilt-decorated in green cloth with all edges gilt. I acquired my copy at a Swann Gallery sale in 1979 for 100 bucks.

Probably the most important other book by Cook is *Eclipse and O'Kelly*, which is about the famous English race horse Eclipse and his breeder, the Duke of Cumberland. The book came out in 1907. I purchased my copy from you in 1979!

I'm on the trail of some original stuff by Will James.

Lots of love,
John

p.s. My 19-year-old grandson, Billy Shull, is in your neighborhood—a sophomore at Skidmore. He's a sweet guy with a warm personality and looks like a Greek god!

* * *

October 11, 1988

Many thanks, my dear, on the information on *The History of the English Turf.*

Have a safe trip south.

Affectionately,
H

Dear John,

Christie's on November 18th is having a sale of John Flemings material and if you aren't going to bid on item 192 (Will James), I thought I would. I would have phoned you but I haven't a number.

Let me know soon.

Affectionately,
H

* * *

[No date]

Dear Helen,

Thanks for your note. I will be *very* interested in what price the Will James Lot 192 brings. I will be bidding thru a friend but will drop out if it goes as high as I think it might. Christie's estimate is typically low.

Love,
John

November 12, 1988

Dear John,

I couldn't find the auction record for what "Sand" sold for in 1976, however the "Lone Cowboy" limited signed original drawing sold in 1976 for $150.

You didn't tell me what your bid was, so I put in one for $800, which I felt was too high. However, good luck to the winner—it wasn't the only copy printed!

Affectionately,
H

* * *

November 23, 1988

Dear Helen,

You probably know that the one Will James book at the Christie's sale went for $1300! George Lowry is very excited about putting our Will James books into a sales catalogue and he should be all the more so after Christie's. We have *fourteen* books plus other goodies.*

I'm enclosing a minor catalogue which I have pulled together to cover a mini-exhibit in a corner of our living room in our new house. It's rather unusual and was fun to slap together in short order for the fall season. I'm trying to plan out a much more serious exhibit for this winter, which I am tempted to make an Izaak Walton show. It would be a lot of work but it would be a stunner.

I hope you have a happy Thanksgiving.

Love,
John

*In an earlier letter to Helen, which is missing, I had described in detail the exciting find that Rob Rulon-Miller and I had made of some extremely rare books by cowboy artist-writer Will James.

Rob had been contacted by a lady hairdresser in rural Idaho. The lady had read an article about Will James in a *Smithsonian* magazine which described Will James and the many children's illustrated books he had written in the 1930s.

The hairdresser's aunt lived nearby. Her hobby was collecting old trunks, and at an auction in California she had been the successful bidder on a trunk which had been owned by Will James's wife. The auctioneer had insisted that the contents of the trunk had to be taken by the successful bidder. The trunk had contained most of the first editions of Will James, in which he had written and illustrated a presentation in the front end-papers dedicated to his wife. There was also a lot of correspondence from Will James and a long horsehair riding coat that was worn at the knees from a stock saddle. The fourteen first edition presentation copies by Will James were extremely unique and valuable.

Rob Rulon-Miller and I agreed to share all expenses. Rob flew out to Idaho and met the hairdresser, who said she hoped the Will James material would sell for enough money for her mother and her aunt to take a midwinter Caribbean cruise. We were able to buy all of the Will James material for the equivalent of two Caribbean cruise tickets. I kept the five most important Will James presentation first editions and we sold the rest of the books, the correspondence, and the horsehair coat through George Lowery at a Swann Gallery book auction.

December 5, 1988

Dear John,

I'm glad all those lovely people came to Mulberry Plantation for Thanksgiving. Youth is wonderful, but this old lady enjoyed a quiet evening by the fireplace with a tall Hennessey brandy.

That's a very fine collection of books you have put together. It sounds as tho you are thoroughly enjoying the new house. I'm not sorry that I didn't win the Will James. I remembered that I had had fifteen first editions for well over three years, some signed, that stayed on the shelf until about three months ago with no interest shown. A dealer came by and I sold him the lot for $5.00 apiece. So why did I bid on James? I did it for a friend. Thank God I haven't completely misplaced my mind.

The book business is strange. Most of the fine books and authors a person wants today are completely forgotten a year from now. End of dissertation.

Do you remember when you asked me about having Walton in your library? I just bought a small library. Nothing exciting. You might be interested in Wayland's *History of Rockingham County, Virginia.*

Affectionately,
H

December 9, 1988

Dear Helen,

Please tell me about Wayland's *History of Rockingham County, Virginia*. All I know is that I don't have anything by a Wayland. Should I?

I've been on a binge of illustrated bullfighting books. It's rather odd. In June of 1987, I purchased a nice oblong folio with twelve hand-colored copperplates of bullfighting scenes produced in Madrid in 1790. More recently—in the last month or so—I have acquired two more books with the same twelve bullfighting prints, one of them hand-colored, published by Ed Orme in London in 1813, and the others published in Granada, not colored but much finer prints—no date, but my guess is earlier. All three are very nice—they puzzle me a little—but they fit into my modest but fairly good collection of books on bullfighting, which includes Hemingway's first and several by Barnaby Conrad. What do you have on "в" for bullfighting?

No, I don't remember asking you about having Walton in my library. Did you say "yes" or "no" or "maybe"? Whatever you did say it may be too late! At last count I have about ninety different editions including the first six editions and some other rare stuff. There are only one or two more Waltons that interest me.

I was sorry to hear that you had given away fifteen first editions of Will James. C'est la vie! Our friend George Lowery at Swann is hot and enthusiastic about the Will James autographed and presentation remarque firsts we have given him to catalogue & sell for us. Maybe it's the gen-u-ine horsehair coat that comes with all that stuff which is adding the sizzle.

What do you think the copy of *Oriental Field Sports* will go for at Sotheby's next Wednesday? The Jeanson copy sold for $35,150!

Take care of yourself and have a lovely holiday season,
Love,
John

Dear John,

I said "yes" to Walton and that it should be represented in your library. Poor Walton, everyone has forgotten about him. It's the day of literature. You must have some fine copies in the Plantation library. Elizabeth Barrett Browning and Edna St. Vincent Millay are hot items right now. So many copyrights on sports books have expired and the publishers are having a great business in the reprint field. Not my dish of tea.

How about Swinburne's *Mary Stuart,* 1881, for $1,000 to prove a point?

To you and your family, have a happy holiday.

Affectionately,
H

Bullfighting:

> Barnaby Conrad, *Matador.* 1952. 8vo. DJ. 1st. Damp stained.
> Angus Macnab, *Fighting Bulls.* 1959. 8vo. DJ. 1st. First published in England under title *Bulls of Iberia.*
> Kenneth Tynan, *Bull Fever.* 1955. Large 8vo. 1st.
> Rex Smith, *Biography of the Bulls.* 1957. An anthology of Spanish bullfighting. Large 8vo. DJ. First edition?
> Barnaby Conrad, *Encyclopedia of Bullfighting.* 1961. Folio. DJ. 1st.

> All the books are illustrated in B&W.

> Motz, an original watercolor, a picture of a bullfighter in the ring. Signed, 1920. Picture 8¾ x 6½ inches. Framed. Brought it back from Madrid.
> John W. Wayland, Ph.D., *A History of Rockingham County, Virginia.* Dayton, VA., 1912. Large 8vo. 438 pp. Brown cloth. First. Some ink notes on endpapers. Index: sheriffs, judges, members of the state senate, marriage records, etc. (famous people). Genealogy.

Dear Helen,

I'd like to get several of your bullfighting books:

> Rex Smith, *Biography of the Bulls*
> Kenneth Tynan, *Bull Fever*
> Barnaby Conrad, *Encyclopedia of Bullfighting*

Did I tell you that I knew Barnaby Conrad & his wife, Mary? Barnaby was a year behind me at Yale, where I knew him slightly. Martha & I got to know Barnaby & his wife when we sailed across the Pacific Ocean together in March of '87. He's a most attractive guy—big & tall & walks with a limp (gored by a bull). He shares my fate in being an alcoholic & has written a very interesting book about his experiences at the Betty Ford Rehab Center.

Barnaby is also a distant relative of Fletcher Christian and was in heaven when we landed at Pitcairn's Island for the day and he had a chance to meet all the great grandchildren of his mutinous forebear. Conrad is working on a novel based on his idea that Fletcher Christian wasn't killed on Pitcairn's Island but escaped, secretly, back to England with the *Bounty*'s gold treasure! Wow!

I hope that you have a very happy and merry and cozy Christmas and that 1989 will bring you good health, prosperity, and happiness.

Love,
John

January 22, 1989

Dear Helen,

Did I tell you that I had acquired a rather disreputable copy of *Oriental Field Sports*, 1807—Tooley 508, Schwerdt II 298, etc.? Sotheby's had sold the Marcel Jeanson copy at the Monaco sale in 1987 for $35,150 and my copy only cost a quarter of that at Sotheby's sale in N.Y. on Deceember 15th. My copy is quite okay even though it has had some "uneducated" handling that put tears in some dozen pages of the text. The prints themselves are bright and clean and it all collates. I'm really just thrilled just to have a good copy which I can afford.

Did you watch the inauguration? I think that George Bush is a very good man—much better than Reagan—and George will do a super job as president.

Love,
John

P.S. I liked the three bullfighting books you sent! Thanks.

Dear John,

I'm glad you acquired the copy of *Oriental Field Sports*. I think
I offered you a first that I brought back from England in May.
If I remember correctly, it was expensive, around $23,000. Some
day you will be lucky and be able to upgrade your copy.

I just sold a lot of Derrydales to a university, which surprised
me as Derrydales haven't been moving. I heard that Crown
is going to reprint fifty titles. It seems a shame, but it is a
reprint world.

The doctor tells me I am going blind. I don't buy it. Vermonters
are never defeated. I'm off this week to Motor Vehicle School
to reduce some of the points on my license. That should keep
me out of trouble for a few days.

Affectionately,
H

[No date]

Dear Helen,

Your "good news/bad news" letter arrived. I'm ever so glad that "Vermonters are never defeated," but I'm sorely tried to hear that your doctor tells you that you are going blind. Don't! Is there anything that you can do? I dearly hope you delay the process forever and never lose your eyesight. So please do whatever you can—and keep me posted.

I did a couple of "bookish" things last week. Went to the Grolier Club annual dinner & saw some old friends. I sneaked out before the business meeting started after dinner because it was going to be a series of very dull reports and I wasn't going to hear anything that I couldn't read later.

The next day I visited the Beinecke Library in New Haven & met with a brilliant young curator who spent some time with me about some of their sporting books. They've got some marvelous things!

Love,
John

p.s. I hope they taught you something about speeding at the Motor Vehicle School!

Dear John,

The list of books in this red envelope are my personal ones that I enjoyed collecting. Most of them are in fine binding and if there is anything that appeals to you, you are welcome. I thought they would be fine for Sherri as she would have been a good book woman, but at my age I think maybe someone else should enjoy them.

If it's not too much trouble, will you please return the list?

So you are a songbird.

Affectionately,
H

P.S. Have you heard that Crown is reprinting fifty Derrydales (I hope on good paper)?

February 18, 1989

Dear Helen,

Thank you so much for giving me the opportunity to study the list of books in your living room from your personal collection. This is a very impressive assembly of rare and beautiful books. Amongst the list I saw a number of old friends—books which I am pleased to have in my own collection.

I also found a number of books that interested me and a few which made me curious. I have made a copy of your list and I have marked with red some of the books that interest me. Could you give me a little more information about them, please?

> *Going to the Fight*, panorama. 17 hand-colored plates. Is this a Spurling book? Is it about horses & hounds? Who is the author? Who is the artist?

> S. Sidney, *The Book of the Horse*. How is it bound? Is there any text? Large leather album of original drawings. What are they of? Who are the artists?

> Katsumi Matoba, *Horsemanship*. Tokyo, 1857. Can you give me more description of this interesting book?

> *Sporting Anecdotes*. London, 1894. First ed. Who is the author? The artist? Please describe.

I would like to start out with these five & learn more about them. I am returning your precious red envelope with the original list. I have made a copy for myself.

Love,
Your "songster" friend

Going to the Fight, panorama. Colored label inside the front cover reads, "Grand Supplement to the Illustrated Sporting News." Merton House, Salisbury Square, Fleet Street, London, ND. Book oblong measures 11½ x 3¾ inches. Panorama measures 3 x 167 inches. With 17 plates of individual views. ¼ red morocco, unmarked but bound by Bayton. Exhibiting the sporting world 100 years ago, in all its varieties of style and costumes. In color, possibly hand-colored. Along the Road to Hyde Park, corner to Moulsey, Hurst. Colored table on back cover reads, "The Original, presented by E. Weston, Esq., Holborn Music Hall as a mark of respect to Harry Brunton." It truly is an unusual item. Every plate is of a different sporting event in England.

S. Sidney, *The Book of the Horse: Thorough-breed, Half-Breed, Cart-Breed; Saddle and Harness; British and Foreign.* Published by Cassell of London, 1880. Small 4to, 604 pp. Full-page colored illustrations and numerous wood engravings. Rebound in fine binding, decorated boards, ¼ red morocco. Sidney, author of *Gallops and Gossips,* was the manager of the Agricultural Hall Horse Show.

Album: Folio. (This is going to be hard to describe.) Dark green silk with 1/4 green leather back strip. Colorful slipcase. Inlaid needlepoint in color, decoration on cover, measuring 4 x 5 inches of two horses with lady riders. Hand-lettered descriptive text on page before each mounted plate. Some of the drawings are in pencil, others hand-colored, all of horses (14 drawings and two photos). Handmade watermarked paper. (I've been told that the drawings are done by a famous artist.) If you'd like to see it, why don't I send it down and you decide if you like it, or return it. I bought it in England from Way.

Katsumi Matoba, *Horsemanship: How to Saddle and Harness Horses (Sho ku ba Ko).* Tokyo, 1857. 2 vols, imp. 8vo. Illus in seventeen colored woodblock (I'd say hand-colored) prints, some double pages. Wraps, on Japanese paper, enclosed in oriental blue linen style case with bone clasps.

Sporting Anecdotes: Original and Select: Including characteristic sketches of eminent persons who have appeared on the turf, extraordinary events which have transpired in the sporting world, by an amateur sportsman. Maclay's *Five Centuries of Sport* gives no author; however, on the title page of my volume, it says "printed for Thomas Hurst, Paternoster Row; J. Harris, St. Paul's Churchyard; and J. Wheble, Warwick; Albion Press, 1804." 8vo. Full orig. gilt-tooled calf with raised bands. First ed. 16 plates.

March 4, 1989

Dear Helen,

Thank you for taking the time to describe in such a careful & detailed way the five books I asked about. I would like to go ahead with four of the books as follows:

> *Going to the Fight*, panorama.
> S. Sidney, *The Book of the Horse.*
> Katsumi Matoba, *Horsemanship.*
> *Sporting Anecdotes.*

As you suggested, why don't you send down the Album: Folio on approval. I can decide then whether to keep it or return it.

Love,
John

* * *

March 11, 1989

Dear John,

I sent the books off yesterday UPS—you are always welcome to return any book to me, for any reason.

I'm sorry that I bitched about quoting. It's something that I don't do well and it defeats me and destroys my disposition. Add the fact that I can't spell and you have the whole picture.

I sent John Lawrence's *The History and Delineation of the Horse to Bath* to be restored, and after three months it has returned. I could have had a holiday in the bloody town for what it cost. However, it looks like it was worth the effort.

Affectionately,
H

Dear Helen,

The four books which I recently purchased from you arrived safely this P.M. They are a nice lot! The Japanese book of horse-manship is a "first" for my collection since I have no other book on horses in that language. The hand-colored woodblocks are beautiful and the blue linen cloth case with the bone clasps (which work!) is very interesting. I'm sure I'm probably reading the book back to front!

The Panorama is quite special, too. I have several panoramas already and this fits right in. I think the date would be first half of nineteenth century. I can hardly wait to get back to Minnesota to compare the Panorama with a small reference book on the subject which was written by Ernest Gee. If my memory serves me right, *Going to the Fight* is described in Gee's book and I think the artist *may* be H. Alken.

I am enclosing my check for the Folio Album which you sent on approval. It is in German and I will find someone to translate the text for me. The date on one of the drawings is 1936, which probably makes the entire book pre-World War II.
I don't recognize the artist, although some of the drawings are signed. The style is similar to Marie Laurencin's and the era is about the same, which is consistent. Someday I'm sure I'll get a better "fix" on the artist. I have a hunch. The artist is talented.

Saw a mutual friend, Babs Cocks, at a party the other night and we talked about you—fondly. Babs & Burley are having a good winter down here and I understand that he has a lot of good horses in training. They are a durable pair of old friends!

Love,
John

March 22, 1989

Dear John,

I think I might have a treasure for you (if you don't have it).

> Jessie Marie DeBoth (compiler), *Famous Sportsmen's Recipes*. Chicago,
> 1940. 12mo, 96 pp. Includes Irving Cobb, Zane Grey, Jack O'Connor,
> Oscar of the Waldorf, Col. Sheldon, and Babe Ruth. A pres. copy to
> Eugene Connett, with a long note. The illus are wonderful.

Also, after reading the Spur that you thoughtfully sent me,
I wondered if you'd have any interest in a pair of Japanese
lacquered stirrups, eighteenth century, that I bought at the sale
of Mrs. F. Ambrose Clark, held at Iroquois Mansion, Cooperstown, N.Y. The sale was held by Christie's, August 10th, 1982.
You bought some books from me that I purchased at the sale.
(They weighed eight lbs.).

I'm glad that you are happy with the books from upstairs. I've
had some of them for over twenty years, and I'm pleased that
you now have them!

Greg Way was here this week and wanted the Album. He remembered that I had it. He told me that some of the original
drawings were by Tattersall, and that is all he remembered.

It must be interesting and busy living in Camden. Do you still
ride?

The accountant tells me to spend money. So I've decided to get
a new Jaguar. I put your checks in my account so you'll own a
wheel of the new car. Don't push that wheel very fast, because I
can't have another speeding ticket.

Affectionately,
H

Dear Helen,

The book about "Famous Sportsmen's Recipes" sounds interesting and I'd like to buy it.

It reminds me of a time a few years ago when a friend of mine was planning to compile a book of recipes for cooking all kinds of wild game. He was soliciting recipes from all of his shooting & fishing pals. I sent him my "Fabulous Wild Duck Sauce" recipe which I feel is a real showstopper. And waited. And waited. And I am still waiting for the damn book to be published. I wonder if Babe Ruth tells you how to cook a planked barracuda?

Take care of your new Jaguar. Can you get the factory to put a governor on it before you take delivery?

Yes, we still do some riding here around the plantation. We have a pair of nice old hunters who are comfortable and relatively docile and are just our speed.

We are being visited by lots of children & grandchildren, now the weather has turned nice & warm. This Saturday is the big steeplechase race meeting here in Camden. The Carolina Cup used to be billed as Carolina's largest cocktail party. They've cleaned up their act and now they call it Carolina's largest picnic. The rites of spring will probably bring out a crowd of 45,000.

Love,
John

P.S. I don't want the Japanese lacquered stirrups. Thank you anyway. I was interested in what Greg Way had to say about the album, but I wonder what Tattersall would be doing in a German book!

HENNESSEY BOOKS

By Christine Corasaniti

Behind Filene, beyond the woods of Skidmore College rests a 1899 carriage house owned by Joseph and Helen Hennessey. Above the side door of the house on Fourth Street hangs a small sign with the inscription "Hennessey Books."

The Henneseys worked in Manhattan during the 1930s and 1940s in the new and old book business. In 1963, while Joseph worked for the Civil Defense Department, the Henneseys moved to Albany. Shortly thereafter, the Hennesseys purchased the carriage house and furnished the first floor with rare books, while making the second story their home.

The brick walls and wood floors of the bookstore maintain the look of the original carriage house. The floors display weaved oriental and Indian rugs. Desks, chairs, and couches form a comfortable resting area for browsers and some buyers. Even the cat, Gin, helps to create the atmosphere of the hidden past lurking within the books and the house. Sporting prints of race horses grace one wall along with some of Helen's riding gear from boarding school. Beyond the prints, the Hennesseys display photos of Sir Lawrence Olivier, Vivien Leigh, Ruth Gordon, and Dorothy Parker, to name a few.

Inside Helen's office hangs a letter from Pulitzer Prize winner William Bolcom, thanking the Hennesseys for their support. Beneath the letter, Helen quickly points out, hangs a bit of British humor, a bumper sticker that states, "Thank you for smoking."

Helen purchased the sticker on one of her many trips to England. Last November, Helen made her twenty-seventh trip to England to collect more books. The Hennesseys have always gotten their books in England because there is a better selection abroad.

The main room of the store holds works by Blake, Keats, Twain, and Joyce. In a separate room, the extremely valuable books are kept, locked away, along with duplicates of works. The prices of the books range from one dollar to a few thousand dollars for the most valuable manuscript. Dating from the sixteenth century, the Italian music manuscript has handmade paper. There are no paperback books. The books are grouped in categories except for first editions, with everything from art to poetry, including a children's section.

To open the business, the Henneseys advertised in the Yellow Pages and joined an antique book association, but today things have changed. "People know where we are if they want us," stated Helen. The busiest time of the year is August during the tourist season. These customers even remain loyal all year round. One gentleman from South Carolina continually keeps in contact with the Hennesseys.

After twenty-five years in business, Hennessey Books is run primarily by Helen, since Joseph has had a stroke. Helen plans on staying in business as long as she can.

The store does not have set hours, just ring the bells or call. If you are looking for rare gifts, first editions of books, or wish to order books, this is the bookstore to explore.

* * *

April 13, 1989

Dear Helen,

Thank you for sending me the very pleasant profile article about you and your book-biz in the March 31st issue of the *Skidmore News.* I thought that the reporter drew a nice picture of you and what you do and where you live. I enjoyed being portrayed as the "gentleman from South Carolina." With a saucy lady like you at the other end, who wouldn't want to "keep continually in touch"?

Christine Corasaniti, the reporter, might find it hard to believe that the gentleman from South Carolina has a grandson who is one of her Skidmore neighbors.

I think that you come off very well in the article, and if I didn't know you so well already, I'd be clamoring to meet this scholarly, well-traveled, well-connected lady who has a nice sense of humor and an impressive inventory of exciting rare books.

My only criticism with the article is a gripe that I have for so many (too many) young people of this day & age who call their elders by their first name in what I consider unneeded familiarity! Why can't the reporter call you Mrs. Hennessey instead of Helen? (g-r-r-r!)

In any event, you go into the scrapbook right away, Helen.

Love,
John

April 20, 1989

Dear John,

I enjoyed your comments on people calling you by your first name. I remember the first time that I resented it—the young man changing the oil in my car addressed me as Helen. I'd never seen him before and I froze. However, I'm learning to accept it—it's called life.

What treasure are you looking for now? I need to have my brain stimulated.

Affectionately,
H

* * *

April 25, 1989

Dear Helen.

I'm afraid that the "treasures" I'm seeking will bore you to tears: Izaak Waltons! Certain holes I'd like to fill, namely, Horne 4, 16, 20, 24, 26, and 27. These six volumes would give me a complete run of Horne 1 thru 30, which would be fun to have. I'm sure there are many other treasures that I'd love to have. Right now I don't have enough spare time to do the much-needed research to come up with other goodies.

Please keep me posted.

Love,
John

May 3, 1989

Dear Helen,

I remembered a little reference book about panoramas by
Ernest Gee that I have in my files. Sure enough, there was the
panorama *Going to a Fight* that you recently sold me! The interesting thing is that it identifies the artist as Robert Cruikshank
and the date, 1821!

It is very early spring here—quite a reversal from S.C. where
the mosquitoes & snakes are all out and the temps are already in
the 90s!

Love,
John

      * * *

May 10, 1989

Dear John,

Welcome to the North Country—you got out of the Carolinas
just before it almost blew away.

I don't know what I can do about your missing Waltons, as I
don't use or have Horne, I only have Oliver, so the numbers
won't correspond. However, I'm not defeated yet. Thanks for
the information on the panorama. I hope it means you are
happy with it. I've had it since 1971. If you don't want it, I'll buy
it back.

Affectionately,
H

June 24, 1989

Dear John,

Thanks for the card. It's nice to be remembered.

I need a holiday and I'd like to go to Australia, but I know that I couldn't sit still for eighteen hours. So I'll probably end up going over to England.

Josy is deteriorating, but fairly healthy, so I'll try not to get restless.

I played in the stock market a couple of months ago—Rochester T&T. It's hell to be old and make money—what can you do with it?

Affectionately,
H

Dear Helen,

I'm glad you got the postcard from Greece. That was a delightful trip. Interesting, comfortable, nice people, just the right
length of time.

No more trips for a while. Next trip will be to the U.K. in
mid-August. Theater and some clothes in London, a week
of touring in Wales, and finally a week of grouse shooting in
Northumberland.

I'm coming down the stretch on my book exhibit project! I have
assembled about sixty of my most exciting and important sporting books into what I'm going to call "The Best." I've almost
completed writing the catalogue. Then I'll send the catalogue to
about twenty-five local bibliophilic friends and invite them to
come out any time in the next thirty or forty days to see the
books on exhibit at their own pace. I do this kind of a show
each summer. It's fun!

I will send you a copy of the catalogue when it's completed.
A number of the books in the show came from you.

Congrats on your financial acumen!

Love,
John

July 9, 1989

Dear John,

Your book exhibit project sounds like a large undertaking. Do I remember that you did this once before?

I think I've decided to go to England in September. It gives me a great deal of pleasure to think about it, and the time will pass quickly.

Do any of your friends raise standard French poodles (not white)? I think I'd like a dog again and I had a poodle once. No one around here has standards, only toys, and I like large dogs.

I'm off to pick raspberries.

Affectionately,
H

Dear Helen,

When you go to England, what do you most enjoy when
you are there? Friends? Book hunts? The theater? Touring?
Or what?

I must say that I love to go to England for many reasons!
We have a couple of favorite hotels and favorite restaurants.
This coming August we will be in London for four nights and we
have already lined up theater tickets for each night we are there.

Then there is my favorite London bookstore—Sotheran's. They
always seem glad to see me and they usually have several nice
books with which they tempt me. This year we are going to
have a fitting of the shooting clothes we ordered from a Savile
Row tailor who visited Camden this spring. I have a four-piece
suit—coat, vest, trousers, and plus twos—to try on, and a new
Inverness cape!

Do you like the museums? How about the food? Any very special dishes and any favorite restaurants? Do let me know!
Sorry, I don't know anything about standard French poodles.
I'm a Labrador retriever man and Martha is "into" Old English
sheepdogs. My oldest daughter goes in for Boykin spaniels.
Does the first edition of the *Big Book* of Alcoholics Anonymous
ever come on the market? If so, how much does it cost?

You are correct. I do at least one book show each summer. But
this year's show is the best ever. My first house visitors came to
see the show this morning. By appointment only. In the next
thirty days, before I strike the set in preparation for our departure
to England on August 22nd, I expect about forty more visitors.
It's hard work but exciting. I learn more about my books than
anybody else.

Happy Bastille Day.
Love,
John

July 21, 1989

Dear John,

When I go to England, I fly into Heathrow and rent a car and go up to Oxford and have a room at the Eastgate Hotel, and to bed for a couple of hours. After driving to Montreal and the trip over, I'm tired (can't sleep on planes). After I've rested a while, I go over to the college library, sit and admire the books. (Sherri went to school there.) Then off up the west coast of England, to Preston and Mr. Halewood, who always has some good books for me. Then off to the Lake District. (I'm still looking for the monster.) Mr. Grant in Edinburgh and then down the east coast to one of my favorite small towns, Berwick-upon-Tweed. I like to stay in small inns. Most of them are Trusthouse Forte and it is interesting to meet the natives. Northumberland has the Duke's castle and a splendid library. Years ago they used to let you handle the books—no more.

Then to London and Sotheran's, which is changing, too. Maybe I notice these things because I'm getting old.

Hurriedly,
H

Dear John,

Brown's Hotel in London is one of my favorites, for food and attractive setting, old England.

We have had several Labradors, but as I don't hunt anymore I thought I'd go back to French poodles. I sold my last gun the other day and that ends that chapter of my life. Moss Hart gave us an Old English sheepdog once, whom the other dogs tried to drown. We lived on the island. To save its life, I gave it to a farmer.

I tried the cookies, and I agree, they are delicious.

Affectionately,
H

July 24, 1989

Dear Helen,

I loved hearing your voice on the phone the other day. It was strong and firm as ever! Thank you for taking the time to let me know about the availability of the first edition of the AA *Big Book*.

I'm amazed that there were 100,000 copies printed for the first edition. Talk about grandiosity! I'm not surprised that they sell for such a high price after all these years of heavy use. As I told you on the phone, I'm not interested for myself, but I have a friend who goes to my AA meetings who wanted to know the price & the availability. Now, when I tell him the score I'm sure that his ardor will cool.

Thank you for your interesting letter about what you enjoy doing when you go to England. It sounds like a well-established & very pleasant routine. When you are in the Lake District, look up my friend David Grayling. David is an antiquarian bookseller who has found some very good sporting books for me over the years. His address is Lyvennet, Crosby Ravensworth, Penrith, Cumbria.

David is also master of a beagle pack and if you're not careful he'll get you out on the fells running around after his beagles. It's strenuous!

In your book travels in the U.K., I'm surprised that you don't call on Joe Allen in London or Greg Way in Newmarket—but I guess you can't be everywhere.

I just came back from a two-day fishing trip on the St. Croix, where I caught forty smallmouth bass on my fly rod. Since it is entirely "catch and release" fishing, my conscience doesn't bother me—just my casting arm & wrist!

Love,
John

July 29, 1989

Dear John,

I've known the Ways for over thirty years. I used to visit and buy from Greg's father when Greg was in college. Mr. Way was a great deal of fun. I remember him breeding a donkey with a horse to see what would happen.

Mr. Allen and I don't like each other. Punctuation!

Sometimes I order from Grayling catalogues. I also used to go to the Head's, but not lately.

Robert Way wrote a book titled *The Garden of the Beloved*, published in 1975. It bends towards religion.

Tell your friend that the *Big Book* is in its third edition. I personally thought it as good as the first. However, what he wants, he wants.

Affectionately,
H

August 4, 1989

Dear Helen,

My friend works for the Hazelden Recovery Center, so he is well acquainted with the *Big Book*. (Yes, the 1976 edition is the third edition, and the twenty-eighth printing was made in 1987). My friend has seen a first edition, but he knows he can't afford one.

Have you read Nan Robertson's book about AA called *Getting Better*? The author won a Pulitzer Prize for some of her articles about AA. She is a reporter for the *New York Times* and I read some of her stuff in the *N.Y. Times* magazine section before I got her book. According to her, the first edition was a run of only 5,000 copies, which rolled off the Cornwall Press in Cornwall, N.Y., in April 1939 and was priced at $3.50—only $1.15 less than it costs today. Most of the copies were unsold for quite a while.

So much for that subject, except to mention to you that I'm still going to meetings and am very grateful to AA for helping to turn my life around, "one day at a time."

I just got my copies of the new bibliography of Izaak Walton's *Compleat Angler*. It is by Rodolphe Coigney, who is a retired director of the World Health Organization and a major collector of I.W. Jim Cummins helped produce & publish the book, which lists 460 editions compared to Horne's 385. I think it may have been unnecessary!

I agree with you that Joe Allen is a difficult person. I haven't had much luck with him for a long time.

Martha & I are going to a reception at the White House on August 14th. Any messages for George Bush?

Love,
John

      * * *

So! You're off to see the President and then England. Have a happy time.

H

August 3, 1989

Dear John,

Have you any interest in a Francis Bannerman *Catalogue of Supplements of Military Goods, guns, flags, drums, bugles, tents, swords, saddles, uniforms, trophies, etc.?* 1911. 362 PP. 4to. Printed wrappers, bound in maroon cloth. Fine condition.

Bannerman's "arsenal" was located on an island in the Hudson River. You see what's left of it riding the train north.

Affectionately,
H

August 7, 1989

Dear Helen,

Thank you for bringing it to my attention, but I don't want the 1911 Francis Bannerman *Catalogue of Supplements of Military Goods*. It's a bit out of my line.

We are going to England & Wales on August 22nd in spite of the fact that our grouse-shooting week in Northumberland the first week in September has been abruptly canceled. The very hot and dry spring & summer has led to an "explosion" of a parasite strongyle worm that has wreaked havoc on all of the best moors in England, and almost without warning, all the shooting for the entire season has been canceled. We are out of luck and out of pocket of our two-thirds deposits, which we had to make the first of the year. We decided to make the trip on an abbreviated basis anyway.

We are very disappointed about the shooting, but may make up for it with a brief foray to Mexico for the white-wing dove.

I have some hot shots from the Minneapolis Institute of Arts coming out to see my current book exhibit tomorrow morning. They want to look me over because they want me to put on an exhibit at their museum about a year from now. It will be an interesting morning.

Love,
John

September 17, 1989

Dear Helen,

As I write this I'm sure you are still touring around England. I do hope that you are having a good time, enjoying good weather, and accomplishing all of the things you set out to do.

Welcome home! This letter will be waiting for you when you get back. We've been back for two weeks now, so all our jet lag clocks are back on local time and we've stopped getting sleepy in the middle of the day.

Did you find any goodies? Please let me know.

My handsome grandson is back at Skidmore for his junior year. He loves it there. Should I have him call on you?

Love,
John

       * * *

September 23, 1989

Dear John,

Nice to hear from you. However, you neglected to list the treasures you found. Needless to say, I haven't made England yet. I have to depend on someone to take care of Josy and that's not always easy. (He objects to some people.)

So-o-o you're off to catch a duck. That ought to be fun. I have sat in a duck blind up on Lake Champlain for hours. It got cold, too, but it was good fun.

Affectionately,
H

October 2, 1989

Dear Helen,

Here I thought that you were in England and you haven't yet gone. I do hope you can find someone to take care of Josy and make the trip before winter sets in. You have so much fun when you do go.

I guess that the two best "treasures" that I found in my travels are a panorama of Queen Victoria's coronation, 1838—but it is twenty feet long!—and a superb, complete set of thirteen volumes of *Annals of Sporting and Fancy Gazette* in excellent condition and with the June 1828 number, which is particularly rare. Since our return, I've found a couple of books on cockfighting and two rare books on coaching, so I'm not standing still.

Martha & I have just come back from a rush trip to South Carolina to survey the damage done by Hurricane Hugo. By some miracle, our new house was almost completely spared while all the trees surrounding the house were knocked down or snapped off. We have lost more than 1,000 big pine trees that were over thirty years old! What a mess!

The eye of Hugo came right over Camden on its way from Charleston, S.C., to Charlotte, N.C., with winds of over 100 miles per hour and with many tornadoes bouncing on and off the ground. It was the tornadoes that flattened great swaths of big pine trees.

We think that a tornado bounced off our mill pond and created a water spout that killed hundreds of our fish! We picked up more than 100 dead fish on the shore in front of our house & hauled them off to stink in the distance.

After that nasty job we went out for dinner with some friends and couldn't bring ourselves to order the crayfish cocktail and the scallops. No, thank you! Just meat and potatoes, please.

Love,
John

October 10, 1989

Dear John,

Have a safe trip south.

Sorry about the trees all down, but I suppose you are in luck about the house.

I have a nice little book titled *Morvich*. Won the Kentucky Derby in 1922. If interested, let me know.

Affectionately,
H

* * *

October 18, 1989

Dear Helen,

I got your note of October 10th and would like you to tell me more about the book titled *Morvich*. Sounds interesting. I have some terrific news, but don't have the time right now to go into any more detail than to tell you that the Minneapolis Institute of Arts has asked me to put on a one-man show of my sporting book collection in 1992! A two-month show and two very large gallery rooms at my disposal.

Help! What should I call the show? What theme should I use? What books to exhibit? What? What? What?

Love,
John

October 25, 1989

Dear John,

You asked for it—so here goes—take some of your Civil War books that I appraised a hundred years ago. Also some framed maps, as well as some your Alken prints. My advice and it is free.

Why not call it the Mulberry Plantation collection? The public will be impressed.

I'm going to send the Morvich book down to you. I think it needs to be seen. If it's not your dish of tea, send it back up.

I just went over to Northampton to the auction of the Joseph D. Bates Jr. estate of fishing books. Your friend Cummins was there. I had gone over for only one book and I don't like to be defeated, so naturally I got the book, Ronalds's *Fly-Fishers' Entomology*, 2 vols and sunken mounts.

Affectionately,
H

Dear Helen,

The two-volume *Fly-Fishers' Entomology* by Ronalds that you
just purchased at the Bates auction is a gem! I was looking at
my copy, which I got in England in 1984 and am so happy to
have. I paid $1,000 five years ago for my copy. What is it selling
for now? Mind telling me what you paid?

Your little book, *Morvich*, arrived in this morning's mail. Most
attractive. My check is enclosed. Thank you for sending it.

By any chance do you have a copy of Ortega y Gasset's English
translation of his analysis of man and hunting? I don't have the
actual title at my fingertips but I think it is *Meditations on
Hunting*. My treasured copy has disappeared and I'd love to
find another copy because the author writes so well about the
basic instincts that man has always had for "the chase,"
whether it's fox or stag hunting, shooting or even fishing.
This is one of the ideas that I'm trying to capture in developing a book show for the Minneapolis Institute of Arts.
"Sporting comes naturally!"

Because it is going to be a show of my own collection of sporting books, I can't include the Civil War books that you
approved of "a hundred years ago."

I'm going up to the Aldeman Library of the University of
Virginia in Charlottesville this Friday for a private showing of
the library's collection of sporting books collected by Marion
duPont Scott. Gerald Strine, who wrote a biography of Mrs.
Scott, is going to give the talk. I will be most interested in seeing the show and hearing the talk because it is somewhat con-
nected with what I'm going to be doing at the Minneapolis
Institute of Arts in 1992.

Mrs. Scott was a great old gal. She was a famous owner of thoroughbred horses. When she died she left the magnificent

Springdale Race Course here in Camden to the State of South Carolina, with an endowment of a million dollars!

Her sporting book collection consists of about 3,000 volumes. I've seen the inventory and it is not very good, except for a wonderful section on cockfighting. She had her own breed of fighting chickens and her own special cockpit on her estate at Montpelier, and she was an ardent competitor up and down the Eastern Seaboard with her chickens. It's funny to think of this tiny, quiet little lady as being so bloodthirsty!

Love,
John

Dear John

You might have just turned sixty-eight, but this kid has ten
years on you. Sherri used to say, when you watch my mother
going down the street, she looks like a kid. Then when you see
her face, you know differently. Nice kid. I wish she was around.

Ortega y Gasset has me stumped. I can't find him in Schwerdt's
or in any of my bloody reference books. Perhaps you can do
better.

I paid $1,485 for the Ronalds *Entomology*. The last one (set) I
had, I sold for $800.

Do you need or want Jordan and Overman's *The Aquatic
Resources of the Hawaiian Islands?* Washington Printing Office,
1905. 3 volumes, 77 colored plates of fish. It's too bad you can't
include some Civil War in your show. It's a hot item at the
moment.

Affectionately,
H

November 7, 1989

Dear Helen,

About four years ago my friend Alex Mackay-Smith asked me to contribute an article about drag hunting to his new book *Foxhunting in North America*. I'm enclosing a copy of the chapter that I wrote because it has a reference to the Spanish philosopher José Ortega y Gasset on page 132. (By coincidence, another foxhunter named Ben Hardaway contributed another article to the book and he also referred to and quoted Ortega—see page 195.) The book is out of print and hard to find, but if you locate a copy please let me know. I really need a copy!

The trip to Charlottesville for the opening of the Marion duPont Scott sporting book collection at the University of Virginia library was well worthwhile. Mrs. Scott left about 3,000 sporting books and a large endowment. Although her books are not very good, the library has been buying some excellent rare books to add to the collection from the income generated by Mrs. Scott's endowment. Eventually, they will have a good collection of equestrian-oriented sporting books. It's very appropriate for the State of Virginia, which has so much foxhunting, horseracing, and cockfighting.

Mrs. Scott's collection was well displayed and I got some good ideas for my future show—especially about adding some personal sporting ephemera!

Ronalds's *Fly-Fishers' Entomology* is a lovely book. The fact that the price has almost doubled isn't surprising because the quality of the book is so good. I believe that high-quality books, like high-quality works of art, are going to continue to be in high demand and will command high prices. The values are so basic.

Thank you for offering me Jordan and Overman's book about fish in the Hawaiian Islands. What are you asking for it? It sounds a bit far out of my field, although I do go in for angling books.

Love,
John

Dear John,

After numerous phone calls to my colleagues, I have been unable
to locate Ortega y Gasset's *Meditations* for you. As a matter of
fact, they laughed at me. They informed me if they had a copy, it
would cost me $200. So as not to be defeated, I found out it has
been reprinted in a paperback. So I ordered one (a week to ten
days for delivery). If you want that, I'll send it on to you. In the
meantime, I'll still keep looking and phoning.

Hurriedly,
H

D.S. Jordan and B.W. Overman, *Aquatic Resources of the Hawaiian
Islands.* Part 1, Shore Fishes. Bookplate of University College, South
Wales, Department of Zoology. (I bought them in England.) All three
volumes have many illustrations.

Bulletin of the United States Fish Commission. Vol XXIII. Part 1, 1903.
Folio, 574 pages. Illus include 77 colored plates, 208 photos & folding
map. Title page, George M. Bowers, Comm. Washington, 1905.

Bulletin of the United States Fish Commission. Vol XXIII, Part 2.
Section II, *The Deep-Sea Fishes,* by Charles Gilbert. Section III,
The Commercial Fisheries, by John Cobb. 44 black & white plates
and endless text figures. 191 pp.

Bulletin of the United States Fish Commission. Vol. XXIII, Part 3. *The
Aquatic Resources of the Hawaiian Islands.* Miscellaneous papers based
on collections and investigations made by U.S. Fish Comm., Steamer
Albatross in 1902, under the direction of Jordan and Overman. Illus of
birds, eggs, porpoises, hydroids, schizopods, starfishes. 433 pp. All vols
uniformly bound in black cloth. Fine cond.

If you should decide to purchase these volumes, it's going to
take you the bloody whole winter to read them. The 3-volume
set weighs 14½ lbs.

November 26, 1989

Dear Helen,

I'm enclosing my check for the 14½-pound, 3-volume *Bulletins* of fish information. This comes to $41.38 per pound of fish book. It sounds interesting.

Also, please send me the paperback edition of Ortega y Gasset's *Meditations on Hunting* and bill me for it. I'm actually more interested in the contents of his book than in getting the old edition.

Thanks for all your good work!

Love,
John

Dear John,

You said that *Meditations on Hunting* was published in 1942. I found a copy that was published in 1972 and I tried to reach you on the phone and the operator said you didn't have a phone. I knew that was wrong, but I wasted so much time fighting with her that the guy sold the book. Send me a phone number.

John Ordeman has a new book out—*To Keep a Tryst with the Dawn.* Published in your backyard. It's a nice-looking book. You might like it.

I'll send the Jordan off today. If it's not your dish of tea, send it back.

I often wonder if your children realize the value of your library—with Sherri gone, somebody is going to have a lot of fun with my library. Oh well, I enjoyed collecting it.

Affectionately,
H

December 7, 1989
Pearl Harbor Day
(I vividly remember where I was on that day. Do you?)

Dear Helen,

My telephone number here is 803-555-1234. I can't understand why the telephone operator told you that I didn't have a phone because I *am* listed in the Camden phone book.

Tell me more about John Ordeman and his new book, *To Keep a Tryst with Dawn*. I don't know a thing about it.

Now, the Jordan. I'm afraid it is definitely not my cup of tea. I really can't find a fit for this u.s. government publication about aquatic resources in the Hawaiian Islands with anything resembling a sporting book. At first, I thought to myself, "My, my, I've made a mistake and dear Helen has sent me a real turkey, but I don't want to hurt her feelings."

And then my Scottish blood got the better of me and I decided to face up to the fact that I didn't want to spend good money on some books I didn't want.

So I'm sending them back to you via ups today, and am asking for a refund. I'm sorry to have put you to all this trouble.

Love,
John

December 11, 1989

Dear John,

I am sorry you are having all the trouble of sending the Hawaiian books back. They haven't arrived yet, but they will. In the meantime, here is my check.

Enclosed is a flyer on the Roland Clark.

Hurriedly,
H

* * *

January 1, 1990

Dear Helen,

Happy 1990! I hope the new year will bring you good health and happiness.

I'm sorry to be so slow in answering your letter of December 11th, but I have been running about very fast in the ensuing time.

I'm finally sending you my check for the Roland Clark book.

Lots of love,
John

February 12, 1990

Dear Helen,

I'm hard at work on the displays for the "Collector's Case" at the Yale-Beinecke Library and pleased with the progress. I've completed one layout on angling and another on bird shooting, and am deep into the third display, which I'm calling Big Game Hunting in the Early Wild West. When that one is completed, I'll have two more segments to go, and those are beginning to take shape. It is a "fun" project for February's winter weather, and I'm pleased with the technique I developed of getting a local cabinetmaker to build me a mock-up of the collector's case. (I don't know whether this makes any sense to you or not.)

Love,
John

* * *

February 24, 1990

Dear Helen,

I'm enclosing my check for Art Buchwald's book *While Reagan Slept*. Maybe in the light of Ronnie's non-testimony for the Poindexter trial, the book should be renamed *While Reagan Keeps Sleeping*!

I went up to Washington, DC, this week for a Business Council meeting. On Wednesday evening we met in the great hall of the Library of Congress for dinner & a speech by President Bush. I'd never been in the Library of Congress before and was very impressed by its splendid decor.

George Bush speaks well and gives me the strong impression that he knows what's going on.

Love,
John

Dear Helen,

I'm so relieved and glad that you are all right—well and happy and all that! When it dawned on my fuzzy old mind that I hadn't heard a word out of you for almost two months, I really got worried. And then I tried to telephone you yesterday—Sunday—and didn't get an answer, so I really got worried.

This morning when you answered the phone was blissful!

I have a couple of things to report in the book field. First, I've shipped nine boxes of sporting books and Leech watercolors up to the Beinecke Library at Yale for the little exhibit they are going to put on beginning in July. The exhibit opens on Tuesday, July 10th, and there will be a small reception that afternoon starting at four o'clock. I'm sending you an invitation, but please don't fight the summer heat by coming. (I can fill you in about the show later.) I did want you to be included.

The other thing is that the big sporting book exhibit at the Minneapolis Institute of Arts, scheduled to open in August 1992, is still on. Things got rather screwed up this winter because I hadn't heard from "the man" at the Minneapolis Institute for almost four months! So I wrote him a rather polite ultimatum —you know—and sent him a follow-up fax and got his attention. So now things are back on track.

Do stay in touch and do stay well.

Love,
John

April 28, 1990

Dear John,

It was so thoughtful of you to phone me the other morning. You go through life not realizing that sometimes people like you.

I had a birthday last week—I hadn't mentioned it to anyone, but had all kinds of surprise parties. I must admit that I was considerably concerned at being eighty.

It was extremely nice of you to think of me for the Yale exhibit, and I would love to be there. However, it is very difficult for me to be away from home overnight.

The book business is changing, as you probably have observed from the catalogues you have been receiving—it's a reprint world. The new generation are not collectors and I'm too much of a snob to learn that field.

Again, my dear, thanks for everything,
H

Dear Helen,

A belated and heartfelt birthday wish. You are a bright and
charming dear friend and I send you my best wishes and love
on your eightieth.

We have just returned from a whirlwind one-week trip across the
Atlantic to Czechoslovakia! It was really a spur-of-the-moment
decision to go over there at the invitation of some Czech friends
whom we'd met in 1988 and had become pen pals with.

I'm so glad we went! It was a very rare and special occasion.
Think of it! Here is a country that has been enslaved by a grim
totalitarian communist government with Russian tanks & troops
to enforce the iron grip since 1968. The commies brutalized and
terrorized these people and mistreated and lied to them. Then,
thanks to their own young people, they had what they call their
"velvet revolution" in November 1989, and they are free!

I'm enclosing a copy of the speech that I gave a week ago today
to 2,000 cheering, flag-waving Czechs in this little matchstick-
making town in western Czechoslovakia. It was a great day.

Love,
John

May 25, 1990

Dear John,

You must have had a wonderful time in Czechoslovakia, and the honor of giving a speech. Now when they update your name in *Who's Who of American Men,* you will have to add this to your list of accomplishments.

There is very little new around here, except for the rain, which has brought the grass up to a tall Indian's ass—in the meantime I've lost the outdoor man, so I'm pursuing the lawnmower, and I might add it's not my dish of tea.

Enclosed is a description of a book I just purchased—have you any interest?

Affectionately,
H

PUBLISHER'S DELUXE BINDING
Dwight W. Huntington, *In Brush, Sedge and Stubble, A Picture Book of the Shooting Fields and Feathered Game of North America.* The Sportsman's Society, Cincinnati, 1898. Imperial 4to. 8 mounted photogravure plates in color, 8 photographic halftone plates, numerous text sketches and photographs. The photogravure color plates are by H.F. Farny (3), W.A. McCord, D.W. Huntington (3), and C.A. Fries. In this copy the color plates by Huntington have been signed in pencil on the mounts. Publisher's full morocco, front cover embossed in blind and gilt, newly rebacked in morocco, light marginal water stain at top edge, not affecting plates or text. The work was issued, at various prices, in a portfolio, in buckram and full leather. A copy of the prospectus has been loosely inserted. First edition. A fine copy with all the printed tissue guards for the plates present.

Dear Helen,

You always say things so nicely. Thank you for your complimentary remarks about my speech-making in Czechoslovakia.
As I gain some perspective about that event it seems like an
unreal experience that happened to somebody else.

Thank you for offering the Dwight Huntington, *In Brush,
Sedge, and Stubble*. I find that I bought a nice set at Swann
Gallery back in 1985.

Please don't give up on me. I usually am delighted to latch on
to your good offerings.

I've been trying to think up a good title for my exhibition at the
Minneapolis Institute of Arts. It should be a catchy title, and I
think I have one. How do you like this?

I HAVE LAID ASIDE BUSINESS, AND GONE A'FISHING.
   —Izaak Walton, *The Compleat Angler*, "Epistle to the Reader"

Incidentally, what you call an "outdoor man" we call a "yard
man." I hope you can hire one soon to keep you off the lawnmower—and keep the Indian's ass uncovered.

Love,
John

        * * *

Your Huntington is worth $1,500 according to Col. Siegel.

H

[No date]

Dear Helen,

I feel even better about the Dwight Huntington to know that Hank Siegel thinks it is worth $1,500. I only paid $560 at Swann in 1985, including commissions! Any way you can triple your money is okay.

I'm rushing around all this week & next putting together a massive sporting book display for a group of about twenty nice ladies & gents from the Minneapolis Institute who are coming out on June 16th to sort of check me out for the big showing of my collection that they are planning to put on for about four months in 1992. Wow! It's lots of fun pulling all the stuff out and arranging it in different categories.

I wish you were here to help me and to see it all.

In haste,
Love,
John

* * *

June 13, 1990

Dear John,

Yes, it would be fun to be there with you helping to prepare your show—we would disagree, but that would stimulate our brains.

I can't believe the prices in the catalogues I've been receiving lately. Maybe we ought to tell the Japanese about the book business in America. Every book that I have had in this library was bought and paid for. I have never taken anything on consignment. But I'm beginning to think that my colleagues do.

Affectionately,
H

June 16, 1990

Dear Helen,

I agree with you about prices. I just got a quote on some twenty-five Henry Alken color plate books and I was shocked. The asking prices were more than twice (sometimes four times) what I'd paid for many of the books only four or five years ago! It makes me feel good about the prices I did pay, but it scares me off from buying additional Alkens.

I'm enclosing a copy of the little program I cooked up for today's visit by some twenty-five museum types who are coming out to see my books. I'm rather pleased with the old Juliana Berner's fisherman and I'm even happier with my Izaak Walton quotation, which suits me to a tee.

Love,
John

    * * *

June 30, 1990

Dear John,

I had a nice letter from Vincent Giroud inviting me to your reception at Yale Library. I would have loved to have attended, but as I explained to you before, it's not impossible, but it's very difficult for me to be away from home overnight. My best to you both.

Nothing exciting on this side of the continent, except the weather leaves a lot to be desired.

The only thing that is any fun around here now is I'm feeding six young stray kittens that the tour bus stops and points out to the lovely old ladies.

Affectionately,
H

July 4, 1990

Dear Helen,

I have a Yale classmate who lives in a large house on the shores of Lake Minnetonka—the area where many of the "swells" reside. During the summer months an excursion boat cruises by each afternoon and through the public address system comes a running commentary about the various inhabitants who live in their big homes along the shore. Alas, when they get up to my friend's house they always pause and say, "That big, gray, three-story house belongs to Mr. ____. He isn't very important."

I'm going to tell my friend about the effects you have been having on your tour bus by feeding six young stray kittens. Who knows? This might solve my friend's problem about his lack of importance. Got any spare kittens?

I know you can't get to the Beinecke Library opening, but I'll be thinking of you and will try to send some photos & a report later on.

Love,
John

* * *

July 22, 1990

Dear John,

Nothing much is happening up here. Five of the kittens have gone to homes. One I kept temporarily so the mother wouldn't be lonely. I had her (the mother) operated on only because the president of Skidmore's wife (who lives next door) thought it was terrible that she was a fertile female. I like animals better than people.

You must be back home from Yale. I'm sure your show was a great success.

Affectionately,
H

Dear Helen,

You are wonderful. When "nothing is happening" you have a great knack for making things happen. Now it's the "cat war" with the wife of the president of Skidmore. Don't ever change. The Yale rare book show got off to a good start. My wife and I flew to Hartford from Minneapolis the Sunday before the opening, which was scheduled for Tuesday afternoon, July 10th. It is fortunate that we went that early because it took almost a day and a half to lay out the exhibition. The results were very pleasing to the eye of both the bibliophile and the collector, and also to the casual tourist.

The "Collector's Case" is at the top of a grand staircase on the mezzanine floor of the Beinecke Rare Book Library at Yale. The case consists of two twenty-five-foot-wide curved glass cases that are back-to-back. There are generally three different shows or exhibits each year of the collections of some of the Yale alumni.

Because the display space is very limited, I only used four categories of sporting books from my collection—angling, foxhunting, bird shooting, western American early big game hunts—and only used about sixty books as well as some original manuscripts and some original watercolor paintings. I'm enclosing a copy of the news release from the Beinecke, which describes some of the books.

The exhibit will run for the next three months. The thing that surprised and pleased me the most is that during the summer a large number of visitors come through the Beinecke Library each day on guided tours. So the exhibit will be seen by many visitors, which is good.

We had a very pleasant two-hour reception on the day the exhibit opened. My brother from New York, a nephew and his wife from Danbury, and a daughter from Washington, DC, came and there were twelve or more classmates from the local area, as well as quite a few "book people," including Yale University Library people and some booksellers that I know from both nearby and from New York. It was a most pleasant and successful "kickoff."

Now I'm back home and beginning to turn my "book attention" toward the longer-range task of preparing for the show I've agreed to do for the Minneapolis Institute of Arts, which doesn't open until March 1992! It really dwarfs the Yale show in size & scope because they have allotted two very large galleries to the show and are going to do an illustrated catalogue. Wow! This is going to take beaucoup time and work to bring off. It's good we are starting now because it is going to take lots of time to select the books and the art and sculpture that are going to be used, and then it will take a long time to do the catalogue.

I've already been "vetted" by the library committee from the Minneapolis Institute who came out—twenty strong—earlier this summer to see my collection. This "preview" gave me an opportunity to put on a major display in our house—but I've already sent you some stuff on that back in June so I won't go into any more details.

Keep cool.

Love,
John

August 4, 1990

Dear John,

I enjoyed your letter. I'm sorry I couldn't make it to New Haven. I wish I had a copy of Seccombe's book. I looked him up and he did a book titled *Specimen of the Harmony of Wisdom and Felicity,* published the same year, sold for $5.00 in 1965.

The racing seasons started yesterday, but I haven't seen Ms. Fout yet. I'm not too fond of the horse trade. They mostly come by to kill time and don't treat the books kindly.

Why do they race horses in this heat?

Affectionately,
H

        * * *

August 10, 1990

Dear Helen,

We're going to England for ten days later this month. A combination of shopping & theater in London, plus our annual week of grouse shooting on the moors.

Do you have any advice about London booksellers? Are there any special ones who handle sporting books that you'd recommend? My favorite is Sotheran's.

Love,
John

August 14, 1990

Dear John,

Quaritch and Maggs are totally different today than they used to be. Even Sotheran's (who is also my favorite) is not the same. It's a first-edition-literature world. As an illustration, how about $14,000 for a first edition of Hemingway's *Farewell to Arms* in DJ? Allen is not one of my favorite people.

    John Head, Salisbury, Wilshire
    G.B. Way, Newmarket, Suffolk

Both of these dealers are special. If you speak to them, give them my best wishes.

Have a wonderful holiday.

Affectionately,
H

* * *

September 5, 1990

Dear John,

I thought that before you left home you would have known that the bloody American dollar was only worth fifty cents, and if you are patient it's going to be worth less.

Never mind the books. I hope you have a successful hunt and a wonderful vacation.

Affectionately,
H

September 10, 1990

Dear Helen,

Our house party cum grouse shoot, Northumberland, England, was the best ever. We had great weather and lots of birds, so our syndicate, which included my wife, a son, and a brother-in-law, shot 504½ brace in four days. (Why do they count grouse in "braces" and foxhounds in "couples?")

We got back to warm Minnesota in time to rehearse for and participate in an all-amateur musical show celebrating the seventy-fifth anniversary of the founding of our local country club. I sang a couple of numbers with some pals, and even though I had a terrible time memorizing my lines it worked out okay.

I'm enclosing a snapshot of my wife, Martha, and me in our costumes for the seventy-fifth anniversary party.

Love,
John

P.S. We have a grandson who is a senior at Skidmore this year.

September 27, 1990

Dear John,

Nice picture of you and Mrs. Daniels. Charming couple.

Bookman's Weekly had a nice piece on your sporting books at Yale Library (September 10th).

I got another speeding ticket. The same judge for the third time. He only charged me $65, and according to motor laws it was supposed to be $200—my brother says he gave me the Senior Citizen rate. I think it was because I appeared in person instead of sending my lawyer.

The kittens have homes, but the tour bus still goes by.

Affectionately,
H

* * *

October 1, 1990

Dear Helen,

I'm happy for you that the judge only fined you $65 for speeding. Take it easy! Please.

Love,
John

Dear Helen,

Have you seen Jim Cummins's new catalogue #27? It has 527
lots and some very good stuff at very, very big prices! The thing
that makes me feel so good in reading his catalogue is that I
already have most of his real treasures and paid only a fraction
of what he is now asking for them!

As to my collection, the Yale University exhibition of some of
my sporting books in the Collector's Case at the Beinecke Rare
Book Library has finally closed after a three-month run. It was
very well received & reviewed and was visited by a lot of people,
so I feel very good about it.

I have spent a lot of time this summer working with the librarian
of the Minneapolis Institute of Arts. My job this summer has
been to develop the "inventory" of books, art, sculpture, and
ephemera which will actually be in the exhibition, so that all
can be catalogued by the museum this winter after we've gone
south. We have selected about 400 books for the first broad
selection to be catalogued, with the idea that this will be culled
to fit the available space some time next summer when we start
working with the museum staff on showcases, spaces, etc.

I really am very pleased and excited about the entire project.
The museum is going to turn loose all of their in-house talent
& personnel in planning the layouts and doing the publicity,
etc., etc. I have to think through & research the introduction to
the catalogue, which I am going to write this winter, and then
eventually I will have to prepare some lecture notes for some
talks I am to give at the opening of the show.

I've got my winter projects cut out for me already.

Thank you for "sitting Roget in your lap" when you wrote me
that last letter. I love your effort and special attention to detail
and I love hearing from you.

Don't speed! *Do* write!

Love,
John

October 31, 1990

Dear John,

Yes, I did watch the series on the Civil War, and I learned a great deal. It was never a subject that I knew enough about—I'm honored to know such famous people.

Don't be so hard on the Colonel—he looks like death warmed over.

I didn't go to the second sale, but I did go to the first one and I went for only one book, Ronalds's *Fly-Fishers' Entomology*. I had had a first and while this is not a first, it's a nice copy. Have a great holiday in New Haven.

Affectionately,
H

Frank Benson, *Etchings and Dry Points*. Compiled and arranged by Adam Paff, first four vols. Folio. All five vols uniformly bound, tan linen spine, gray boards. First editions.

Vol 1. MDCCCCXVII. Original signed etching, ltd. 275 copies, no. 12.
Vol 2. MDCCCCXIX. Original signed etching, ltd. 275 copies, no. 80.
Vol 3. MDCCCCXIII. Original signed etching, ltd. 525 copies, no. 18.
Vol 4. MDCCCCXXIX. Original signed etching, ltd. 600 copies, no. 27.
Vol 5. By Arthur W. Heintzelman, Keeper of Prints, The Public Library of the City of Boston (Benson was dead). MCMLIX. Ltd. 400 copies, no. 334. DJ.

I don't know if Paff vols came with DJ—however, I've never seen one. All vols in fine condition.

Dear Helen,

Yale defeated Princeton in the pouring rain on Saturday, and I got very wet but had a lovely time. After getting into dry clothes I joined seven other Yale Whiffenpoofs at a friend's house and we sang for two wonderful hours!

Now I'm back home, trying to get caught up on a Sunday evening. Thank you for letting me see the material on Frank Benson. I've decided not to go for them and I'm returning the pamphlet you loaned me.

I went to Sotheby's when I was in New York & got a preview of some of the sporting books they're going to be offering in December from John Schiff's collection. It's fantastic!

Affectionately,
John

      * * *

November 21, 1990

Dear John,

Belated Birthday Best Wishes—you're only a kid. Josy was ninety-five yesterday.

Sotheby's had somebody hand deliver the Xerox sheets to me on the Schiff sale, about three weeks ago. The catalogue had not been printed yet. Why I was so honored I have no idea. However, twenty years ago I would have had a wonderful time with the Riviere bindings, but I have almost made up my mind not to accumulate any more stock.

Have a happy Thanksgiving.

Affectionately,
H

[No date]

Dear Helen,

Many thanks for your B.B.B.—at my age all birthday wishes are treasured. There were some peep shows and panoramas at Swann Gallery recently, but they were sold for amazingly high prices—especially in the light of their very bad condition. I missed out!

We are flying down to Yucatan on Saturday with some friends to do a week of bonefishing with fly rods. It's a lovely, exciting spot—all catch and release.

Dick Francis, the British ex-jockey & whodunit writer, was here recently for our Colonial Cup Steeplechase. He told a couple of ripsnorting, shady stories, which were very funny, & got away with them. I got him to autograph *Sport of Queens*.

I'm going up to N.Y. for the Schiff auction on December 11th. It will be an exciting and very rare event.

Fondly,
John

December 12, 1990

Dear Helen,

On Tuesday, December 11th, I had a record good time as a collector of sporting books. I made a special trip up to New York to attend Sotheby's auction of the John Schiff library.

As the saying goes, "I was on a roll." I literally got all the books I wanted at about fifty percent of what I was willing to pay. It included two unpublished manuscripts by Surtees (his autobiography and his biography of Nimrod), an unpublished manuscript of Hunting Songs by "Phiz" with twenty-one original drawings, a group of fouteen autographed letters signed by John Mytton to his financial advisors as he was going "down the tube" drinking himself to death, an original manuscript of a poem about grouse shooting by Robert Burns, *and* a twenty-page autographed manuscript by Teddy Roosevelt of an article he wrote for the *Century Illustrated Magazine* about drag hunting with the Meadowbrook in 1886!

Not bad for an old fellow, don't you think? I saw our mutual friend, Judith Bowman, as well as some others.

Affectionately,
John

Dear Helen,

I was glad to hear your voice and learn that everything is okay. I hadn't heard from you since before Christmas and just wanted to check in to make sure you are well and haven't been getting any speeding tickets.

After buying the R.S. Surtees manuscript of his autobiography, I had stars in my eyes about publishing it. Tilt! E.D. Cuming scooped me in 1925! Have you been glued to the TV like me? I'm fascinated by the coverage of the war. When is Saddam going to "blink"? What will be Israel's way of striking back? What will happen if there's an offensive on the ground by our troops? History in the making has never been more vivid.

Affectionately,
John

P.S. My grandson is Willard (Bill) Shull, in case he turns up.

* * *

January 25, 1991

Dear John,

Very thoughtful of you to phone. Physically, I'm fine . . . mentally, I'm depressed. Could be the war, or almost anything. I'd planned on England, but I think I'd better hold off on that voyage.

No business and that annoys my brain—however, the whole world is in the club.

Affectionately,
H

Dear Helen,

No wonder you feel depressed at times. This war is no joke,
but you have been through wars before and this one is going to
be quite short (three months) and victorious—believe me, I'm
an expert (ha ha).

I'm enclosing a copy of Kiplinger. It's the most optimistic thing
I've read in weeks.

I don't think the economy is going to pick up until the war is
over. If the war ends by spring, I think we'll see a rapid recovery.

No, I'm not smoking anything—I just feel good and optimistic.

Affectionately,
John

            * * *

February 8, 1991

Dear John,

So you think the war will be over soon—I'm a gambling
woman, so I'll bet you ten dollars it won't be. This is a political
performance and they have a large audience.

I hope Bush isn't one of your favorite people.

If you reprint your Surtees, it will no longer be one of a kind.

Affectionately,
H

February 11, 1991

Dear Helen,

I *will* bet you ten dollars that the war will be over before the end of June 1991. I consider that to be a short war! We have a bet.

George Bush *is* one of my favorite people. I think he is doing a *great* job as our president & our leader in battle. I'm enclosing a copy of the latest Coleman/Bartlett letter which says the same thing, better.

Love,
John

* * *

February 20, 1991

Dear John,

It seems your favorite friend is a monument of indecision.
So I think my ten dollars is safe.

I think I'll put Cuomo *and* Bush in a large paper bag and give them to the garbage man when he comes by on Tuesday.

Affectionately,
H

Dear Helen,

In your note of February 20th you sound as if you are pissed off about the world and especially Cuomo and Bush. Well, there are days like that for all of us.

I have some good news. My grandson, Bill Shull, who graduates from Skidmore in May, got a job offer from my old company, Archer-Daniels-Midland Co. I am urging him to accept. If he goes to work for ADM, he will be the 4th generation with the company. His great-great-grandfather—my grandfather—founded the company ninety years ago.

Love,
John

* * *

March 3, 1991

Dear John,

Congratulations—you see that wasn't hard. I'm defeated, but I don't think Saddam Hussein is. He's still got the gas that the journalists talked for hours about.

February's *ABMR* had a piece titled "New Partnership for Joseph's Heritage Bookshop and James B. Cummins."

Burlington Gallery in London is having a show of Cecil Aldin material. He is a favorite of mine and I have quite a lot of his books.

For all the years we have been writing to each other, I never knew what your profession was. Just think by your not telling me how much money I didn't make.

Affectionately,
H

March 4, 1991

Dear Helen,

Thank you for being so very prompt in paying off your bet about the duration of the war. I'm clearly elated by the fact that it was such a short war with so very few casualties. Thank God.

Although I'd like to give you a chance to get your money back, I certainly hope it doesn't revolve around betting on another war—ever again.

Cecil Aldin is also a favorite of mine and I have quite a few of his books. I am enclosing a copy of my index cards on the Cecil Aldin's that I possess, in order to find out if you might have any others you would want to offer me.

Incidentally, I erred. My grandson, Bill Shull, the Skidmore senior, will be the fifth generation (not fourth) to work for ADM if he takes the job offer. My informants tell me that he is about to accept!

I didn't think about your not knowing what I did for a living. I certainly wasn't trying to keep it a secret, and I'm obviously proud of having been President & Chief Executive Officer of Archer-Daniels-Midland Co. I ran the company for ten years.

Keep me posted.

Affectionately,
John

Dear John,

You have a very nice collection of Cecil Aldin. Some I have
had. Burlington Gallery lists fifty-seven titles, and I suppose
there are more. If you are interested, I have *Forty Fine Ladies* by
Patrick R. Chalmers. Spottswood and Eyre, London, 1929.
Illustrated by Cecil Aldin. 4to, vellum-backed brown cloth, TEG.
One of 250 copies, #63. Signed by Chalmers and Aldin. Fine
copy. Bookplate of Nancy Goddis Heller.

I also have two children's books:

> Walter Emanuel, *A Dog-Day*. Dutton, N.Y., 1919. 12mo. Illustrated by
> Aldin. Color. Not a first. Fair condition.

> S. Sutton Smith, *Stories from Puppyland.* Donohue & Co., Chicago, no
> date. Charming small oblong 12mo. Illus by Aldin in color. Interior
> fine.

I'm still trying to get Sotheby's to send me the post-sale results
of the John Schiff sale. Two phone calls and one letter. Maybe
Cummins should buy the bloody place.

Affectionately,
H

March 21, 1991

Dear Helen,

Alas, I already have Chalmers's *Forty Fine Ladies*. Please send me:

> *A Dog-Day* by Walter Emanuel
> *Stories from Puppyland* by S.S. Smith

Both illustrated by Aldin. My check is enclosed.

I have to tell you about my "great discovery." In March 1989, you sold me a panorama—*Going to the Fight*. Two years later (1991) another bookseller sold me a small pamphlet by Pierce Egan titled *Key to a Panorama*. You won't believe it but they fit! Reunited after all these years, the Pierce Egan pamphlet describes each scene in the panorama! It is a real breakthrough!

Love,
John

* * *

March 26, 1991

I found another book with Cecil Aldin illustrations: Walter Emmanuel, *The Dogs of War*. Scribners, 1906. 8vo. Illus by Aldin, color & B&W. Brown cloth, rear hinge cracked, but binding tight. First. Fair cond.

Hurriedly,
H

April 1, 1991

Dear Helen,

Enclosed is my check for the Cecil Aldin illustrated *Dogs of War.* I hope you had a happy Easter.

Fondly,
John,

* * *

April 12, 1991

Dear John,

Have you any interest in the medals and decorations book enclosed—Fernandez's books have very good auction records. I have a birthday next week. I'd like to ignore it, but I'm afraid my fan club is doing something.

Affectionately,
H

* * *

April 16, 1991

Dear Helen,

Thanks, but I am not interested in Fernandez.

Fondly,
John

June 3, 1991

Dear Helen,

That's a very nice newspaper article, and you came off like a star! Thank you for sending me a copy.

My grandson, Bill, who just graduated from Skidmore is coming for dinner & I'll show him the article.

Love,
John

* * *

"OLD AND . . ."
Society mavens, bootleggers, hippies, and yuppies have called this home

Helen Hennessey's house used to keep horses. Now it holds books about [150,000? of] them.

Her home is a carriage house, which she proudly has left to its original shape—minus the straw and other horse paraphernalia, of course. Her living quarters are on the second floor, and the book store is on the first.

The store is discreet—only a small hanging sign announces its presence, and a smaller sign asks that customers please ring bell before entering. Inside hardcover books sit on walls and on shelves, tables, or cabinets. But no paperbacks: "They disintegrate very quickly, they turn yellow," she says.

Amidst it all is a shiny, new Jaguar, looking strangely out of place.

"Don't be envious, kid," she says, "I've earned it. I've worked since I was fourteen."

Hennessey, eighty-one, has kicked back a bit since her serious working days. She has lived, along with her husband Joe and her books, in this house for thirty years.

The shape of the carriage house is perfect for her bookstore—especially since she specializes in books on horses. And she likes the neighborhood, with the president of Skidmore College on one side and deep, green woods on the other. Her only problem is the students parking on the road, but even that concern she shrugs off.

"The roads belong to the city, so how can I be cross about it?" she asks.

Photo caption: Helen Hennessey, owner of the Hennessey Book Store, poses with her cat Gin. Hennessey lives in another converted carriage house, but left the first floor—except for the straw, of course—as it was.

—*The Saratogian*, May 27, 1991
Saratoga Springs, N.Y.

* * *

July 22, 1991

Dear Helen,

I haven't heard a word from you in more than a month & I'm writing to see how you're doing. How is the summer going for you? No speeding tickets, I hope.

My friend Jim Cummins sold me an unusual sporting book recently. The thing that struck me so forcefully is that it was published by the American Historical Society, Inc., New York, in 1932. This the same bunch of crooks who victimized my grandmother in 1934 (two years later) and conned her into paying an outrageous amount of money for an almost identical looking, fancy-tooled leather binding, deluxe ego book about my grandfather. Have you ever heard of the American Historical Society? They were very smooth operators who got a lot of money out of wealthy widows in the 1930s. I wonder what happened to them.

Write soon and let me have a few pearls of your charming wisdom.

Affectionately,
John

July 28, 1991

Dear John

I don't think you are going to be happy hearing from me. I'm in a foul frame of mind. It started with the Webb sale, which upset me, because the Shelburne family found it necessary to sell a very fine library for lack of funds. Calumet Farm in trouble—no estate in Saratoga anymore. Galbraith House in Saratoga for sale. I could go on with a few more paragraphs, but . . .

My brother had a heart-bypass operation and they didn't feed him enough oxygen on the table so he has brain damage and doesn't know me or his children. This took place in Burlington, VT. However, the police like Jaguars and haven't ticketed me yet.

The binding on your book reads wonderfully. I have no reference on publishers that early.

Have a fine holiday in England.

Affectionately,
H

August 1, 1991

Dear Helen,

As you know, I've been working long & hard with this guy at
the Minneapolis Institute of Arts developing the catalogue of
the sporting books that will go in the big exhibition next year.
We have finally cut the last book out of the show and will end
up with 180 catalogue entries plus some great original art (oil
paintings & watercolors) by Cecil Aldin, Lionel Edwards, John
Leech, Edith Somerville, and others. We are going to select
twenty-four full-page illustrations to go in the catalogue tomorrow, as well as the illustrations for the front & back covers of the
catalogue, & we'll be done with that key step. It's going to be
wonderful. I'm very pleased & excited. We open the exhibit
April 18th, 1992.

Affectionately,
John

     * * *

August 18, 1991

Dear Helen,

We depart for England next Sunday for a two-week stay.
London for a couple of days and a couple of shows, then
Yorkshire for five days and finally a week of grouse shooting
in Northumberland.

Take good care of yourself.

Affectionately,
John

September 18, 1991

Dear John,

Nice picture of you and your bride. It's great that you enjoy doing things together.

Affectionately,
H

* * *

September 28, 1991

Dear Helen,

I have twenty-seven packages waiting for the truck from the Minneapolis Institute of Arts to pick them up on October 8th. It's a year's worth of assembling the 199 books to go in the exhibition.

Glad you like the picture.

Affectionately,
John

Dear John,

The countryside here is beautiful. Skidmore Woods out my kitchen window is very colorful; however, I can't find anyone willing to rake leaves. I might just leave them there—

Are you going to bid on Swann's sale, November 7th— Freeman's *Observations of the Horses' Foot*? I'd like it, but horse books are asleep.

Affectionately,
H

* * *

November 11, 1991

Dear John,

So you had a birthday. You're just a kid—wait until you are eighty-one. Eighty was all right, but my brain is tired now. Nice to have a large family to celebrate your own holiday with.

Josy Hennessey celebrated ninety-six years last week—we only let him have one drink though.

I hope there are many happy days ahead for you.

Affectionately,
H

December 4, 1991

Dear Helen,

Thank you for your note about my big seventy. Sure, I'm still just a kid. I love it!

Hope you had a good Thanksgiving.

Affectionately,
John

* * *

December 21, 1991

Dear Helen,

Martha and I are simply thrilled to have the polo picture "Backing the Ball" by your talented daughter, Sherri. You are so generous to part with such a treasure. Thank you so very much for a lovely and very special Christmas present.

I'm going to get it framed and plan to hang it here in my office where I can enjoy it—and think of you—every day.

The old year is about to run out of days. I hope it has been a good year for you and that 1992 will also be a good one.

This is the time of year when I think how lucky I am to have such good friends like you.

Much love and thanks,
John

January 4, 1992

Dear John,

So it's a new beginning. Business is very slow and a bit of a bore. Most dealers want you to negotiate, and I promised myself when I went into this business that I wouldn't do that. What you see in the back of my books is what you pay—less ten percent to dealers. The British are making fun of us dealers over this subject.

I'm glad you liked Sherri's picture—she was a fairly good artist, a hell of a kid, naughty, but I wouldn't have had her any other way.

Affectionately,
H

    * * *

January 11, 1992

Dear Helen,

Happy New Year! I hope you have good health, happiness, a minimum of speeding tickets, and all the prosperity in the world! Please keep your letters coming this way. You are my favorite pen pal because you never let me get away with anything and because you sign your letters "Affectionately." I like that.

Love,
John

February 6, 1992

Dear John,

I enjoyed the picture of the dogs. When we lived on the island we had five dogs. Dorothy Parker sent up her Standard poodle to be bred and she had six children. At night it was an argument over who was going to sleep with whom—after we sent Dorothy's dog back. Maggie the cook won the six children. I like animals better than people.

I wonder if you are keeping a record of the increased value of your library—for example, 4 vols of Schwerdt has an auction record of $3,500 now. I don't remember what you paid me for it, but I know it wasn't that figure. It is important that you keep a record.

Affectionately,
H

* * *

[No date]

Dear Helen,

Just to make you feel good, I paid you $3,650 for the 4-volume Schwerdt in May 1981! I looked it up in my card file and there it is. Incidentally, I've always been very pleased and proud to own that magnificent set. You see, I *do* keep records of all the books in my collection and I agree with you that over the last twenty years my collection has greatly improved in value.

So how are you? I hope you're getting through this long cold winter in very good shape!

We are going to fly down to the Bahamas next week for some super fly-fishing for bonefish. I'll send you some pictures.

Affectionately,
John

Dear John,

You must be back from your voyage to the Bahamas. Hope you had a great time.

The book business is very quiet, but as it has never fed me except mentally, I only become bored when it is quiet.

Do you realize the inheritance your children are going to be taxed on your library? I just decided to give mine to Sherri's college. However, I haven't told them about it.

Affectionately,
H

March 31, 1992

Dear Helen,

You're 100 percent correct. What to do with a valuable collection? Give it away? Sell it? Do nothing?

If I could find the right college that wanted it, I think it would tempting to give it.

But! I had so much fun collecting all those books from *you* and others that it would be nice to think about other collectors having the same opportunity, and you know darn well that a college will lock up the "goodies" forever. So it is tempting to sell them.

The "ego" thing—i.e., recognition—has been pretty well satisfied by the Beinecke exhibition and the forthcoming—really exciting—show at the Minneapolis Institute of Arts. (Incidentally, I have seen the proofs of the catalogue for my show and it's going to be very good. Just as soon as I get the finished catalogue I will send you one.)

So, in my case, the "jury is still out." I think about it, but I haven't decided which way to go. What is your advice?

Love,
John

P.S. It is wonderful and very appropriate to give your collection to Sherri's college.

Dear John,

Thank you for my invitation to the Minneapolis Institute of
Arts. I'd like very much to attend, but I can't, of course.

Don't your children have any lust for your books? Sherri was a
very possessive kid—she never wanted me to sell things we
inherited from Woollcott. When she died, I sold a Toulouse
that I had been carting around for fifty years and bought my
first Jaguar.

Life plays funny tricks on you. Regardless how you plan your
life and possessions, things won't turn out that way. Skidmore
has a rare book room that no one is allowed in—that's the
height of stupid.

I'm a poor kid beside you, however my ego is stimulated. I have
a bank balance that I didn't have twenty years ago that I made
in the stock market and probably a couple hundred thousand in
sporting books. But if Josy and I end up in the home for the
aged, I doubt if we have enough money to pay our way.

Aren't you glad you asked me for a letter.

Affectionately,
H

[no date]

Dear Helen,

I enjoyed reading your letter about so many interesting things. The Woollcott "Toulouse" must have been fun to transform into a Jaguar sports car. You have so much fun out of life—I applaud you.

I didn't know that Skidmore never lets anybody into their rare book room. How ridiculous!

At my alma mater, the Beinecke Rare Book Library is meant for scholars to use.

Incidentally, while on the subject of Skidmore, I have a second grandson who is probably going to start there this fall. A very nice young man named Cedar—like the tree.

We're heading for Minneapolis on Tuesday and I'll get my first look at the sporting book exhibition, which is displayed in a large two-room gallery. I'm enclosing a copy of a four-page article about the show which appeared in the April edition of *Arts,* the news magazine put out by the Minneapolis Institute of Arts. I'm sure you will recognize the illustration of the panorama you sold me a few years ago.

"Break a leg" is the show biz greeting & salutation to someone who's show is opening.

Wish me it.

Love,
John

Dear Helen,

You deserve a special note of appreciation for all of the goodies you have made available to me over the years. I'm sure you will recognize many of your books.

Please let me have your reactions to the catalogue.

Affectionately,
John

＊ ＊ ＊

June 5, 1992

Dear Helen,

That grandson I wrote you about this winter has been accepted by Skidmore and will be going there in the fall. He's a fine young man and we're going out to Denver today for his graduation from Colorado Academy.

I hope things are okay and you're not flirting with traffic cops too blatantly.

What are your summer plans? Are you going to England again? We're going out to Seattle this month for a World War II Army reunion, and then are sailing from Vancouver, B.C. for a cruise up to Alaska. Do write soon!

Affectionately,
John

June 26, 1992

Dear John,

Some young men stole some books a couple of weeks ago. My colleagues told me when they offered the books to them— They had forgotten to erase my prices in the back of the books. They took only fine bindings & hand-colored plates—The loss of the books didn't upset me as much as the fear of getting hit on the head and really cleaning me out—The police now come by twice a day to see if this old lady is safe. How do you like that story?

I'm thinking of getting a new Jaguar—England is only making 300 of this one, and none for America. If I decide to have one, I'll have to go over and have it sent back by ship. I've had a lot of fun thinking about this—I wouldn't be surprised if I did it.

Affectionately,
H

* * *

August 12, 1992

Dear John,

Of course I'm not in your homemade catalogue—I haven't quoted you a book in a couple of years—The last book I quoted you was Benson's four-vol set. Writing about quoting, are you interested in Rockwell Kent's *Wilderness, A Journal of Quiet Adventure in Alaska*?

The city is busy with the races—polo has had to be postponed several times because of the weather. The horse sales are off forty-three percent. That's all from here.

Affectionately,
H
August 15, 1992

Dear Helen,

Glad to hear from you & know that your summer season is going full tilt. Speaking of polo, I'm subsidizing a researcher who is looking up all the details & history of polo in Camden, S.C., where I played so much in the 1930s, '40s, & '50s. The Camden Polo Field dates back to 1898, which makes it one of the oldest polo fields in the u.s.

Please tell me about Rockwell Kent's *Wilderness, A Journal of Adventure in Alaska*. I'm only interested if it's got shooting and/or fishing in it. Thanks.

Affectionately,
John

* * *

August 14, 1992

Dear John,

Rockwell Kent, no hunting or fish. Peary, yes.

I have sold over the years lots of books on polo and have been a member at the Polo Club since it first came to Saratoga.

Edgar Queeny is a *fine* copy of a bear hunt.

Hurriedly,
H

> Edgar M. Queeny, *Cheechako*. New York, 1941. The story of an Alaskan bear hunt. Introduction by Nash Buckingham. Tall 8vo. Illustrated with black and white and color photographs by the author. Heavy buckram, gilt labels on cover and spine. First edition, limited. A fine copy.

> Robert Edwin Peary, *A Narrative of the Polar Expedition of the Peary Arctic Club*. N.Y., 1907. 8vo, 411 pages. 67 plates, plus map. Orig. cloth. Signed letter, part typewritten, rest handwritten. First edition. Book signed by Peary. Fine condition.

August 31, 1992

Dear Helen,

I have the Queeny book. Please send me the Peary book. My check is enclosed.

Glad to see polo is alive & well in Saratoga. Our Camden Polo Club is pretty slow even though it's approaching its 100th anniversary, having been founded in 1898. I'm working with a researcher doing a history of the club, which I hope to publish within a year. I look forward to your good letters.

Fondly,
John

* * *

September 8, 1992

Dear John,

If you're not happy with Peary, send him back.

Do you need U.S. Polo Association yearbooks for 1934 and one for 1938, references for your polo book? Capt. E.M. Daniels is in 1934 as a one-goal man.

Polo for August wasn't a success in Saratoga. The weather defeated them.

Affectionately,
H

September 12, 1992

Dear Helen,

I'm quite pleased with the Peary book. An interesting slice of history.

Thank you, but I have an almost complete set of u.s. Polo Assn. yearbooks going back to the 1930s. My father was a rated player as far back as 1931, and I think I got my first rating (zero) in about 1934 or 1935. My father's name was Thomas L. Daniels & he played for the Twin Cities/Fort Snelling team.

I played polo for about thirty-five years. I was captain of the Yale Varsity Team. We won the indoor intercollegiate and the outdoor while I was at Yale. Over the years I had a grand time with the game.

Affectionately,
John

＊ ＊ ＊

November 14, 1992

Dear John,

I have a letter from you written many years ago, asking me if you should have Walton in your library. My answer to you was—He should be represented. Do I get credit for that advice?

Nice piece in the newsletter.

Affectionately,
H

November 20, 1992

Dear Helen,

Thanks for your note. I'm pleased that you liked the recent article that appeared in the National Sporting Library newsletter.

Yes, you most certainly do get credit for advising me some time ago that Walton should be "represented" in my collection. I took your advice and have avoided slavishly collecting any & all Waltons. I have tried to get only quality copies & not "overload." But out of curiosity I have just run a quick inventory on my Waltons. Guess? Ninety different editions, but a complete run from Horne 1–30 and fifty percent below Horne 100.
Not bad. What say?

Love,
John

    * * *

December 23, 1992

The world seems in such an unhappy state that it's hard for me to become enthusiastic over Christmas. So I'm celebrating Hanukkah. I went to the liquor store and bought a case of Hennessey Brandy for my friends—Perhaps they will have me over for a drink—It doesn't matter. I only increased my allowance.

Merry Christmas.

With my compliments,
H

January 28, 1993

Dear John,

Nice pictures of the family. You must have had a wonderful holiday. Many years ago I read a book on the Galapagos Islands and remember how I thought I'd like to visit the islands—Now, of course, I can't remember who wrote the book—But I vaguely think it was one of our presidents, perhaps Roosevelt.

Affectionately,
H

* * *

February 1, 1993

Dear Helen,

Many thanks for your gracious note about our photo-card.*
We are still getting rave reviews from our children because they are so pleased that the experience drew everybody in the family closer together—an unexpected dividend!

There have been so many books about the Galapagos Islands that it's hard to find really worthwhile texts. The good news is that the Ecuadorian government is taking good care of the environment as the pressure from tourism quadruples every few years.

We're getting ready for another trip! A Yale University Alumni Association trip through the Panama Canal and to the National Parks of Costa Rica. A nice little interlude in February.

Thanks for offering the "Oglethrope." I'm not interested.

Affectionately,
John

[*All twenty family members on our trip to the Galapagos Islands to celebrate our fiftieth wedding anniversary.]

February 18, 1993

Dear John,

Have a wonderful voyage. I took a frigate many years ago from California to New York with a Standard French poodle and three paying guests. . . . Made a lot of money playing poker. . . . The things I did in my youth are fond memories today. So I've seen the Panama.

H

* * *

July 24, 1993

Dear John,

Nice to hear your voice and to have your letter. I've never been to Russia. When Sherri and I went around the continent, I don't know why, but I didn't want to go to Russia.

I approve of Cummins—it's just that I have nothing in common with him. He earns his living in the book business and I don't. I still buy books for their contents rather than their sale value. Josy and a young man, Edward Lazare (Lazare owned *Book Prices Current* years ago), were in the rare book business in N.Y., many years ago. When we came to Saratoga thirty years ago we started our library to stimulate our brains.

I have a new friend—a crow who comes every morning for breakfast. He doesn't like brown bread, only Pepperidge Farm apple and walnut bread. Gin, the Siamese cat, was upset with him at first, but now they are friends.

Enclosed is a xerox copy of a book that I may have quoted you before.

Affectionately,
H

July 28, 1993

Dear Helen,

Thank you for your interesting letter. I guess that we all get our kicks in different ways, and it's probably very much the case in the book collecting game. Jim Cummins makes a very good living because he is very aggressive and takes risks that most conservative booksellers would never dream of. I saw him buy in some very expensive lots when Sotheby's ran their sale of the John Schiff sporting books. I know that he made a lot of money by holding on to some of the manuscripts until he found just the right buyer. He's pretty flamboyant at times, but I've had some great successes buying some unbelievably rare books that he's come up with, and I'm happy to deal with him because I've learned when to say no.

Your new friend, the crow, sounds like a good communicator! How did it tell you it only liked Pepperidge Farm apple & walnut bread? That's even difficult for me to say. A good crow like that is pretty smart, so take good care of it.

The morning TV news carried a story about Saratoga & the racing season. It looks wonderful. Do you get out and participate?

I'm enclosing my check for the Vernon Admiral 1749 book, *Considerations Upon the White Herring & Cod Fisheries.* It sounds good.

I had lunch yesterday with an old friend who is regarded as the dean of the bibliophiles in this community. Harold Kittleson is eighty-eight and still going strong. He encouraged me to put on my little summer book show again and to star some of the new gems in my collection. I'll get to work on it next week.

It's always good to hear from you, my love.

Affectionately,
John

August 3, 1993

Dear John,

Nice to have your letter. I sent the book off to you this morning. If you aren't happy, post it back. I bought that in 1977—never offered to anybody. My age has made me feel less the possessor.

Racing in Saratoga has changed a lot. They have loud music and tents filled with strange entertainment—totally different than it used to be. I stopped going last year. A great many of my old friends who had fine stables are no longer coming up. Polo has changed also. I've been a member for years—last year I only went over once. Some of the players aren't coming back this year.

God, this letter reads as though I were a repulsive old lady. I guess I am. However, Mr. Crow still loves me and Gin the cat thinks I can do no wrong.

Affectionately,
H

Dear Helen,

Thanks for your letter about Saratoga racing and polo. Our racing in South Carolina is going stronger than ever, but our polo is almost inactive. I've been paying a local historical research person to develop a written history of the Camden Polo Club, which was started in 1898! I've finally been able to persuade this historian that he has done all the research he needs (and I'm going to pay for) and it's time for him to start the writing phase. With luck I hope to get the MS completed by the end of 1993 and then will get it published. We have all kinds of photographs to go with the history, and I think it will be of local interest in our area when we finally get the book out.

I'm enclosing a copy of my homemade catalogue of my mini-book show, which opens this Sunday and will run for a month. I'm also enclosing a copy of the invitation that I've sent out to about fifty local bibliophiles and friends who are interested in my collection. I've been doing this almost every summer for the last fifteen years, and in a very small way it has been very well received. As you will see, the show is quite small and covers a broad range of sporting books that I've acquired, mainly in the last twelve months. It's actually a handsome-looking show the way it turned out. I would welcome your comments.

Love,
John

August 16, 1993

Dear Helen,

Many thanks for your brief note. I'm having fun with the mini-show. Lots of friends are dropping by to see it.

I was interested in the Saratoga Polo Association material you sent. Three or four high goal games a week in August is a very busy schedule! I was surprised to see that the games don't begin until 6 P.M. With daylight savings time, it's possible and it's cooler by then, so it makes sense. In my day game time was usually 3 P.M.

Our Colorado grandson—age twenty, a sophomore at Skidmore—has been visiting us this past week. He is a fine young man. This summer, to earn money and to get college credits, he got a job selling cutlery. He put on a demonstration for me and my wife that was so impressive that we've purchased more cutlery than we ever thought possible! He's going back to Skidmore in early September and will live off campus.

Love,
John

* * *

September 8, 1993

Dear John,

Nothing exciting around here. All the horse people have left and the town is nice and quiet again. Mr. Crow has brought some of his friends for breakfast and they talk up a storm. However, I enjoy it.

Have you any interest in General Grant's *Arabian Horses*, 1885?

Affectionately,
H

Dear Helen,

I'd guess that lots of the steeplechase horses that are leaving Saratoga, plus their owners, trainers, jockeys, hot-walkers, and hangers-on, will end up in my hometown, Camden, before too long.

We head for France for the first two weeks in October. In France we're going to become culture-vultures and spend a lot of time in museums looking at impressionist paintings with our son-in-law, who is an expert on these things, a good lecturer and a nice guy.

I also plan to go wild in some of those wonderful French restaurants. Bon appétit!

Sorry, I'm really not interested in General Grant's *Arabian Horses*, 1885, but thank you anyway.

Please stay in touch.

Ciao & love,
John

* * *

[no date]

Dear John,

You are a very fortunate gentleman, to have children who love you and enjoy spending time with you. I'm very envious.

Be careful about the eating, it may not be so much fun trying to return the belt back to its original hole.

Have a wonderful time.

Affectionately,
H

October 17, 1993

Dear Helen,

How did you know that I'd put on 6+ pounds eating French cuisine? That was the only bad part of our trip to take in the Fête des Impressionists. The museums and the travel in southern France near Nice were superb. We were also very proud of our daughter Jane and her husband, who led the trip.

So now we're back home on a crash diet.

I've taken on a new project this winter. Another major book show at my old prep school, Exeter. It should be fun to organize and put on because it will consist of only the very best from the 1992 Minneapolis show, plus some new rarities I've acquired since then. The show opens March 28th and will run through June 5th. Time to get it done properly if I dig in now! I hope you're well and enjoying a nice autumn—

Love,
John

Dear John,

So you are doing another book show. I have a suggestion—
although I should probably mind my own business since I don't
like to be defeated . . . bu-u-u-ut . . . take something else with
you besides sporting books. If you have some memorabilia from
your days at Exeter and a rare American History . . . In other
words, something for the portion of the public that has no
interest in sporting records.

Well, at last I've gotten the leaves raked—How about $25 an
hour? Every time I think of it I laugh.

I just saw a fox go up the road and into Skidmore. Student?

Affectionately,
H

      * * *

November 15, 1993

Dear Helen,

Your suggestion about the Exeter show is worthwhile. Many
thanks!

You must have a banker raking your leaves! Down here we
could get a tosspot of layabouts to rake all day for twenty-five
bucks.

Be careful what you say about Skidmore students! I have a
grandson going there & he's a nice guy.

Love,
John

November 13, 1993

Dear Helen,

I didn't realize that Eve Fout was a pal of yours! I had a nice visit with her yesterday evening and your ears should have been burning! I have known Eve and Paul for years and years. They are both down here again for the big Colonial Cup Steeple-chase this Sunday. They are such nice people.

How are you? I hope all goes well and you haven't had any speeding tickets lately. I am having fun working up the new show that will open at my old prep school—Exeter—on March 28th. Exactly 100 of my best books, manuscripts, illustrations, and ephemera. It's coming together quite well and I'm pleased. You are only 200 miles from Exeter as the crow flies. Any chance of your driving (slowly) over?

Love,
John

* * *

December 10, 1993

Dear John,

Nothing exciting happening around here. The doctor tells me I am going blind and while I don't want to agree with him, he's probably right. I'm farsighted, so it's reading that's giving me a problem.

Oh well, something good always comes out of a problem—I can't see the dirt in the house!

The Fouts are old friends—nice that you had a conversation together.

Have a happy holiday,
H

Dear John,

So it's a new year. I call it the reprint year. This generation isn't interested in first editions. I wonder what will happen to all the wonderful books we both have collected all these years. Why did the Derrydale family sell the copyrights on their books?

You mentioned the Second World War—I passed all my examinations for Officers Training until the last one that I took, my physical, which I failed.

So I went to Hartford, Connecticut, Pratt and Whitney, and was the first woman they hired to make airplane motors. Had a wonderful experience.

Have a great New Year.

Affectionately,
H

* * *

January 16, 1994

Dear John,

It seems our president needed or needs (past or present tense) a great deal of sex. That, or the women he chose weren't very satisfying. I find it hard to visualize his sex life in Washington. I couldn't read the piece in one sitting, after a while I got bored. I don't mind pieces about living people as they are able to defend themselves. I do object to dirt about people who are dead, such as Kennedy, who can't protect himself. I'm off to shovel the path. We have snow up to a tall Indian's ass.

Affectionately,
H

February 15, 1994

Dear Helen,

You are going through one of the worst winters I've ever seen. Our yard man back in Minnesota writes to tell me that for the first time in seventeen years Lake Superior is FROZEN ALL THE WAY ACROSS! About ten days ago the historic mill pond that we live on here in South Carolina was FROZEN ALL THE WAY ACROSS for the first time that I can remember, and I've been coming down here to South Carolina for fifty-five years! Things in Saratoga must be rugged. I hope that you are surviving and are of good cheer.

I have been putting the finishing touches on the preparations for my sporting book show that opens in Exeter on March 28th. All of the books have been chosen, checked, researched, listed, and finally wrapped and shipped from S.C. to New Hampshire. (They all got there safely, all 124 of them!) Now I'm having fun putting the frosting on the cake by assembling a catalogue for the show. Instead of the fancy, four-color, printed job that I slaved on for the Minneapolis Institute Show in 1992, this is "homemade" using the materials at hand and doing my own typing when needed. I have worked out an arrangement with Kinko's to produce the catalogues for the Exeter show. It will be ready by the end of the week and I plan to send you a copy as soon as I can.

About one-quarter of the books and manuscripts in the Exeter show are "goodies" that I have acquired in the last two years since the Minneapolis show was put together. Of the many things that were in the Minneapolis show I have only picked out the very, very best. So the Exeter show is going to be fresh and I believe of interest to the wide variety of students, former classmates of mine, school faculty, and others who will see the show between March 28th, when it opens, and June 10th, when it closes.

Some of the new things are pretty rare and interesting. One is a *Game Book* kept by Captain Carmichael, who was aide-de-camp to the larger-than-life governor of Bombay, India, in 1921-23. His Excellency, Sir George Ambrose Lloyd, G.C.I.E., D.S.O., and his beautiful wife were typical British career diplomats, ruling one of the best roosts of the British Empire at the height of colonialism, when the sun never set on the British Empire. Captain Carmichael was a dashing British officer and a deadly shot. *The Game Book,* which I'm quite sure was kept for the Ambassador by Carmichael, is a punctilious record of all the ducks, geese, bear, and deer that His Excellency and his top honchos killed. The absolute best entry in the book describes the day when the Brits were the guests of the Nawab of Jungadh on a lion hunt! Both Sir George and Captain Carmichael shot a lion, and, of course, His Excellency's lion is six inches longer than the Captain's. To top it off there is a very large, formal black and white photograph of His Excellency and Captain Carmichael in their lion-shooting attire, guns at hand, wearing pith helmets and standing beside their two lions! It is a magnificent and evocative time capsule of the glories of a bygone era.

Oddly enough, another treasure in the Exeter sporting book show is a handwritten manuscript by the Royal Gamekeeper who was running all of the royal shooting in 1814, an amazing year that began with Napoleon on the French throne and ended with Louis XVII sitting on the throne. In precise and fine penmanship, every detail of the Royal Chasse is listed. The names of each of the 300 men who took care of the royal game in the five royal forests of Louvre, Versailles, Rambouillet, Fontaine-bleau, and Compiégne. Every expenditure is itemized and the grand total cost for the year came to 445,000 francs. The 200 hounds are listed by name and so are the eighty-three grooms and kennel keepers. A total of 1,878 animals were killed by the royal hunts in 1814 and these are broken down by types—stag, deer, roebuck, wild boar, etc.—and by the forests they were from. You wonder how Napoleon had time to fight the Battle of Waterloo with all of this venery going on!

There are a lot of other manuscripts, such as John Taintor Foote's *The Look of Eagles* and Nash Buckingham's *Ole Miss*. And even though there is a great deal of variety, I think the show will be understandable and not confusing because it breaks down into logical and well-identified segments. I'll be very interested in getting your reaction after you have a chance to look at the catalogue.

Meanwhile, I hope you get a rest from shoveling snow!

Love,
John

* * *

February 19, 1920 [sic]

Dear John,

February the first I fell on the ice and broke my hip—I'm in a geriatric center. God love me if I survive this ordeal. I had just put Jo Hennessey in the Veteran's Hospital five days before.

Affectionately,
H

March 2, 1994

Dear Helen,

Here is a Walkman tape player and some tapes to try. The tape player comes with fairly simple instructions. I have put two AA batteries in the tape player and tested it and it is working. There is a volume control on the side. When all else fails, get a friend who knows about tape players to show you how to work it. I had some fun picking out some of my favorites. Two are nonfiction and the other three are fiction. This is what they're about.

Barbarians at the Gate—by *Wall Street Journal* reporters Bryan Burroughs and John Helyar. It is a fascinating account of the real-life financial war over the takeover or RJR-Nabisco. My real-life friend Ross Johnson is the "star" of the story. Ross is on our Board of Directors.

Den of Thieves—By another *Wall Street Journal* reporter, James B. Stewart. This is a true story about the corporate thieves Ivan "the terrible" Boesky, Michael Milken, and others.

Remains of the Day—The improbable author is Kazuo Ishiguro. Made into a major motion picture in 1993. Both Anthony Hopkins and Emma Thompson could win Oscars if *Schindler's List* doesn't win them all.

Longshot—by Dick Francis, my favorite English mystery writer and former jockey for the Queen. (If you enjoy Dick Francis there are many other of his books on tape.)

The Firm—by bestseller author John Grisham. This is a first-rate action/adventure story about crooked lawyers.

I really hope you haven't read all of these and that you will have some fun with books on tape. (If there are any of these that you have already read just send them back.)

I hope that this letter finds you back from the hospital and feeling a lot better than you sounded on the telephone yesterday. I'll stay in touch.

Love,
John

April 7, 1994

Dear Helen,

Here are a couple of books on tape which I hope will amuse you. Please let me know if you have any special requests and I will try to locate them.

It was so nice to hear your voice on Easter Sunday. You sounded strong and I hope that your are getting along all right and "mending."

It is amazing to think that in all the years we have only met once. I think it was at the Swann Gallery sale where I struck out (fortunately) in bidding for the first edition of Izaak Walton's *Angler*. Your pal Judith Bowman was the high bidder. I think that you and I shared a cab up to Grand Central station, where you were catching a train back home. We had time for a visit and a drink and I remember that you ordered "Old Hennessey."

I have kept all your letters. I feel very lucky and grateful to have you for a pen pal and especially as a good friend.

I'm thinking of you and send you my love.

As always,
John

Dear John,

I loved your letter that you sent with the tapes—No one has ever said such things to me before except my daughter—She'd fight with anyone that criticized her mother. I saved all your letters also.

I let all the hired help go. I'm living alone with a Siamese cat who loves my company.

Josy is at the Veteran's Home in Bennington, VT. Bloody expensive, and he doesn't know me. Why doesn't God let people go to sleep?

Affectionately,
H

p.s. Do you know a Robert Burke in Camden?

April 19, 1994

Dear Helen,

I was very touched by your lovely letter and have reread it several times. I have had such a good time as your pen pal. You always write something that is incisive and to the point. Over the years you have told me quite a lot about yourself so that I feel very well acquainted with you and cherish your friendship. Right now I wish I could be of more help than your Siamese cat. Does it know what a large responsibility it has to keep you good company? It is an important job!

There is a Robert J. Burke Sr. who lives here in Camden with his wife, Jean. We are members of the same little Springdale Hall Club, but I'm sorry to say I don't know him. I am told that he is a professional horseman and that he buys horses, mainly show horses, for his customers and has to do a lot of traveling. They say he is a "nice guy." In his sixties. Does this sound like the same person you asked about?

Babs and Burling Cocks live in Camden and we see them from time to time. He is still running a steeplechase training stable in Camden in the winter, although their son, Winkie, has to do most of the work because it is so hard for Burling to get around. Babs is a "character" and a good old friend of ours. Babs and I often talk about you because she remembers visiting you on several occasions when they were up in Saratoga in the summertime.

We have a grandson who is a sophomore this year at Skidmore. He is a very quiet and sincere chap, and I know that I could get him to run some errands for you if you needed someone special. I think he is of legal age now so he could even locate some "Old Hennessey" if you felt thirsty.

Jim Cummins has found me some very special books lately. He just came back from a pleasure trip to Russia, where he and some other pals played a series of hockey games. They were clobbered! Even a bunch of high school kids skated circles around his team!

I'll be staying in touch. Take good care of yourself and I'll be telephoning soon.

Love,
John

* * *

April 18, 1994

Dear John,

Your nephew* arrived yesterday afternoon from Skidmore with a beautifully wrapped package of Hennessey cognac—was that for my eighty-forth birthday? My friends gave me a surprise birthday party yesterday.

Many thanks,
H

[*My grandson, Cedar Daniels, a student at Skidmore]

April 24, 1994

Dear John,

How thoughtful of you to phone me yesterday.

Do you realize that we have only met once and that was years ago in N.Y.? How do people enjoy each other with only one face visit? I think we should get medals.

My leg is nearly healed, but I have lost so much weight that it is an effort to walk across the room. Everyone is wonderful to me, but paid help cannot take the place of family—Josy and I have no family.

Many thanks for my Walkman. I enjoy it and the tapes.

Affectionately,
H

* * *

April 28, 1994

Dear John,

Josy left this world last night. Thank God He finally let him go to sleep. He had a full life—ninety-seven years.

I'm sending the medal* off to you tomorrow.

Hurriedly,
H

[*The medal commemorates the seventy-fifth Anniversary of World War I. The reverse side "A GRATEFUL NATION REMEMBERS" 1918–1993. It was presented to Joseph Hennessey who was an Army veteran of that war.]

Joseph Hennessey

SARATOGA SPRINGS—Joseph P. Hennessey of Woodlawn Avenue died Wednesday, April 17, at the Vermont Veterans Home in Bennington. He was 97.

Born Nov. 20, 1896, in New York City, he lived in Castleton, VT., from 1933 to 1950, and was elected town representative in Castleton in 1945.

He moved to Saratoga Springs in 1963, and with his wife, Helen, owned and operated Hennessey Books on Woodlawn Avenue. A former Manhattan book dealer, he also repaired prints and provided framing and matting services.

He was the assistant director of the New York State Civil Defense Commission in Albany, and was later promoted to director. Mr. Hennessey was an Army veteran of World War 1, and later frequently traveled to Europe. He was secretary to Alexander Woollcott, a noted author, movie critic, and writer, and assisted Gerald E. McLaughlin in Vermont.

In an article published in 1977 in *The Saratogian*, Mr. Hennessey recounted New York City in the 1930s, when notables, literary folk, and the general population mingled more easily.

He had a particular interest in books about fishing and hunting, he told a reporter then.

One daughter, Sherri B. Hennessey, died before him.

He is survived by his wife of 52 years, Helen Burt Hennessey.

Services will be at the convenience of the family in Whitehall.

Arrangements are by the William J. Burke & Sons Funeral Home, 628 N. Broadway.

—*The Saratogian*, Thursday, April 28, 1994

May 9, 1994

Dear Helen,

From what you have written to me in your letters, your husband, Josy, had been in very bad shape for quite a long time, so it must be a blessing for you to know that, as you said, "God finally let him to go to sleep." And you have all of the good memories to cherish after fifty-two years of marriage.

I, nevertheless, send you my deepest sympathy over your bereavement. It is a tragic and sad final moment.

The article which you sent me was very interesting. He had an eventful career and from what you have already told me it was a stimulating life that you shared. It must have been exciting to have been associated with so many distinguished and colorful friends.

Thank you, again, for the medal, which I treasure.

I hope that you are getting around more easily and comfortably. You've been through enough this winter. I'm thinking of you and send you my best wishes and my love.

John

* * *

July 4, 1994

Dear John,

I haven't heard from you in quite a while—Does that mean that you are having an exciting and interesting summer?

The only thing new here is my leg is cured, but my brain got lost in the process—Did you write me something about children's books?

Affectionately,
H

July 10, 1994

Dear Helen,

I was so glad to hear your voice over the telephone yesterday.
I'm sorry that I had been out of touch for so long. It was very
reassuring to talk with you and to know that you are getting
along all right in spite of all the eye and heart problems we all
seem to be coping with these days.

We depart at the end of August for a three-week trip to Europe.
We will spend a few days in London en route to Lisbon, where
we will board one of these new, small, deluxe cruise ships that
have a crew about the same size as the seventy-person passenger
list. Our voyage from Lisbon to Istanbul will take two weeks
and we will make stops at many of the places we have always
wanted to see.

This morning I got my wife to sit through a trial run of the
speech that I'm making on Thursday at the University of
Minnesota about illustrated children's sporting books. My wife
okay'd the slide talk and has made some good suggestions. I feel
pretty good about the way the lecture has come together.

Please take care of yourself. I'll be in touch again sooner rather
than later.

Love,
John

July 29, 1994

Dear John,

I'm sorry about your hospital visit—Join the club. They tell me I have congestive heart failure. Breaking my leg didn't help it. The only thing that aggravates me is the things I've done for years that I can't do anymore, such as pushing the vacuum cleaner . . .

I went to Wells, Maine, for three days with some friends—I thought I was going to the country, but the bloody place was wall-to-wall people. Every house for miles was business. Glad to be home.

I see that Cummins is looking for a book on ballooning. Didn't I sell you one? I have another one.

Affectionately,
H

* * *

September 11, 1994

Dear John,

I'm sure your mini-book show was a great success. It was a wonderful catalogue—Now I'll flatter myself I have most of the books on your list. I never tried to sell them. I keep them for my own pleasure—I wonder what will happen to them—sporting books are being reprinted and sell for $35, so the youth today don't enjoy first editions, just paperbacks.

Things in Saratoga are falling apart, horse sales are down, track attendance way off, and they sold the polo field—This is a nice cheery letter—However, have a fine voyage.

Affectionately,
H

Dear Helen,

A few years ago in one of your letters you asked me about what
I planned to do with my collection. At the time I answered, I
acknowledged that I hadn't yet made up my mind. I said that I
was tempted to put it all up for auction so that other collectors
could have the same fun as I have had in buying rare books.
The other alternatives were to give the collection to an institution or simply avoid making any decisions and let my heirs
figure it out. Well, I have come to a decision and I can't tell you
how pleased and excited I am. The National Sporting Library
in Middleburg, Virginia, has enthusiastically accepted my offer
to give them my entire collection! This is a perfect home and
repository for all of my books. They are going to build a new
library building and I think they will eventually be the leading
reference library for sporting books in the entire country. Rather
than completely losing the identity of my collection, as would
happen in the vastness of Yale's Beinecke Rare Book Library,
the collection will become the centerpiece of the National
Sporting Library.

I'm enclosing a news release which gives more details. All of the
treasures that I acquired from you over the years—the Schwerdt
4-volume bibliography, the panorama *Going to the Fight*, and
the ballooning book, and so many more—will now have a permanent home where they will be well cared for and thoroughly
appreciated.

I hope you'll be pleased even though I'm out of the book collection game.

Love,
John

July 23, 1995

Dear John,

Thank you for your note and the newsletter. It's a wonderful thing you are doing with your library—You are going to be lonesome. *Smart Aleck* can be a bloody bore sometimes, but if you go to the index, you only need to read about the people you enjoy. Those were great days in my life.

Affectionately,
H

* * *

July 29, 1995

Dear Helen,

Thank you for steering me to Howard Teichmann's book, *Smart Aleck.** I especially enjoyed the chapter about Neshobe Island, and the picture of and description about your husband. He obviously was a terrific person.

Many years ago you sent me a copy of *Vermont Life* (Summer, 1984) with the article about "where I used to live," which quotes Helen Burt and brings back so many old memories.

It is amazing to me that the "glory days" at Bomoseen have a great deal of similarity to the "glory days" of Camden, South Carolina. I am writing a book (with the help of a researcher and a hired re-write man) about *The First 50 Years of Polo in Camden, 1898–1948,* and during those years Camden was a big winter resort for Yankee visitors. Today, all the resorts are gone in Camden, just they way they went in Bomoseen. I hope to complete the book this year and will send you an autographed presentation copy.

Love,
John

[*Howard Teichmann's book, *Smart Aleck,* is a vivid account of the life of Alexander Woollcott. It is also, inadvertently, an important document about the Hennesseys. Helen Burt met Joe Hennessey on Alex's eight-acre party property, Neshobe Island, in Lake Bomoseen, Vermont, during the glory days of Woollcott and his brilliant and amusing gang of authors, actors, and playwrights from the Algonquin Hotel's Round Table, in the 1920s.

Joseph Hennessey was fourteen years older than Helen. He was born in New York City in 1896 and enlisted in the Army in 1916 after graduating from high school. After serving with distinction in World War I as a machine gunner, he owned a bookshop in New York. He was hired by Herbert Swope to run his Long Island estate when Woollcott hired him away from Swope to be his personal secretary. Joe Hennessey was running Neshobe Island when he met Helen Burt, a local Vermont woman. They were married in 1942. When Woollcott died, he left Neshobe Island and other valuable property to Joe Hennessey.

The Hennesseys eventually sold Neshobe Island and in 1963 moved to Saratoga Springs, where they bought an old carriage house at 4th and Woodlawn. Here, they opened an antiquarian book business. The Hennesseys lived on the second floor of the carriage house and operated their business on the ground floor. Helen learned the book business from her husband.]

November 30, 1995

Dear John,

Sixty years more or less ago I learned to play golf in Boca
Raton, Florida, with Sam Snead. He taught me that the game
was won or lost on the putting green. I was pretty good then
and made money there. When we got back to Vermont there
were only a few golf courses, but we had a Piper Cub small
plane and would fly around the country, but mostly to the
Equinox in Manchester, VT. I have wonderful memories of
those days. I had to give up playing ten years ago because of my
hands. I had some special clubs made, but they really weren't a
success. Practice your putting.

Affectionately,
H

p.s. I think you should buy Item 105 in Cummins catalogue #51,
only because you have empty shelves.

Dear Helen,

Nothing should surprise me about you because I don't have many antiquarian bookselling friends who get speeding tickets like you. But, I'm still very impressed to learn of your golfing prowess! Sam Snead taught you? *Well!*

We're off to Minnesota today for about a week. I have to go into the shop (i.e., hospital) up there to get my heart fixed. Not an emergency, but a necessity. Don't worry, I'm okay.

Love,
John

[Note: In December 1995, I had a sextuple heart bypass that laid me low for a while. By May 1996, I was fully recovered, so Martha and I could go to Saratoga, N.Y., for our grandson Cedar's graduation from Skidmore College. During our visit to Saratoga, we called on Helen Hennessey in her carriage house at 4th and Woodlawn—just behind the house and grounds of Skidmore's president. This was only the second time that Helen & I met face-to-face. Helen was looking forward to our visit. She welcomed us when we rang the bell at her front door. She gave us a complete tour of the ground floor, where her books and her Jaguar were stored, and then of her living quarters on the second floor. Most of the walls on both floors were hung with framed photographs and memorabilia. Although she had already sold at auction much of her most valuable book inventory, there were still hundreds of books on her shelves. Helen insisted that I take a framed print of a polo game at Jerome Park in 1876. I subsequently used the polo print as endpaper illustrations for my book *Nothing Could Be Finer.*

January 22, 1996

Dear John,

Nice to hear from you. I'm glad they put your heart back together. They want to play with mine, but I said no. At eighty-five, it's earned a rest.

Nice article about the National Sporting Library. You did a wonderful thing when you gave them your library—

Affectionately,
H

* * *

One summer day in 1924, Woollcott was driven up from New York City to nine-mile-long Lake Bomoseen by his financial advisor, Enos Booth, who owned property on the lake overlooking Neshobe Island. Woollcott immediately fell in love with the island, visualizing it as the perfect getaway for members of the Algonquin Round Table during the hot summer months. So with his friends he purchased the island and proceeded to establish what became known as the Neshobe Island Club.

Over the next twenty years, regular summer visitors to Neshobe Island included Harpo Marx, playwright George S. Kaufman, Helen Hayes and her husband, Charles MacArthur (who, with Ben Hecht, wrote part of the script for *Wuthering Heights* on Neshobe), Vivien Leigh, Laurence Olivier, actress Ruth Gordon, Alfred Lunt and Lynn Fon-tanne, Noel Coward, Walt Disney, Rebecca West, Dorothy Parker, Oscar Levant, Gertrude Lawrence, illustrator Neysa McMein (a favorite magazine cover artist of that time), Robert Benchley, and the editor of *The New Yorker*, Harold Ross. Political commentator Joseph Alston completed a book on the island, as did Thornton Wilder. Actresses Ethel Barrymore and Cornelia Otis Skinner could be found (as John E. Williams wrote in the August 1980 *Yankee*) "shouting the lines of new stage roles into the wind off Lake Bomoseen."

Mr. Chandler, a retired executive of Xerox Corporation and a native Vermonter, reclaimed Neshobe Island for his home state more than thirty years ago by purchasing it from Alexander Woollcott's business manager, who had taken it over after Woollcott's death in 1943.

—Yankee Magazine, October 1996
from "Vermont Island Famous New Yorkers Adored"

[Note: Although we did not exchange any letters in 1997, I continued to stay in touch with Helen by making frequent telephone calls. Helen always sounded pleased to get my phone calls and she occasionally telephoned me to see how I was getting along. She was particularly interested in hearing about the progress being made with the plans and drawings for the new National Sporting Library building in Middleburg, Virginia. In late May 1997, she sent me a copy of the May 25th feature article about herself and the plans to auction the remainder of her books.]

WOMAN TO SELL TREASURED BOOK COLLECTION
Helen Hennessey, legendary city dealer, prepares for auction

"I was kind of fussy about the books I had. Most people knew I was a snob about books."
                                            —Helen Hennessey

SARATOGA SPRINGS—Her hands are weathered by time the way good leather improves with age—soft and wrinkled, but strong. If you offer her yours, she will return a firm grip.

The hand she extends forward has held many of her favorite English cigarettes, lifted more than a few glasses of brandy, greeted the likes of Groucho Marx, Dorothy Parker, and Laurence Olivier.

Helen Hennessey, at age 86, will sometimes complain about being old. She will tell you she doesn't have a favorite anything anymore. But when she did, it is safe to say books were among those things most cherished.

People cannot exist without books to read, Hennessey often said. It is clear from how she spent the past 36 years that books, rare and treasured, are a pillar of her own existence.

Hennessey and her late husband, Joseph, sold fine books for more than three decades from a store within their 1899 carriage house on Fourth Street. In recent months, thousands of the books have been auctioned off as the silver-haired widow prepares to move to Pine Manor, a group home for the elderly in Ballston Spa.

On June 8, the Albany County Auction Gallery will auction off more than 200 books from the Hennessey's private collection under a tent on her property's front lawn. It is the first on-site auction at the home, which is tucked just south of Skidmore College off North Broadway.

"I was kind of fussy about the books I had," she said on a recent afternoon. "Most people knew I was a snob about books."

The collection includes a first-edition of Lt. William Bligh's *Mutiny on the Bounty,* dating back to 1790. The book, leather-bound with tattered pages, is perhaps worth as much as $10,000, Hennessey has estimated.

Auction dealer Robert Meringolo, who is handling the Hennessey collection, said the couple was known among other antiquarian booksellers for their expensive prices.

He says the Hennessey collection is the most valuable he has ever handled in his career as an auction dealer. Meringolo also will auction off most of the home's antique furnishings, artwork, and Kurdish and Oriental rugs that have had a place for years in the cozy, three-bedroom apartment above the old barn and bookstore.

Most days, Hennessey's place is on a chair by the window in the kitchen where she watches the occasional passerby on the street below or the birds that perch on a feeder for seed.

"This is my favorite spot," she said, leaning forward. She is dressed in dark dungarees that are faded at the knees. Her petite frame looks even smaller under a bulky, Kelly green sweatshirt.

As she chats about book dealing, she reaches for a 1984 copy of *Vermont Life* under a stack of rare book catalogues on the window sill.

"If you turn the page, that is where I am from," she said, handing the magazine to a guest.

A full-color photograph captures sweeping vistas of Neshobe Island, which sits in the middle of Lake Bomoseen in western Vermont. The resort island in the 1920s and 1930s was witness to Glenn Miller's Orchestra, art critic Alexander Woollcott, Vivien Leigh, and some personalities from the Algonquin Round Table.

Hennessey met her husband-to-be at the Neshobe Club, where they hobnobbed with the who's who of literary and art circles.

"In those days, you didn't consider them famous," she said of her acquaintances. Black and white photographs of Woollcott, Parker, Leigh, and Olivier throughout the home reveal her camaraderie with the in-crowd.

"Dorothy Parker—we hated with a passion," Hennessey said with a sharp tongue not unlike Parker's, a writer known for her outspoken nature.

Outspoken and brash on occasion, Hennessey has been known to hang up on those callers she does not want to talk to on the phone. But she sounds a little sweet as an 11-year-old Siamese cat walks into the room.

"That's the president of the house," she said as the pet called Gin brushed against her chair. "I wish he were younger."

Though she doesn't smoke anymore, reminders of her former vice also reveal her wit: "Thank you for smoking" signs hang on the walls where her collection of books used to be.

The store, with its empty shelves, is more like a skeleton these days. Memories hang around like ghosts.

The couple opened the bookseller shop in 1961 after Joseph Hennessey retired as an assistant director of civil defense in Albany. The collection grew to include all subjects, specializing in sporting books.

The Hennesseys set up the store's office in one of the old horse stalls. Letters and caricatures on yellowed paper are still taped to the wall by the rotary phone.

Several oriental rugs dress the hardwood floors. Nearby in the garage, Helen Hennessey's blue Jaguar is parked when she is not taking it out for an occasional drive down Broadway.

Hennessey is also a snob about England. She loves anything British—from Pall Mall cigarettes to the large 18th-century clock hanging in her living room. She has been there 27 times.

"The English are better bookmakers—better pages and more ink," she said. "Americans economize on the ink."

Hennessey has friends visit her a few times each week. They are mostly other booksellers. Folks she knows from the business. She realizes in some ways her time has passed, recalling her past status as a respected member of the Antiquated Booksellers Association.

"Now I'm called an honorary member," she said, her bright blue eyes still shining from behind large-framed glasses. She turned the pages of the association's catalogue, stopping at the one where her name is listed.

"This is where I am now," she said. Members emeritus.

The Albany Co. Auction Gallery will hold its auction of the Hennessey book collection and furnishings beginning at 10:30 A.M. June 8, at the couple's 4th Street carriage house. For more information contact the gallery at 432-7093.

Picture caption: Helen Hennessey holds her cat, Gin. Hennessey, who with her husband, Joseph, sold fine books for more than three decades, is preparing to sell 200 books from her collection.

—*The Saratogian,* May 25, 1997

SARATOGA SPRINGS—As a Skidmore College student in the 1970s, Mark Walp enjoyed visiting the bookstore Joseph and Helen Hennessey ran in their carriage house. But Walp, a painter and history student, said he was certainly no regular of the 4th Street shop.

Still, fond memories of the Hennesseys' store brought him back to Saratoga Springs 20 years after graduating from the college that sits only yards away from the store. Walp now owns his own bookstore in Chestertown, and was in town Sunday as the Hennesseys' diverse collection of rare books, artwork, Persian rugs, and antique furniture was auctioned off.

"It was a very beautiful and comfortable shop," Walp said. "She certainly had amazing and wonderful books."

The Hennesseys sold the books, many of them antiques, for three decades from the carriage house on their property at North Broadway and Fourth Street. The books ranged in subject matter from history to travel to art, and the store specialized in sporting books.

But Joseph Hennessey has died, and 86-year-old Helen is preparing to enter a group home for the elderly. So the task of dismantling the formidable collection fell to the Albany Auction Gallery.

Sunday's auction attracted high-powered antique dealers, small-time collectors, and plenty of the merely curious.

The Hennessey's Persian rugs were laid out on the lawn and their furniture was displayed in the carriage house, while first the books were auctioned off under tent on the lawn.

Robert A. Meringolo and Joan Bohl, co-owners of the auction house, said the sale was strong, with many items selling for more than their estimates. For example, Bohl said, one library table estimated at $1,500 sold for $4,200.

On the other hand, however, a 1790 first edition copy of William Bligh's *Mutiny on the Bounty*, expected to sell for as much as $10,000, sold for only $2,500. Meringolo said the book was found to be missing four pages, accounting for the disappointing price.

At first, he said, he feared that a dealer had taken the pages in order to buy the book cheaply and repair it. But experts assured him the pages have been missing for years, he said.

Total revenue from the auction will not be calculated until this morning.

Walp's first purchase was *The Discovery and Conquest of Mexico 1517–1521*, a 1942 book by Bernal Diaz Castillo.

There was no competition for the book, so he was able to buy it for $10. "Cheap enough," Walp said, laughing.

When the auction was completed, Walp had purchased six books for a total of about $200. He called it "bottom fishing," admitting he was "definitely not a player on this scene."

At the other end of the spectrum, however, David Block was the very definition of a "player."

The Greenwich, Conn., book dealer bid on 13 lots, spending a total of $17,000 on the books. His most expensive purchase was $2,000 for *Hunting Hawking Shooting,* a 1937 four-volume catalogue of book manuscripts.

"It was a beautiful copy," Block said. "It was a spectacular copy."

For the most part, Block was not spending his own cash, but rather buying on behalf of his clients. "I bought virtually nothing for stock because the prices were too high," he said.

Block, who regularly attends book auctions in New York City and London, called collecting an "unnatural behavioral act." He criticized amateur collectors at the auction, saying they paid too much for many of the books.

"They feel they must acquire things," he said, loading his purchases into the trunk of his car. "People are out here looking for bargains."

But the buyers did not seem to care.

"I don't know if that's a good bargain or not," South Glens Falls resident Jacqueline Kelly said of the $310 she successfully bid on two art books. "I just hope these are good books."

Kelly was hunting for books to give to her son, a University of Maryland professor of Renaissance architecture who has a passion for Italian art books. She said she knows nothing about her purchases other than the fact that they deal with her son's interest.

If he does not want the books, Kelly said she will gladly add them to her own collection.

While the auctioneer goaded buyers to increase their bids under the tent, others perused the goods that would be auctioned off later in the day.

Greenfield resident Moussa Pessar had his eye on two Persian rugs, which he said were made in the 1930s. Pessar, a private collector, said he was willing to pay $3,000 for one and $5,000 for the other, but he was anticipating tough competition from professional dealers.

"These are very unique, by the size and pattern, and they're very well kept," Pessar said. "You can't find anybody today who can make this kind of material. The material is totally handsome."

—*The Saratogian,* June 9, 1997

SARATOGA SPRINGS—On "Old Master" painting was stolen from Helen Hennessey's carriage house in the days leading up to the auction, the head of the auction house said Sunday.

The painting was valued between $3,000 and $5,000, said Robert A. Meringolo, co-owner of Albany Auction House.

The painting was to be auctioned off Sunday with the remainder of Hennessey's items. It was stored, with the other items, in the carriage house at Fourth Street and North Broadway.

A pre-World War II camera valued at $300 also was stolen, he said.

The carriage house was not secured well, Meringolo said.

He said he reported the theft to city police. No further information was available Sunday.

—*The Saratogian*, June 9, 1997

* * *

[Some time after the auction in June, Helen and her beloved cat, Gin, moved out of the carriage house and into the Pine Manor Nursing Home in Ballston Spa, outside of Saratoga. In September 1997, I learned from Helen's friend, Robert Kearney, a bookseller from Saratoga, that Helen had broken a hip and was in the hospital in Saratoga. I spoke with her in the hospital several times, and she sounded pleased with the flowers I had sent, but even more pleased to tell me that she was getting out of the hospital and rejoining her cat at the Pine Manor Nursing Home. In October, Robert Kearney telephoned me to say that Helen had died. Robert Kearney sent me the copy of Helen's obituary.]

Helen Hennessey

SARATOGA SPRINGS—Helen Burt Hennessey, formerly of Fourth Street and Woodlawn Avenue, died Wednesday, Oct. 22, at Saratoga Hospital. She was 87.

Mrs. Hennessey was born on April 18, 1910, in Vermont.

She and her late husband, Joseph P. Hennessey, owned and operated Hennesseys' Books in their carriage home for several years. She was known for her knowledge of vintage books and collections, and there was an auction of the store's inventory in July.

Her husband died in 1994. A daughter, Sherri Burt Hennessey, also died before her.

She is survived by several nephews and a niece.

Graveside services will be in Whitehall at the convenience of the family.

There are no calling hours.

Contributions may be made to Community Hospice of Saratoga, 179 Lawrence St., Saratoga Springs, N.Y. 12866.

Arrangements are by William J. Burke & Sons Funeral Home, 628 North Broadway.

—The Saratogian, October 24, 1997

Afterword

In my life as a book collector, Helen Hennessey became one of my favorite friends. She helped in my developing knowledge of fine, rare, old sporting books and shared and abetted my great respect for them. She found and made available to me many of the outstanding books of my collection. If she is looking down at us in her usual sharp, observant manner, I hope that she is pleased that some of her personal treasures, unusual rare works such as the panorama, and the Japanese book on horsemanship, and the four-volume bibliography by C.F.G. Schwerdt are already the valued possessions of The National Sporting Library in Middleburg, Virginia. This new, state-of-the-art library is to be completed by the first of May, 1999, and at that time the rest of the fine sporting books I acquired through her will, as well as from Jim Cummins and others, be unpacked and displayed.

Helen loved to gamble. She preferred poker, not bridge. Once, many years ago, she spent the whole of a journey from California to New York playing poker with three paying guests on a frigate ship—and she won a lot of money. She would challenge me frequently—five dollars that the selling price of a book of Munnings's paintings would go for more than a thousand dollars, ten dollars that the Falklands War would drag on and on, and ten dollars that "Desert Storm" would not be over quickly. If she were alive today, I'm sure she would be betting me that the new library would not be finished by May first.

Helen was a survivor. Her beloved daughter died tragically and unexpectedly in the prime of life. Her husband, Josy, suffered a stroke about the time I had started a correspondence with the Hennesseys. He was a helpless, bedridden invalid for twenty years. Throughout these family tragedies she remained courageous, tough-minded, and defiant. Her strong, rebellious streak manifested itself in her many escapades with her proudly flaunted Jaguar sports car, and they earned her fifteen traffic tickets and a penalty session at drivers' education school.

Her trajectory from her rural childhood in Vermont took her to the edges of the fast lane traversed by the members of the famous Algonquin Round Table. We don't know what the glamorous writers, thinkers, and humorists on Alexander Woollcott's guest lists at Neshobe Island thought of Helen, but she remembered many of them as old friends, others as less than they thought themselves to be. (I knew Helen only as a very old woman, so I was delighted when I finally saw a photograph of her as a winsome beauty in her thirties.) Helen and Josy were lovers who had to wait for Josy's boss, Woollcott, to die before they dared to marry.

A bout with cancer nearly cost Helen her life, and she fought her way back to health at great expense over a fifteen-year period. She rose above that trial with dignity and fierce pride. Unable to get into the armed services during World War II, she spent those years working in an airplane factory.

Josy taught Helen everything he knew about the book business. He did a good job; she became a skilled and proficient antiquarian bookseller. With her native Vermont acumen and her strong competitive nature, she was an outstanding though unlikely success story in the book world. She had learned to love fine sporting books, and was both proud and possessive about her personal collection.

Helen worked hard at her business. She made twenty-seven trips to England to buy new stock. She considered it a game to be won. Fiercely competitive, she enjoyed gossiping about her rivals. Sometimes she acted like an aging courtesan with her customers. "How can I tempt you?" or "What treasures can I find for you?" Only toward the end of her life, after she came to like me and trust me, did she start offering me some of the real gems of her own private collection. Sherri was gone, and Helen had no close family, so I supposed that she was casting about for a good home for some of her prized sporting books.

We had become very good friends. I stood up to her occasionally brusque manners and I confided in her. She enjoyed our banter as much as I did, and she was compassionate in response to my frankness. As she began to fail physically, and our letter writing tapered off, we began to communicate more and more frequently by telephone. She always seemed pleased when I called. I thought it was important for both of us that Helen knew that I cared a lot about her.

During her last trip to the Saratoga Springs Hospital after she had fallen and broken her hip, we were close via the telephone. My bouquet of flowers brought a warm and cheerful response. The last time I spoke with her she was about to be dismissed from the hospital, which she loathed. She had nothing good to say about hospitals, which wasn't at all surprising. But she was finally going back to Gin, her cat, and things would be better.

A few days later Bob Kearney, Helen's friend, called me from Saratoga Springs to tell me that Helen was dead. I grieved.

GLOSSARY OF ABBREVIATIONS AND TERMS

There is a lingua franca used to describe and catalogue books. Although there are many variations and no "official" standard terms, most books are described in a series of abbreviations. Following are definitions of most of the abbreviations.

ads or adverts	advertisements
AEG	all edges gilt
bk	book
boxed	book is in a specially labeled and decorated cardboard box
BP	bookplate
C or ca	circa, about
calf	leather binding
cased	book is kept in a special (folding) case or container, often decorated
Coigny	Rodolphe Coigny, the most recent cataloguer for Izaak Walton's *Compleat Angler*
dec	decorated
disbound	no covers because they have come off
D/W or DJ	dust jacket or dust wrapper
ed	edition
end papers	the plain or decorated papers at the front and back of a book
fine	near mint condition
folio	a very large book
front board	the front, hard cover of the book
G or good	adequate condition, probably worn because of hard use or age
Horne	Horne catalogued Walton before Coigny
illus	illustration(s) or illustrated
ins	inscription
levant	leather binding
lg	large
ltd	limited number printed
miniature	small book three inches or less in height
mint	brand-new condition

mor or morocco	leather binding
ND or nd	There is no identification of when the book was published, also can indicate there is no pagination
NF	near fine condition
numbered	an edition where each copy is consecutively numbered
obl	oblong
octavo	standard size book
orig	original
o/w	otherwise
parchment	animal skin
pp	[number of] pages
PP	privately printed
pub	publisher or published
quarto	large (often square) book
raised bands	found on the spine; originally covered binding threads, now ornamental
reading copy	book in very poor condition, but legible
sg	signed
sm	small
sq	square
spine	the back of the outside of the book
TEG	top edge gilt
ttsp	top and tail of spine
uncut	the edges of the book not trimmed smooth
unopened	pages still folded together and not cut open
vellum	animal skin
vg	very good condition
wraps	paper covers
½ leather	only the spine covered with leather
¾ leather	the spine and front corners covered with leather
1st	first edition
4to	quarto
8vo	octavo
12mo	smaller than standard size book
16mo	very small size book